Cooking and Baking the Greek Way

ANNE THEOHAROUS

Cooking and Baking

THE

GREEK

WAY

Holt, Rinehart and Winston · New York

Published simultaneously in Canada
by Holt, Rinehart and Winston of Canada, Limited.

LIBRARY OF CONGRESS CATALOGING IN PUBLICATION DATA

Theoharous, Anne.
Cooking and baking the Greek way.

Includes index.
1. Cookery, Greek.   I. Title.
TX723.5.G8T47   641.5'9495   76-29917
ISBN 0-03-017521-6

First Edition
Designer: Mary M. Ahern
Drawings by Lawrence Marek
Printed in the United States of America

10 8 6 4 2 1 3 5 7 9

For the happy years of growing up
with love and understanding
I humbly dedicate this book to my father,
Isideros Mavrotheris, and Foundoúke

Wherever they may be

Contents

Preface

Why another Greek cookbook?

More people are traveling to Greece than in any other period in history. As they become acquainted with Greek foods and pastries, they want to add a bit of Greek flavor to their daily menus and dinner parties. But many have been reluctant to try, and I can't blame them. The recipes are unfamiliar and often seem complicated.

I have collected and used most of the Greek cookbooks printed in English throughout the years, but I found myself very often in the middle of a recipe that suddenly became unclear. Either the instructions were not complete or they were too complex. I set out to discover what was missing or what *I* was doing wrong. Most of these books seemed to take for granted that the reader was Greek (I was) and had watched her mother making every dish in Greek cuisine while growing up. Unfortunately many young Greeks had other things on their mind. I was no different.

I discovered through trial and error that many of these cooks were reluctant to tell you how much time was involved, and that shortcut methods and substitute ingredients were provided. This may indeed save time, but it does not give you authentic cooking. Many of my American friends, having absolutely nothing to compare with, were slaving over strange concoctions and calling them Greek all because they were relying on recipes that just didn't work.

As I watched Greek recipes I had known and loved from

childhood disappearing with the older generation and being mis-interpreted by my generation, I decided to stop complaining and write my own version of what a Greek cookbook should be.

In this day of instant mixes for cakes, casseroles, gravies, sauces, and frostings, one can spend hours in the kitchen and still end up with almost totally artificial food. There is a time and place for these mixes, I suppose, but I am disturbed that our taste buds have become so numbed that we don't try to wake them up and give them a thrill any longer. Somewhere deep in my Greek psyche, the concept that the preparation and cooking of food is an art still prevails.

So, in my own kitchen I tested and retested and wrote and rewrote until each one of these recipes was as clear and foolproof as possible. After a while it actually got to be fun trying to figure out why certain recipes looked so right on the page but wouldn't work out when you tried to use them.

There is no such thing as a bad cook, only one who won't take the time to learn. Don't be afraid of fine Greek cooking. It's like painting. You start timidly at first, and as you proceed the strokes get bolder, the colors more vivid, the subject bigger. Suddenly you find yourself softening certain lines, muting some colors, accenting others. Then you sit back in amazement. You have created a beautiful picture. A marvelous, tasty dish.

Some of these recipes may appear at first glance to be lengthy. Don't let that frighten you. I am trying to anticipate every question you might have, every small problem that may arise during preparation, cooking, or serving, even reheating or freezing. I have come to know the pitfalls often encountered.

"Add flour until dough is of the right consistency." (What is the right consistency?) "Pour batter into pan and bake." (What size pan?) "Cook over medium heat until done." (Well, if you haven't made that recipe before and you have never eaten it, how would you know when it was done?) How long is it going to take? How many people will it serve? I resolved to answer these questions carefully in this book. The time involved became tricky in some instances. In Moussaka, for example, where most of the time is spent in preparation, I have broken down the recipe to encompass a three-day period.

When I have found a recipe that freezes well I have included this information. Some recipes require line illustrations to make clear an intricate technique, and I have included step-by-step drawings where necessary.

In this period of high prices in a vast meat-consuming country such as America, these recipes will be of intrinsic value, economically and nutritionally, to every cook. Since Greece does not have a lot of grazing land, much of the meat is imported, and a little meat must of necessity go a long way. You will find that the Greeks transform even small portions of lamb, veal, pork, beef, and poultry into culinary delights with their rich variety of flavorings and artistic combinations learned over the centuries.

The Greek vegetable dishes should be of particular interest to vegetarians and others concerned with natural foods. They are not merely dull side dishes but flavorful and satisfying meals in themselves. Protein, fats, carbohydrates, mineral salts, and vitamins all are contained in vegetables. The Greeks add wedges of cheese, and perhaps unconsciously the principles of protein enrichment are followed.

Yogurt with its refreshing taste is a favorite food. It's low in calories and has always been regarded as a cure for all intestinal ailments. Nuts, nut pastes, and seeds are prized not only for their availability and taste but also for their concentrated protein and fats. Honey, used so frequently over Greek desserts, is a highly concentrated food and more easily assimilated than sugar. So if one looks carefully into the Greek diet, one sees that the people's love of these foods has also given them a high sense of nutrition.

Greek foods and especially the exquisite pastries lend themselves beautifully to parties and great dinners, so why not have a *gléndi* (celebration), and to all of you, even at your most simple meal, *Kali orexi* (Hearty appetite)!

Cooking and Baking the Greek Way

A Little about Greece
Past and Present

Eating and Drinking in Ancient Greece

In ancient Greece, a professional cook was regarded as an artist by the intellectuals. When these cooks invented special dishes, they were honored in front of huge crowds and given rewards of titles as well as money and lands. The Athenian baker Terion was so renowned that he was mentioned in the writings of Plato and Aristophanes. By the fifth century B.C. Greeks knew how to bake more than twenty different kinds of bread. The earliest traces of grapes date from 4000 B.C., and the Greeks were using sophisticated cooking utensils by 1000 B.C., as evidenced by drawings on pottery.

When the Greek empire was finally eclipsed by the Roman, the Greeks took their culture and culinary arts to the conquerors. While Aesop was cooking as a slave, he was also writing in his veiled, suggestive way so as to elude political censorship. From the fifth century B.C. on, the Romans employed Greek tutors for their children and Greek cooks in their kitchens.

In the Middle Ages many intellectuals, who in the true Greek tradition were fine cooks, found their way into Orthodox monasteries to escape Byzantine overlords. They donned black robes and created extravagant dishes for the delighted monks who had before subsisted on austere Spartan fare. To distinguish

1

themselves they wore tall white hats instead of the black ones worn by their colleagues. To this day, we identify that tall white hat with a master chef throughout most of the Western world.

The Individuality of Greek Cooking

People who think Greek cooking has no character of its own believe that most Greek food is really Turkish or similar to Italian cuisine. This could not be further from the truth.

The Turks, being Muslims, do not use wines or liquors in their foods; the Greeks do. It is true that many Greek dishes have Turkish names, but Greeks shudder when they hear their coffee being called "Turkish coffee." Greece was occupied by the Turks for nearly four hundred years, and Greeks were forced to refer to their dishes in the Turkish language. It is amazing that the Greek language itself survived. (My own father, who was born on the island of Chios, was forced to learn Turkish in grade school.)

Greek food also differs from Italian. Italian cooking very often uses salt pork in which to sauté vegetables and meats. The Greeks never use salt pork, preferring instead butter or oil. Italians love veal; the Greeks favor lamb. Italians use tomatoes freely, the Greeks sparingly, relying more on eggs and lemons.

Greece Today

When asked what Greece is like today I think first about the hospitality of the people and then about their individualism and their enormous capacity for living to the fullest. Toward friends and strangers alike, hospitality has always included the ritual of eating and drinking. It is considered rude not to offer something to a guest, as it is considered equally rude for a visitor to refuse food. In the tiniest of villages, the poorest of houses, if you cross the threshold you will invariably be served something sweet with the proverbial demitasse cup of strong coffee and a glass of cold water as a welcome. In the small villages of Greece one still sees the tradesmen bringing their food to the door of each house— the Koulouri (roll) vendor, the fishman with freshly caught fish, the baker, the vegetable man. In the large towns and Athens, of course, one must go to grocery stores or large open-air markets.

Greeks eat their one large meal in the middle of the day. With the exception of Sundays and holidays, daily breakfast consists of coffee and a Koulouri if the boy has got to the kitchen door before the man of the house leaves for work. If he hasn't, the man picks up a Koulouri from a corner vendor who sells nothing else and munches it on the way.

Lunch is fairly late by our standards. All shops, museums, theaters, and offices close around one in the afternoon and the employees go home; the meal is followed by a three-hour siesta. Thus refreshed, they go back to work at five; everything closes at about eight or nine o'clock.

Dinner is always late. It is served at ten or eleven and is, of course, fairly light—a salad, a glass of wine, cheese, and fresh fruit. Throughout the day, however, the Greeks do a lot of nibbling. The Americans have their coffee breaks, and the Greeks do too. With their coffee they buy cheese tarts (Tiropetes), clams or sea urchins on the half shell, various pastries, or tiny bags of salted pistachio nuts, which are sold everywhere. Such snacks, gathered together and served with Ouzo at a taverna or at home in the late afternoon, are called Mezethes, or hors d'oeuvres. The recipe section that follows appropriately starts with these tasty traditional foods.

APPETIZERS

Mezethes, the Appetite Teasers

The cocktail hour to most people means an apéritif and a few hors d'oeuvres before dinner. The cocktail hour to the Greeks usually means one or two hours of nibbling endless varieties of foods to whet their appetites while sipping a glass or two of Ouzo or Retsina wine to sharpen their wits. Then they go to the theater or shopping. Dinner is always much later in the evening and is extremely light.

This nibbling usually takes place in a taverna. Some tavernas, large and well lit, provide entertainment as well as food. These are always found on the main street, focal points for looking and gossiping. Then there are the small variety, sometimes only one room plus kitchen. Their success is determined by the quality of Ouzo, Retsina, and Mezethes provided by the owner. These tavernas are always hidden on offbeat streets or sometimes even miles from the center of town. Occasionally music blasts from a phonograph.

A salient characteristic of all Greek cities and towns is the noise. Because wood is scarce and marble isn't, almost everything is made of marble or tile. If you drop so much as a fork it can be heard outside. Now imagine a tiny smoke-filled room, a phonograph blasting modern music, tiny marble-topped tables, and the endless clatter of glasses, dishes, and silverware; add to it groups of Greeks sitting shoulder to shoulder heatedly discussing world affairs, monetary problems, art, philosophy, music, literature, and romances, and all trying to be heard above the din; you begin to get the picture.

In the summer these tiny tavernas move outdoors and the tables and chairs are crowded onto small paved courtyards or even in the owner's garden, but most of the year it is these indoor, noisy, crowded little tavernas that are popular with the young Greeks. There they nibble on Mezethes: olives, freshly baked bread, various cheeses, Taramosalata, fried chicken livers, bits of grilled lamb or beef, beans, small pieces of broiled fish, fried baby squid, dried figs, all sorts of roasted nuts and seeds and fresh fruit. All are served on little dishes, a seemingly endless array of them.

If a Greek decides not to go to a taverna he still will have a Meze before dinner with his Ouzo or glass of wine. If his is a humble home, Mezethes may consist of a few olives, a small piece of cheese, and some fresh crisp radishes. In a sophisticated home (especially if having company) Mezethes become much more elegant; Cheese or Spinach Cheese Puffs (Tiropetes or Spanokopetes) may be served, or Rice-Stuffed Grape Leaves (Dolmathes), or both.

Is it any wonder that dinner during the week is very late and very light?

CHEESE TRIANGLE PUFFS
Tirópetes

YIELD: 35 to 50 puffs
TIME: 1½ hours

At Greek diplomatic parties, one nibbles on Tiropetes while sipping champagne. They are the perfect Meze (hors d'oeuvre)—elegant to serve and a delicacy to eat. Tiny triangles of hot, flaky pastry with a wondrous cheese filling, they should be served warm from the oven, puffed and buttery, with napkins, since they're finger food.

Another great thing about them is that they freeze well; if you double this recipe you can make a large number of these elegant appetizers in advance. When someone unexpectedly drops in, all you have to do is take a few out of the freezer, pop them into a hot oven, and in a few minutes they are ready. Guests will eat as many as you have on hand. Ouzo served as an apéritif would be an excellent accompaniment.

Many countries in the Near East fry versions similar to Tiropetes in hot oil and call them *bourekakia* or cheese *boreks*. The Greek version is, in my opinion, lighter in taste and texture.

Many Greek homes serve Tiropetes as a main course, in which case they are made as large as apple turnovers and served with sliced tomatoes and cucumber (see recipe for Family-style Tiropeta).

As the first course of a formal dinner, serve two Tiropetes on a small plate (with knife and fork) with a couple of black shiny olives and a wedge of ripe red tomato for garnish. Whichever way you serve them, don't compete with them by serving other cheeses or cheese-based sauces at the same meal.

½ pound Feta cheese
6 ounces pot cheese or pot-
  style cottage cheese
¼ cup finely chopped fresh
  parsley

3 medium eggs
¼ pound unsalted butter
½ pound Phyllo, at room
  temperature (see page 9)

1. Rinse the Feta cheese with cold water to rid it of excessive saltiness. Pat dry with paper toweling, and crumble into tiny pieces into a bowl.

2. Add the pot or cottage cheese and mix both cheeses.

3. Add parsley and mix well.

4. Beat the eggs with a wire whisk or fork for a few minutes and add to the cheese mixture. Beat mixture with a whisk or fork until well blended. Set bowl aside.

5. Melt butter in small saucepan over very low heat. Do not let it brown. Set aside.

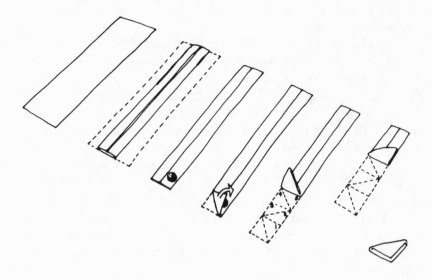

6. Gently unfold the Phyllo sheets and cut into thirds lengthwise, using scissors and cutting through the entire stack at one time. Wrap two-thirds in plastic wrap or waxed paper to prevent drying out and refrigerate until needed. Drape another piece of wrap over remaining third.

7. Remove 1 Phyllo sheet at a time, lay it on the counter, and with a pastry brush coat it lightly with melted butter. Fold the two long sides toward the middle, making a strip about 2 inches wide and 11 inches long. Brush with melted butter again.

8. Place a teaspoon of cheese mixture at the bottom left corner of the strip. Pick up corner with the filling and fold over (see illustration) so that the bottom edge meets a side edge and forms a right-angle triangle. Continue folding over from side to side into neat triangles until you reach the end of the strip. Brush finished triangle with butter and place directly on an ungreased baking sheet. Do not let triangles touch, since they will puff up quite a bit during baking.

9. Bake in a preheated 425° oven for 12 to 14 minutes or until plump, crisp, and golden. Do not turn over while baking.

10. Follow this process with remaining Phyllo that you've refrigerated. Arrange Tiropetes on an attractive plate and serve.

Baked Tiropetes can be frozen. When cool, wrap in foil or put in a plastic bag. To reheat, put baked frozen triangles into preheated 425° oven and bake for 10 minutes.

To freeze uncooked Tiropetes, brush finished triangles with melted butter and place, without touching, on cookie sheets lined with waxed paper or plastic. Place in freezer. When completely frozen, pack Tiropetes into a freezer box or plastic bag, seal, and return to freezer. To serve, place frozen Tiropetes on ungreased cookie sheet. Do not crowd them. Bake, without turning over, in a preheated 400° oven for 25 minutes or until golden and puffy. Break one open and taste before serving to make sure they have been thoroughly heated. Allow them to cool about 5 minutes before serving.

PASTRY LEAVES
Phýllo

Phyllo, sometimes spelled Filo or Fillo and pronounced fee/low, is the Greek word for leaf. Phyllo is made of flour and water, mixed to a stiff paste. Pieces about the size of an orange are broken off, and an expert pastry chef rolls and rolls them until they become as thin as tissue paper. He then tosses them skillfully onto a revolving large metal disk, where they are stretched into an unbelievable paperlike thinness that homemade Phyllo cannot compete with.

Making thin Phyllo is one of the high arts of the pastry world. It is usually sold frozen in 1-pound packages of 20 to 50 sheets, depending on the thickness (box labeled #4 is the most popular, since the sheets are very thin). The size of the sheets will sometimes vary according to the manufacturer, but they are always trimmed to a uniform size (16 by 18 inches), stacked, folded, and frozen. Then they are slipped into plastic bags and packed into long flat narrow boxes. Always allow frozen Phyllo to defrost in its plastic wrapper for at least two hours at room temperature before using.

Phyllo sheets are wrapped around meat, cheese, and poultry fillings. As many as 10 to 20 sheets of leaves are used for the top and bottom crusts of the famous Greek pastries. The Greeks use Phyllo the way Americans use pie crust.

Raw, defrosted Phyllo is white and very flexible; the sheets must be peeled off carefully. When a recipe requires Phyllo to be cut into thirds, cut through the entire stack at one time, using a sharp pair of scissors. When Phyllo is baked it is golden, crisp, and fragile because each sheet has been brushed with melted butter before going into the oven.

If the edges of commercial Phyllo sheets hang over a baking pan or casserole, never trim off as you would a pie crust. Butter these edges and fold them in. Always keep a piece of plastic or slightly dampened towel over Phyllo as you work to prevent it from drying out too fast and becoming brittle.

Defrosted Phyllo should never be refrozen. Wrap it loosely in plastic wrap, lay flat, and refrigerate. It will keep this way for about one week.

Purchase Phyllo in any of the grocery stores listed in the Shopper's Guide, or ask a gourmet shop or local bakery to order you a pound of strudel pastry sheets. These are excellent substitutes for Phyllo, but use less, since strudel leaves are thicker. (For example, if a recipe calls for ½ pound of Phyllo, you will use approximately 10 sheets of commercial Phyllo or 6 of the strudel or homemade leaves.) Some shops in the United States are beginning to carry unfrozen Phyllo or strudel pastry sheets. Make sure as you take them home that the box is lying flat in the bottom of your bag; they will rumple if put in upright.

Finally, for those who want to make Phyllo with their own hands, here is a recipe.

HOMEMADE PASTRY SHEETS
Phýllo Tou Spetioú

YIELD: Approximately 1 pound
TIME: 1½ hours

Pastry sheets made at home can never be rolled out as thinly as the commercial variety; so this recipe applies only to pan-made dishes such as Family-style Tiropeta or Spanokopeta. Recipes such as Baklava, Tiropetes, or Spanokopetes really demand the paper-thin commercial sheets.

3 cups all-purpose flour	1 cup lukewarm water
1 medium egg	Cornstarch
1 tablespoon oil	1 tablespoon unsalted
½ teaspoon salt	butter

1. Place flour in a large bowl, make a well in the center, and drop in egg, oil, and salt. Slowly stir in the lukewarm water until you have a fairly soft dough.

2. Knead the dough on a board sprinkled with cornstarch for at least 15 minutes, or until dough feels silky and pliable.

3. Cover a table completely with a sheet sprinkled with cornstarch. Put dough in the center and roll it out as thinly as possible in all directions. Melt the butter and brush the dough with it.

4. Start pulling gently but steadily, working around the table until the evenly pulled dough is almost tissue thin. Cut off any thicker edges hanging down. Cut into the size needed for the pan you are using and brush with warm melted butter if using immediately.

REFRIGERATING OR FREEZING

Allow entire sheet to stiffen for 15 minutes; then, using scissors, cut into desired size. Omit brushing with butter. Store by laying the Phyllo sheets on top of each other, fold, and wrap tightly in plastic.

Phyllo will keep in the refrigerator four days. If frozen, it will keep for three months. Always remember to bring it to room temperature, still wrapped, before using.

SPINACH CHEESE PUFFS
Spanokópetes

YIELD: 70 to 100 puffs
TIME: Approximately 3½ hours

Spinach is glamorous when presented in Spanokopetes; even people who ordinarily refuse to eat spinach seem to like it prepared this way.

If you are also serving Tiropetes (see recipe) shaped in triangles, make these into little rolls so your guests will be able to distinguish between the two. Freeze them as you would Tiropetes and reheat in a 425° oven for 25 minutes.

2 packages (10 ounces each) frozen whole-leaf spinach or 2 pounds fresh spinach
6 tablespoons olive oil
6 whole scallions, minced
1 pound Feta cheese
12 ounces pot cheese or pot-style cottage cheese
½ cup finely chopped fresh parsley
⅛ teaspoon white pepper
1 teaspoon dill
6 medium eggs, well beaten, at room temperature
½ pound unsalted butter
1 pound Phyllo, at room temperature (see page 9)

1. Thaw frozen spinach at room temperature for two hours or wash fresh spinach well. Drain and chop into small pieces, discarding any coarse stems.

2. Heat oil and sauté scallions until soft and wilted. Add spinach and simmer until moisture evaporates.

3. Rinse the Feta under cold water, drain, and crumble it into a bowl. Blend in pot or cottage cheese, parsley, pepper, and dill. Add beaten eggs and mix well. Add spinach and scallions and mix well.

4. Proceed from step 5 in the Tiropetes recipe (page 7) in the shaping of the pastry. For main course, see recipe for Family-style Tiropeta.

MAKING ROLLS

To make rolls instead of triangles, cut sheets of Phyllo pastry into quarters crosswise. Brush each quarter sheet as you use it with warm melted butter. Place 1 teaspoon of spinach-cheese mixture 1 inch from bottom edge of pastry sheet. Fold an inch margin over cheese mixture, then fold long edges in toward the middle. Brush with warm melted butter and roll loosely to the end. Brush each roll with warm melted butter as you place it, seam side down, in a baking pan. Bake at 425° for 12 to 14 minutes or until crisp and golden. Do not turn over while baking or they won't puff properly.

RICE-STUFFED GRAPE LEAVES
Dolmáthes

YIELD: Approximately 36 stuffed leaves
TIME: Approximately 3 hours

Nothing can compare with the fragrance of grape leaves cooking. If you have never used them in any of your recipes, you are in for a wonderful surprise. You can buy grape leaves in glass jars at almost all gourmet shops. Some American supermarkets in the larger cities and most of the stores listed in the Shopper's Guide carry them.

In Greece grape leaves are gathered when they are young and tender. If you decide to pick them and can them yourself, choose only unblemished ones, about 6 inches across at widest point.

CANNING GRAPE LEAVES

Wash leaves well in cool water several times. Snip off stems with scissors and arrange in stacks of 15 leaves, all facing the same direction. Roll up tightly into rolls and tie with string. Bring 2 quarts of water to a boil and add ½ cup salt. (You could do up to 200 leaves in this amount of water.) Drop the bundles of leaves into the boiling water and remove each bundle with tongs, one at a time, after 2 to 3 minutes. Cool leaves slightly, and arrange bundles tightly in sterilized pint jars. Pour the boiling salted water to top of jar and seal tightly. They don't have to be refrigerated. Use as you would the store-bought variety.

If you wish to use them immediately, rinse under cold water and then blanch them in boiling water to cover for 2 to 3 minutes. Drain, allow to cool, and use.

Grape leaves stuffed with rice are always eaten chilled or at room temperature with a sprinkling of lemon juice. Make sure, therefore, that you use a fine imported olive oil (not butter!), as this does not congeal. They are usually served on a large platter and picked up with the fingers. Dolmathes resemble shiny, fat little sausages in shape and are dark green in color.

A 12-ounce jar of grape leaves contains about 50 leaves. Of these, you will find at least 10 that are too large and coarse to use, or too small and torn. In my experience, a 12-ounce jar should wrap about 36 Dolmathes.

Guests will easily eat three or four Dolmathes, or Dolmathakia, as they are more affectionately referred to. Make up to 2 days ahead of time for a party and cover loosely with waxed paper in the refrigerator.

For meatless dinners or lunches (especially good in the summertime), serve as a main dish with knife and fork. Serve six to eight Dolmathes for each guest with plain yogurt on the side or spooned over them, Greek style.

¾ cup olive oil
  3 large onions, very finely
    chopped (about 2¼ cups)
  6 whole scallions or 6
    shallots, very finely chopped
  1 teaspoon salt
  ¼ teaspoon black pepper
  2 tablespoons pine nuts
    (optional)
  1 cup long-grain rice

1 tablespoon finely
    chopped fresh dill or
  1 teaspoon dried dill
½ cup finely chopped fresh
    parsley (reserve the
    stems)
¾ teaspoon very finely
    crushed mint
  5 tablespoons lemon juice
12-ounce jar grape leaves
Lemon wedges
Parsley sprigs

1. Heat half the olive oil and sauté onions and scallions or shallots over low heat until soft and transparent. Add salt, pepper, pine nuts if you wish, and rice. Cook for 10 minutes, stirring occasionally.

2. Add dill, parsley, mint, 2 tablespoons lemon juice, and 1 cup of water. Cover and simmer until liquid is absorbed (about 10 minutes). The rice will be slightly undercooked. Taste for seasoning. You may wish to add a little salt. If you do, make sure you mix it in very well.

3. Drain brine off grape leaves. Thoroughly rinse leaves in cool water several times. Blanch by dipping them in boiling water for 1 minute, then drain. When cool enough to handle, separate leaves carefully and spread gently on flat surface. Cut out any

thick stem, even if it should run into body of the leaf itself.

4. Place the parsley stems on bottom of a 4- to 6-quart pot in a crisscross fashion.

5. Place a heaping teaspoon of the filling at the base of the underside (the dull side) of a leaf. Fold the bottom up, then fold in the sides; roll toward the point of the leaf (see illustration). Each one should look like a shiny little sausage. Place closely in layers over the parsley stalks in the pot. Repeat the process until you have used up all the filling. Make Dolmathes as small as possible and don't use too much wrapping—if a leaf is unusually large, trim or discard it. Do not wrap too tightly; remember, the rice must expand as it cooks. Mix remaining oil, 2 tablespoons lemon juice, and 2 cups water, and pour into pot.

6. Weight Dolmathes with an inverted plate so they cannot move while they are cooking. The water should barely cover the plate. If you don't have enough, add a bit more. Cover pot and

bring to a boil. Reduce heat and simmer for 1½ hours, until most of the liquid is absorbed.

7. Remove pot from heat. Allow Dolmathes to stay in pot, covered, until they have cooled, at least 2 hours or even overnight if you wish.

8. Remove plate on top of Dolmathes. Place each one carefully, one at a time, so that leaves do not come apart, on a serving platter. Serve at room temperature or slightly chilled. Sprinkle with remaining tablespoon of lemon juice just before serving. Garnish platter with lemon wedges and parsley sprigs.

FREEZING

Lay a sheet of plastic wrap on a cookie sheet. Arrange cooled Dolmathes in rows like little soldiers, next to but not touching one another. Place in freezer. When frozen, pack in freezer container or bag with sheet of plastic wrap between layers. When planning cocktails, remove as many as you will need and allow them to defrost at room temperature, about 4 hours.

FISH ROE PÂTÉ
Taramosaláta

YIELD: 1½ cups
TIME: 40 minutes

Taramosalata is one of the most popular of all appetizers among the Greeks today. Tarama—salted roe from gray mullet, tunny fish, or carp—is the main ingredient. They say the best comes from the carp, and luckily this is readily available in the United States in any of the stores listed in the Shopper's Guide. It is bright orange in color and sold in small jars. It is inexpensive.

Taramosalata is a creamy pâté. It can be served as a spread for canapés, as a dip with raw vegetables around it, or on small wedges of toast as a first course at lunch.

If making canapés, always remember to butter the crackers or toast before spreading on the Taramosalata to prevent moisture from making the canapés limp and soggy.

There are many ways of making Taramosalata. Some people like a lot of onion, others none at all. Some use bread as the main extender, others mashed potato. Some use a well-beaten egg yolk to make the purée lighter and creamier, others just a little water. I have tried many versions and can honestly say they are all good. I am including here a recipe I use often, and I hope it suits you. Once you have made this, however, you may wish to experiment with different combinations. Just remember that the bright-orange roe should be beaten with the other ingredients until the color is a very pale pink and the texture is light and creamy, like a soft purée. It should always be served chilled. Leftover Taramosalata can be used as a dressing over a green salad.

4 ounces Tarama	1 cup olive oil
4 slices white bread	1 small onion, finely grated
¼ cup lemon juice	1 teaspoon chopped fresh dill (optional)

1. Soak Tarama in water for 5 minutes to remove some of the salt. Drain.

2. Trim crusts off bread, soak bread in ¼ cup water, then squeeze dry.

3. Place Tarama, bread, lemon juice, oil, onion, and dill in blender container or bowl, and blend or mix with electric beater until smooth, light, and creamy. Or, if making by hand, mash Tarama, bread, onions, and dill with a fork. Blend in olive oil and lemon juice slowly, stirring constantly, until thoroughly combined. Beat with a whisk until pink and creamy. Chill.

TARAMA MOUSSE
Taramosaláta Formazméni

YIELD: Approximately 15 servings
TIME: 2½ hours preparation;
at least 5 hours to set

This very mild version of Taramosalata takes time and patience. The end result is so attractive, however, that it's well worth the effort.

Garnish this mousse with greens from your garden or with sprigs of fresh parsley and olives. Have a tray of crisp assorted crackers alongside. Spread the mousse on crackers with a small knife.

If you wish to vary the decoration of the fish mold, use canned black truffles (sliced very thinly) in place of olives, or use long thin strips of carrots in place of pimiento. Garnish platter with various shapes cut from jellied aspic, or the salad itself may be unmolded onto a bed of beaten aspic for a glittering effect. Sprigs of watercress interlaced with wedges of hard-boiled eggs would complete the picture.

2 tablespoons unflavored gelatin	Dash cayenne pepper
¼ cup cold water	½ cup finely grated onion
2 cups boiling water	5 large black pitted olives
4 ounces Tarama	A few strips pimiento
1 cup mayonnaise	Black truffle slice or
1 tablespoon lemon juice	anchovy filet
1 cup soft bread crumbs	8-ounce package cream
(see p. 19)	cheese, at room
	temperature

1. Place a 3-cup metal fish mold in freezer for 1 hour.

2. Sprinkle gelatin in ¼ cup cold water to soften. Add 2 cups boiling water and stir until all the gelatin melts. Set in refrigerator for 10 minutes.

3. Blend Tarama, mayonnaise, lemon juice, bread crumbs, cayenne pepper, and grated onion in blender or mixer. Blend in 1 cup of the gelatin mixture, then refrigerate. If doing it by hand, mash the Tarama in a bowl with a fork; add the mayonnaise, lemon juice, bread crumbs, pepper, and onion, and beat with a wire whisk until light and fluffy. Blend in 1 cup of gelatin mixture and refrigerate.

4. While the Tarama mixture is getting cold, remove mold from freezer. Pour ¼ cup of the remaining gelatin mixture into mold and tip it to make sure it spreads into all the crevices of the mold. Put fish mold back into freezer for 15 minutes.

5. Slice olives thinly (crosswise), then cut each slice in half. Slice the pimiento into long slender (lengthwise) strips.

Arrange olive halves overlapping in mold to represent scales. The eye of the fish could be a slice of aromatic truffle or a curled anchovy filet. Arrange the red pimiento strips to represent the fins and tail, then return mold to freezer for another 30 minutes.

6. Pour ¼ cup more of the gelatin mixture into decorated mold at the end of that time, and tip gently to spread into all the crevices. Try not to disturb your arrangement of olive slices and pimiento strips. Return mold to freezer for an additional 30 minutes. (This will set your pattern beautifully, and from here on you are home free.)

7. Mash cream cheese with remaining gelatin mixture and then blend well into the refrigerated Tarama mixture. Fill the fish mold and refrigerate for at least 5 hours or overnight. (The platter on which your Tarama mousse will stand should also be refrigerated.)

8. Just before serving, dip mold in hot water for just a couple of seconds. Place chilled serving platter over mold and quickly turn both over at the same time.

TO MAKE SOFT BREAD CRUMBS

Use 2- to 4-day-old bread. Cut off crusts and tear into 1-inch pieces. Grind for a few seconds in a blender or crumb it lightly with your fingers. To measure soft bread crumbs: Always pile lightly into a measuring cup and do not compress.

OLIVES AND CAVIAR
Eliés Me Haviári

Simple, but terribly good. Serve with any type of drink from Ouzo to champagne. A platter of crisp raw vegetables with Eggplant Purée (Melitzana Purée; see recipe) and another of hot buttery Cheese Triangle Puffs (Tiropetes; see recipe) would complement this nicely.

10 large black Greek olives
1 heaping tablespoon (1 ounce)
imported black caviar

Remove olive pits with a special utensil or a knife or buy already pitted olives. Stuff with caviar, using a paper cone or a pastry bag.

LAMB'S LIVER WITH LEMON JUICE
Sikotákia

YIELD: 15 pieces or 4 to 6 servings
TIME: 10 minutes

This is an appetizer that I guarantee will delight you, and it takes only a few minutes to prepare. Although Sikotakia implies lamb's liver to a Greek, it is equally delicious made with calf's liver.

> ½ pound lamb's or calf's liver
> 2 tablespoons butter
> 2½ tablespoons lemon juice
> Salt
> Oregano

1. Cut liver into tiny bite-sized pieces, wash, and pat dry. (It will be easy to cut if you freeze it briefly.)
2. Fry quickly in hot butter.
3. Sprinkle with lemon juice. salt, and oregano, and serve hot speared on cocktail picks.

CALF'S LIVER IN WINE SAUCE
Sikotákia Me Krassí

YIELD: 4 servings
TIME: 1 hour marinating;
30 minutes cooking

To me, the Yankee way of sautéing calf's liver with bacon and onions is tops. For those who really enjoy liver, try this Grecian way of preparing it. The Greeks use lamb's liver, but calf's liver is as good if not better for this recipe.

Serve this as a hot appetizer on wedges of toast before a light dinner. If using as a main course, serve with creamed potatoes, a hot green vegetable, and a salad.

1 pound calf's or lamb's
liver, thinly sliced and cut
into 1-inch pieces
½ cup dry red wine
1 teaspoon salt
¼ teaspoon black pepper

¼ cup all-purpose flour
¼ cup olive oil
3 medium onions, thinly
sliced
1½ cups boiling water
Sprinkling of oregano,
marjoram, or rosemary

1. Rinse liver and marinate for 1 hour in the wine. Remove liver and reserve the wine. Sprinkle liver with salt, then pepper, then flour.

2. Heat the oil in a large frying pan. Sauté liver quickly (about 10 minutes) and remove it from pan.

3. Add onions to the pan, cover, and cook over low heat for 5 minutes. Add reserved wine, boiling water, and herb, and cook for a few minutes, scraping in all the browned bits sticking to the bottom of the pan.

4. Return liver to the pan, lower heat, cover, simmer for an additional 15 minutes, and serve.

FRIED CHEESE
Saganáki

YIELD: 4 servings
TIME: 10 minutes

This is traditionally served as a light lunch, an appetizer, or an after-theater snack. Half a pound of cheese will serve four people. A crisp green salad, sliced tomatoes, crusty bread, and chilled white wine would be the perfect accompaniment.

Saganaki is always served on small heated plates (with knives and forks). In an emergency a good Parmesan cheese may be substituted.

½ pound Kasseri or Kefalotyri cheese
All-purpose flour
¼ pound butter
2½ tablespoons lemon juice
Oregano

1. Cut slices of cheese, about ½ inch thick.
2. Dust lightly with flour.
3. Fry in *very hot* butter about 30 seconds on each side.
4. Sprinkle with lemon juice and oregano and serve piping hot.

FRIED CHEESE CUBES
Kasséri Tiganitó

YIELD: 30 pieces
TIME: 20 minutes

How often have you been handed a cocktail or a lovely wine in a crystal glass, then suddenly found yourself confronted with a plate of cut-up salami or store-bought cheese dip and crackers?

Here is a tangy hot appetizer you can serve (inexpensively) to make your guests feel truly welcome.

½ pound Kasseri or
  Kefalotyri cheese
1 egg, slightly beaten
½ cup milk

1 cup crushed zwieback
  crumbs or unseasoned
  dry bread crumbs
¼ pound butter
2½ tablespoons lemon juice

1. Cut cheese into bite-sized cubes. Dip cubes first into slightly beaten egg, then into milk; roll in crumbs.
2. Fry in hot butter quickly (a few seconds on each side) until golden. Drain on paper toweling and serve, speared with cocktail picks, on a warmed platter. Sprinkle with lemon juice just before serving.

CHESTNUT AND CHICKEN SPREAD
Kástana Me Kóta

YIELD: Approximately 3 cups
TIME: 1½ hours

This unusual recipe for small canapés or sandwiches is perfect for afternoon receptions and with cocktails.

12 chestnuts, fresh or dried
  2 cups ground or finely
    minced cooked white chicken
    meat
¼ cup finely chopped celery

Approximately ½ cup
  mayonnaise
1 teaspoon salt (optional)
¼ teaspoon white pepper
  (optional)
Assorted breads, plain or
  toasted

1. Cut an X in the flat side of each chestnut shell with a small, sharp knife. Cover the nuts with water, bring to a boil, and simmer 45 minutes to 1 hour, covered. Drain and, while still hot, peel them. If you use the dried shelled chestnuts available at foreign grocery stores, you must soak them in warm water for 1 to 2 days. Then simmer, drain, and use.

2. In a blender, mix chestnuts, chicken, celery, and enough mayonnaise to make a spreading consistency. Scrape into a bowl and add salt and pepper if necessary; mix in well. Refrigerate until cold. If you do not want a puréed spread, combine in a bowl instead of using a blender.

3. Using a sharp knife, cut crusts off breads. With cookie cutters, cut bread into various shapes, wrap tightly in plastic, and refrigerate.

4. Just before serving, spread bread with cold chestnut and chicken mixture.

GREEK SAUSAGES
Loukánika

YIELD: 4 dozen appetizers;
       3 dozen lunch-size patties
TIME: Overnight for marinating;
      15 minutes for cooking

If you've never tasted Greek sausages, you are in for a delightful surprise. The combination of flavorings (including orange rind, savory, and allspice) gives them an unforgettably zesty and pungent taste. An easy way to always have some on hand is to form them into patties and freeze as you would hamburgers, individually wrapped in plastic.

Serve them plain with a salad or with fried eggs or even between bread.

1½ pounds coarsely ground pork (leg of fresh pork, pork shoulder, or pork butt)
½ pound ground beef
1 teaspoon salt
1 garlic clove, crushed
1 teaspoon ground cinnamon

2 teaspoons savory
1 teaspoon allspice
Rind of 1 orange, finely minced
8 black peppercorns, cracked
½ cup dry red wine
5 tablespoons lemon juice

1. Mix all ingredients except lemon juice and knead well. Refrigerate overnight to give spices a chance to permeate the meat.

2. For parties, form into small meatballs or sausage shapes. Fry or broil (no fat is necessary) until well done and very brown. Sprinkle with lemon juice and serve on a hot platter with cocktail picks. For light meals, form sausage meat into larger patties as you would hamburgers. Fry or broil over medium heat. Brown quickly, then cover and cook about 10 minutes on each side or until done. Or you may place sausages in a hot frying pan and add ½ cup boiling water. Cover and simmer for 10 minutes. Pour off liquid and brown sausages well over low heat, shaking the pan to prevent sticking.

MAKING SAUSAGES IN CASINGS

If you wish to stuff sausage meat into casings, order 1 pound of pork casings from butcher. Soak in cold water overnight and then rinse. Run water through each casing, then cover with water and gently simmer for 5 minutes. Using proper attachment on meat grinder for stuffing, force mixture into casings, tying string about every 12 inches. Prick casing with a fork and refrigerate, freeze, or hang up to dry in a very cold place for 1 week. Use as needed. Cut into 1-inch pieces and broil or fry until well done.

ARTICHOKE HEARTS POLITA
*Angin**á**res Pol**í**ta*

YIELD: 5 appetizers
TIME: 15 minutes preparation;
30 minutes cooking

According to legend, the true artichoke came from one of the Aegean Islands, Zinari, where a beautiful girl named Cynara lived. Unfortunately her beauty so enraged a jealous goddess that she turned her into an artichoke.

In this recipe I have specified frozen artichoke hearts, which are easy to cook and, of course, available all year round. Do not substitute butter for the oil in this recipe; the taste will be drastically changed.

1 medium carrot, thinly
  sliced
25 fresh or frozen tiny pearl
  onions, or 2 large
  onions, coarsely chopped
12 small potatoes, peeled, or
  3 large potatoes, peeled
  and quartered
4 whole scallions,
  finely chopped
½ teaspoon salt

⅛ teaspoon white pepper
½ tablespoon dried dill,
  or 1 tablespoon fresh
Pinch sugar
½ cup fine olive oil
3 tablespoons lemon
  juice
2 tablespoons flour
9-ounce package frozen
  artichoke hearts,
  thawed

1. Put carrot, onions, potatoes, scallions, salt, pepper, dill, and sugar in a 4-quart saucepan. Add water to just barely cover the vegetables. Bring to a boil, then cover pan and cook over low heat for 15 minutes.

2. Beat olive oil, lemon juice, and flour until well blended, then pour over vegetables. Cook gently for 7 minutes with pan covered until sauce is slightly thickened.

3. Add artichoke hearts and bring to a boil. Reduce heat, cover pan, and simmer for 8 minutes or until all vegetables are tender. Allow to cool in the sauce and taste for seasoning. Serve at room temperature or slightly chilled as a salad or appetizer.

EGGPLANT PURÉE
Melitzána Purée

YIELD: Approximately 3 cups
TIME: 1½ hours

For a different taste, try serving this exotic vegetable appetizer at your next party. Because the color of cooked eggplant is so unassuming, find a bright red, green, or yellow bowl to serve it in. This purée also makes a good addition to a cold buffet.

As a dip, serve Melitzana with sesame crackers and garnish it with green bell pepper and red tomato slices all around the bowl for buffets.

As an appetizer, for each serving put 2 tablespoons purée on lettuce or spinach leaves. Arrange a slice of ripe red tomato, a black Greek olive, and a couple of sesame crackers around it. Sieve a little hard-boiled egg yolk over the eggplant purée on each plate. This will give you a most unusual and colorful appetizer.

Eggplant purée can be frozen. Thaw out at room temperature and whip just before serving.

1 large eggplant or several small ones (approximately 2 pounds)	¼ teaspoon dry mustard
	1½ teaspoons salt
	¼ teaspoon black pepper
½ cup unseasoned dry bread crumbs (see page 27)	¾ cup olive oil
	1 tablespoon lemon juice
1 small onion, roughly grated	2 tablespoons wine vinegar
1 garlic clove, crushed	¼ teaspoon oregano
1 tablespoon chopped fresh parsley	½ teaspoon mint

1. Slice and discard at least 1 inch off each end of eggplant. Place eggplant on a baking sheet and bake in preheated 375° oven for about 1 hour if using a large eggplant. If using several small ones, bake until eggplant skin becomes wrinkled and the flesh is quite soft to the touch.

2. Dip eggplant into a pot of cold water, peel quickly, then allow to cool on a platter.

3. Cut up peeled eggplant and put into a blender along with bread crumbs, onion, and garlic. Blend until smooth.

4. Add everything else and blend until consistency is like a stiff mayonnaise.

5. Refrigerate overnight. Always serve very cold.

TO MAKE DRY BREAD CRUMBS

Bake several slices of bread in a 375° oven until hard and golden. Crush with rolling pin or put into blender.

SOUPS

Traditional Favorites

Very often soup will be the entire meal in a Greek household, particularly if the soup is a thick one, like Lentil Soup. Fresh bread, a seasonal vegetable, and a few olives accompanying it make no other course necessary.

The Greeks often prepare a vegetable, meat, fish, or chicken stock, toss a handful of rice into it, and just before serving squeeze a little lemon juice into it or blend in their famous Avgolemono Sauce.

Friday was always "Soup Day" while I was growing up. Since my father's paycheck was cashed on Saturday, I suspect economics played a part in establishing this particular custom at our house. Yet how we looked forward to those full-flavored soups!

Beef or lamb bones left over from a roast were simmered, the broth strained, and then the magic would start—turning the broth into a hearty soup. As children, my sister and I would eat our soup, enjoying not only the taste and warmth but also the sense that our family was really together on that night. Watching my father's face, I could see the work pressures of the week melting away with each spoonful. Watching my mother's face, I could always see the Cheshire cat smile at her own special brand of alchemy that had stretched father's paycheck one day more with such delicious results.

Starting with chicken stock, here are some of the wonderful soups I remember and still make.

HOMEMADE CHICKEN STOCK
Kotózoumo

YIELD: About 2 quarts
TIME: 3 to 4 hours

1 stewing hen, approximately
  5 pounds
3 quarts cold water
  (to cover)
1 teaspoon salt

4 peppercorns
1 large carrot, sliced
1 large onion, sliced
1 large stalk celery,
  including leaves, sliced

1. Rinse chicken and place in a 4- or 5-quart pot. Cover with cold water, add salt and peppercorns, and bring to a boil. Lower the heat, cover pot, and keep chicken simmering, taking the lid off from time to time to remove the foam.

2. When no more foam rises to the surface, add vegetables, cover, and simmer over very low heat until chicken falls off the bones easily (about 3 to 4 hours).

3. Remove vegetables with slotted spoon and discard. Remove chicken. (Chicken breast may be cut up into tiny pieces, heated in stock, and served in the soup if desired. The rest of the chicken may be made into a chicken salad or croquettes.)

4. Strain stock through a fine sieve into a large bowl and refrigerate.

5. You can keep stock refrigerated for about 6 days if you do not remove the fat that congeals on top. This keeps out the air and helps preserve the stock. Always remove hardened fat just before using the stock.

FREEZING

Pour strained, cooled stock, along with fat, into covered containers and freeze. You can use a wide-mouthed glass jar with a tight screw top if you leave at least 4 inches at top for expansion. When defrosting any foods that are in glass, place jars in cold water until contents are loosened. Remove fat before using.

CHICKEN AVGOLEMONO SOUP
Kotósoupa Avgolémono

YIELD: 6 servings
TIME: 30 minutes

Eggs give a creamy white texture and lemon juice brings a refreshing tang to this most popular of all Hellenic soups. Avgolemono Soup can also be made from lamb, beef, or fish stock. The egg and lemon sauce is mixed into the soup just before it is served. The rice should not be added until the last 30 minutes before serving, or it will get soggy.

You can use any kind of pasta instead of rice. Greeks prefer rice, with Orzo (see page 96) or extremely fine noodles as a second choice.

6 cups chicken stock
3 tablespoons long-grain rice
4 large eggs, separated, at
   room temperature
⅓ teaspoon salt

4 tablespoons lemon juice
Freshly ground black pepper
   or finely chopped fresh
   parsley

1. Bring chicken stock to a boil, add rice, cover pot, and cook over medium heat until rice is tender (about 15 minutes).
2. Remove pot from heat. Take out 1 cup of stock and reserve.
3. Using an electric beater or wire whisk, first beat egg whites with the salt until stiff. Add yolks while still beating, then add the lemon juice very slowly. Add the reserved cup of stock, also very slowly, continuing to beat.

4. Pour sauce into soup and return pot to very low heat. Stir this over very low heat about 2 minutes and remove from heat.

5. Serve with a bit of freshly ground black pepper or ½ teaspoon finely chopped fresh parsley over each bowl. If you are reheating the soup, do it over very low heat and stir all the time or the egg in the sauce will separate.

HOMEMADE BEEF STOCK
Vothenós Zoumós

YIELD: 6 to 8 cups
TIME: Approximately 6 hours

4 to 5 pounds beef bones
(knuckles, neck, marrow
bones)
1 to 2 pounds lean soup meat
(optional)
2 tablespoons olive oil
½ tablespoon salt

3 quarts cold water
6 peppercorns
1 stalk celery with leaves,
sliced
1 carrot, sliced
2 large onions, sliced

1. Preheat oven to 350°. Rinse bones and brown them in oven along with meat, if you're using it, in a roasting pan with the olive oil for about 30 minutes to give stock a good brown color. Drain off all fat that accumulates in pan and discard.

2. Place bones, meat, and salt in a 5- to 6-quart pot with 3 quarts cold water and bring to a boil.

3. Lower heat and cover pot. From time to time, skim off foam that rises to the surface and scrape off foam that sticks to sides of pot.

4. When no more foam rises, add peppercorns, celery, carrot, and onions. Bring to a boil, reduce heat, cover partially, and simmer gently for about 5 hours. Discard bones. Meat may be diced and later used in soup if desired. Discard the vegetables.

5. Strain stock through a fine strainer and clean cloth and refrigerate. When ready to use, remove hardened fat from surface.

GREEK BEEF SOUP
Kreatósoupa

YIELD: 6 to 8 servings
TIME: Approximately 40 minutes

6 to 8 cups homemade
  beef stock
¼ cup long-grain rice or Orzo
  (see page 96) or 1 to 2
  cups diced cooked meat

4 large eggs, separated,
  at room temperature
⅓ teaspoon salt
4 tablespoons lemon juice

1. Heat all but 1 cup of the stock until it boils; then reduce heat, stir in rice or Orzo, cover, and simmer for 20 minutes or until rice or pasta is cooked. If you wish to use the diced cooked meat instead of the pasta, add it to the stock when it boils; then lower heat and let it simmer a few minutes, just until it is heated through.

2. Meanwhile, prepare the sauce: Using an electric beater or wire whisk, first beat egg whites with the salt until stiff. Add yolks while still beating, then add the lemon juice very slowly. Add the reserved cup of cool stock, also very slowly, continuing to beat.

3. Add this sauce mixture to the stock, stirring constantly over low heat about two minutes, until soup is slightly thickened.

LENTIL SOUP
Fakeé

YIELD: 6 servings
TIME: 2 hours

Aristophanes' *Plutus* mentions a man who suddenly became so rich that "he didn't eat lentils anymore." That's a pity, for lentils contain more protein than any other vegetable and are flavorful as well. The Greeks most often prepare them as a hearty soup. If you have some beef bones, you can make a rich beef stock and use it in place of water. This soup is so savory, however, that it can be entirely vegetarian.

Serve this soup with Greek Garlic Cheese Bread (see recipe) and a green salad garnished with anchovy filets and shiny black Greek olives. Although this may not be considered a "rich man's dish," he will envy you.

1 pound lentils	1 tablespoon tomato paste
2 stalks celery, finely chopped	1 large bay leaf
1 large carrot, finely chopped	½ teaspoon oregano
2 tablespoons finely chopped fresh parsley	½ teaspoon Tabasco or ⅛ teaspoon black pepper
2 large onions, finely chopped	3 beef bouillon cubes (optional)
3 cloves garlic, very finely chopped	½ tablespoon salt (optional)
½ cup olive oil	3 tablespoons wine vinegar or tarragon vinegar
2½ quarts water or beef stock; see previous recipe	

1. Wash lentils carefully, then soak them in 4 quarts cold water with pot covered for about 30 minutes. Discard any lentils that float to the surface. Drain and rinse with fresh cold water. Drain in colander.

2. Sauté celery, carrot, parsley, onions, garlic in olive oil over very low heat in a large frying pan for about 15 minutes.

3. Meanwhile put water or stock on to boil in a 5-quart saucepan. When boiling, turn heat very low and cover.

4. Add tomato paste, bay leaf, and drained lentils to sautéing vegetables. Continue to sauté for 10 more minutes.

5. Add vegetable mixture to boiling liquid. Simmer, pot covered, until all vegetables are very tender, at least 1½ hours.

6. Add oregano and Tabasco or pepper, stir, and continue to simmer. If you have used water rather than beef stock, add 3 beef bouillon cubes to the pot and stir well to make sure they dissolve completely. If you are not using bouillon cubes, add ½ tablespoon salt at this point. Taste the soup. If it needs a bit more salt, add it now and remove from heat. Stir vinegar into pot of soup.

FISH STOCK
Psarózoumo

YIELD: 6 to 8 servings
TIME: 1½ hours

If you wish to make fish stock for some simple soups using left-overs, this is how the seaside villagers do it.

2 to 3 pounds uncooked fish
heads and tails, plus shrimp,
crab, or lobster shells if
available
1 tablespoon salt
½ cup dry white wine

6 peppercorns
2 large onions, sliced
1 celery stalk
1 bay leaf
Pinch thyme
Handful fresh parsley

1. Wash fish parts and shells thoroughly under cold running water. Place in a piece of cheesecloth (approximately 36 inches square), tie both ends, and place in 5-quart pot. Cover with cold water (at least 2 quarts) and bring to a boil.
2. Add remaining ingredients. Boil gently for 45 minutes.
3. Using slotted spoon, remove most of the vegetables and the cheesecloth pouch and discard. Strain stock through a clean cloth or fine strainer. It will keep several days in the refrigerator or several weeks frozen.

IDEAS FOR QUICK FISH-STOCK SOUPS

Heat stock, add 4 chopped tomatoes and ¼ cup olive oil, and simmer for 30 minutes, partially covered. Serve with a wedge of lemon to be squeezed over each portion.

Heat stock, add ¼ cup long-grain rice, and simmer with pot covered about 15 minutes or until rice is cooked. Serve wedges of lemon to be squeezed over it. Or, after rice is cooked, you may wish to make Avgolemono Sauce (see recipe). Add it just before serving the soup.

GREEK BOUILLABAISSE
Kaccaviá

YIELD: 8 servings
TIME: 2½ hours

This most famous of all fish soups got its name from the earthenware pot in which it was always cooked. Greek fishermen would cook their freshly caught assorted fish in lots of water, olive oil, and lemon juice. Gradually the recipe became more refined.

The flavor of bouillabaisse varies according to the different types of fish used. Just remember that the freshest fish cannot be ruined, but a stale fish will ruin even the greatest recipe. The following recipe is made in Greece with ocean fish, but if you live in an area where only fresh-water fish are available, by all means use them instead.

A fresh fish should be used the day it is bought. The body should be almost stiff (not limp), and no imprint should remain when you touch it. Do not buy a fish that has too strong an odor. The eyes should be slightly bulging, and the scales should lie close to the skin.

The following recipe calls for 3 pounds of fish; a variety is traditional but not imperative. The fish can be sea bass, porgies, whitefish, halibut, cod, swordfish, flounder, or any fresh ocean fish; I would not recommend mackerel, herring, or salmon, since they are very oily and have too strong a flavor. You could also use a large ocean fish, weighing about 3 pounds, that has had the head removed and has been washed, scaled, and cut into serving portions. Red snapper, if available locally, is wonderful. Include the head in the cheesecloth pouch in order to give your soup a finer flavor.

For tips on removing fish odors, see page 77.

2 medium onions, thinly sliced
2 small potatoes, peeled and diced
2 small carrots, diced
3 celery tops, chopped, or 1 stalk, peeled and chopped
½ cup finely chopped fresh parsley
1 clove garlic, minced

4 ripe tomatoes, peeled and
   chopped, or 4 canned
   tomatoes
½ cup olive oil
2 quarts water
1½ teaspoons salt
⅛ teaspoon black pepper
1 large bay leaf

¼ cup dry white wine
3 pounds fish
½ cup all-purpose flour
½ cup long-grain rice
¼ teaspoon powdered saffron
2½ tablespoons lemon juice
Croutons
Lemon wedges

1. In a large soup kettle sauté onions, potatoes, carrots, celery, parsley, garlic, and tomatoes in oil for 15 minutes, until almost soft but not brown.

2. Add water, half the salt, the pepper, and the bay leaf, and bring to a boil.

3. Add wine and simmer for 20 minutes, keeping the soup kettle partially covered.

4. Lightly sprinkle fish with remaining salt and roll in flour. Wrap fish (plus any heads) in a piece of cheesecloth approximately 36 inches square. Tie the ends of the cheesecloth together loosely and lower the pouch into the kettle. Simmer covered for 10 minutes.

5. Add rice and saffron, and simmer until rice is tender (about 25 minutes).

6. Carefully remove cheesecloth pouch with 2 large slotted spoons and place on a platter to cool.

7. When cool enough to handle, untie the cheesecloth ends. Remove fish skin and bones gently, and put the fish pieces back into pot. Add lemon juice and taste for seasoning.

8. Serve soup hot with croutons floating on top and a wedge of lemon on the side for those who prefer to squeeze a little more into their soup.

MAKING CROUTONS

Croutons are small squares of bread that have been fried in very hot butter until crisp. Only then will they float on top of a soup properly.

EASTER SOUP (AUTHENTIC)
Mayerítsa

YIELD: 12 to 14 servings
TIME: Approximately 2½ hours

The traditional Easter soup called Mayeritsa is prepared only once a year—from the head, heart, liver, lungs, and intestines of a freshly killed young lamb. A bit of rice and fresh dill is added, and Avgolemono Sauce pulls it all together. Being squeamish, my sister and I wouldn't go near the kitchen when it was being prepared, let alone eat it, but I have to admit it smelled delectable.

According to relatives and friends I have consulted, this is how it is made if you really are a purist at heart. Following it is my recipe for Mayeritsa, American Style.

PREPARING THE LAMB

1 lamb's head, including brain, split in two
1 lamb's heart
1 lamb's lung
1 lamb's liver
½ pound lamb's intestines
2½ tablespoons lemon juice
10 cups cold water
1 tablespoon salt
½ teaspoon pepper
3 bunches scallions, finely minced
½ cup chopped fresh dill
2 sprigs fresh parsley, finely chopped
1 cup chopped celery leaves
3 tablespoons butter
½ cup long-grain rice

1. The lamb's head should be split in half and tied with string by the butcher. Soak for 3 hours in cold water to clean thoroughly; rinse well and retie with string.

2. Wash brain, heart, lung, and liver thoroughly in cold water. Run clean water from faucet through intestines to wash very well. Soak cleaned head and internal organs in cold water mixed with lemon juice for 1 hour, then drain.

3. Place all lamb parts in a large kettle with 10 cups cold water, add salt and pepper, and bring to a boil. Remove foam as it forms on top. Boil over medium heat until meat is tender (about 40 minutes) with the pot partially covered.

4. Sauté scallions, dill, parsley, and celery leaves in butter over low heat until limp.

5. Remove head from pot; this may be discarded or roasted with a sprinkling of oregano and used with a salad as another meal. Remove intestines and brain, chop finely, and set aside. Remove heart, liver, and lung and chop meat finely, discarding any cartilage or membranes, and set aside. Strain broth and return it to the pot setting aside 2 cups for the sauce. Bring to a boil, add all of the finely chopped meats and sautéed vegetables, and cook over medium heat for 1 more hour.

6. Add rice and boil gently with pot covered until rice is cooked (about 15 minutes).

MAKING THE AVGOLEMONO SAUCE

5 medium eggs, at room temperature
2 tablespoons lemon juice

Just before serving make Avgolemono Sauce: Beat eggs until thick. Beating continuously, slowly add lemon juice, then, slowly, the 1 or 2 cups warm broth. Quickly pour into hot soup, stirring furiously for a few seconds, and remove from heat at once.

NOTE: You may reheat any food containing Avgolemono Sauce slowly over low heat, but stir constantly and do not boil.

EASTER SOUP, AMERICAN STYLE
Mayerítsa Tis Amerikís

YIELD: 10 to 12 servings
TIME: Broth: 3 hours;
soup: 40 minutes

1½ pounds lean lamb
Uncooked lamb bones
    (if available)
½ pound lamb's liver
    (optional)

10 cups cold water
1 teaspoon salt
1 onion, sliced
1 carrot, sliced
1 stalk celery, with leaves,
    sliced

PREPARING THE LAMB BROTH

1. Rinse meat, bones, and liver, and place in large kettle with 10 cups cold water. Add salt and bring to a boil. Remove all foam as it appears. Add vegetables and simmer with kettle partially covered for about 3 hours.

2. Discard bones if you've used them. Remove meat and chop finely, eliminating any bits of sinew, fat, or gristle. Cover and refrigerate. Remove vegetables and discard. Strain broth into a clean bowl, cover, and refrigerate. Before making the soup, remove any fat that has formed a hard layer on top. You may do the broth a day or so in advance.

MAKING THE SOUP

3 bunches scallions, finely minced
2 sprigs fresh parsley, finely minced
½ cup finely minced fresh dill

1 cup finely minced celery
1 teaspoon salt
⅛ teaspoon black pepper
½ cup long-grain rice

Bring prepared lamb broth to a simmer in a large pot, then measure; add a little water if you don't have at least 8 full cups. Return broth to pot and bring to a boil. Add reserved cooked meat, scallions, parsley, dill, celery, salt, pepper, and rice. Bring rapidly to a second boil, then reduce heat, cover partially, and simmer for 30 minutes (or until rice and vegetables are completely cooked). Remove 1 or 2 cups of broth (without vegetables, rice, or meat) and set aside to cool. Remove pot from heat.

MAKING THE AVGOLEMONO SAUCE

1 tablespoon cornstarch
1 cup milk, at room temperature
3 egg yolks
2½ tablespoons lemon juice

In a blender, blend cornstarch in milk. Turn on machine and keep it on throughout; first beat cornstarch-milk mixture, then add egg yolks, then lemon juice, then the 1 or 2 cups slightly cooled broth, slowly. If beating by hand, first blend the cornstarch and milk in a mixing bowl with a whisk. Then beat in the egg yolks slowly and add the lemon juice and the broth gradually. Beat until smooth. When sauce is ready, immediately pour into hot soup, stirring furiously with a large spoon for a minute over low heat until soup starts to thicken; then remove pot from heat. Do not cover pot once sauce has been added, and do not allow soup to come to a boil. Serve at once.

HEALTH FRUIT SOUP
Heeló

YIELD: 6 to 8 servings
TIME: 30 minutes

If you have prepared Memorial Wheat (Kolliva; see recipe) for church, you have reserved the broth of the strained wheat you cooked. This broth makes a unique porridge-like soup full of nutrition. Sugar, fruit, tahini, and spices are added to taste, and it is then eaten hot.

Tahini resembles peanut butter in texture and consistency, but it is made of pounded sesame seeds in their oil. It can be purchased in the stores listed in the Shopper's Guide, health food stores, or gourmet shops.

Mastic, or *Mastiha*, is an important and unusual Greek flavoring. It comes from the mastic trees grown on the island of Chios, where my father was born. In August and September, the five million mastic trees are tapped by incising the bark and branches to make the trees "cry." A layer of fine sand is sprinkled on the ground around the base of each tree to catch the "tears." These tears, resembling bits of clear yellow glass, are then washed and pounded to a powder for use in cooking. Tiny packets of the crystals are sold as chewing gum on street corners in Greece.

Mastic is one of the main Greek exports, and in the days of the Turkish occupation the ladies of the sultan's harem were given the money from the proceeds of the mastic sales. Chios became so important as a money-earning island through its mastic plantations that it was granted its own parliament, but it was punishable by death for a Greek harvester to keep any of the mastic.

Widely used as a "sweet" flavoring, mastic can be purchased in the stores listed in the Shopper's Guide.

This soup is very easy to prepare. It may be served for breakfast, lunch, or as a soup course preceding a light dinner.

6 to 8 cups strained wheat broth
1-pound jar tahini
1 cup white seedless raisins
½ cup diced dried apricots

1 tablespoon cinnamon
1 teaspoon nutmeg
1 teaspoon ground Mastiha (optional)
1½ cups sugar (or to taste)

1. Bring wheat broth to a simmer in a 4-quart pot. Add tahini and stir until blended.

2. Add raisins and apricots and simmer until fruit is plump (about 8 minutes). Add spices and sugar to taste, stir well, and serve hot.

CUCUMBER YOGURT SOUP
Tzatzíki Soúpa

YIELD: 4 small servings
TIME: 10 minutes

This is an interesting thick soup to serve chilled during the hot summer days. If you chop the cucumber coarsely, instead of grating it, it may then be served as a salad.

1 large cucumber
2 cups plain yogurt
1 tablespoon olive oil
¾ tablespoon wine vinegar
¼ teaspoon salt or to taste

½ teaspoon finely chopped fresh mint
1 small clove garlic, crushed
Chopped fresh parsley

1. Peel cucumber and grate finely.

2. Blend together yogurt, olive oil, vinegar, salt, fresh mint, and garlic.

3. Add grated cucumber, stir well, and chill for at least 1 hour.

4. Sprinkle chopped parsley over the top of each serving.

SAUCES

Hot and Cold

Sauces play an important role in Greek cooking, and they are on the whole simple and very savory.

The two main cooked sauces are the Egg and Lemon (Avgolemono) and the basic White, or Béchamel, Sauce to which grated cheese or eggs are added, depending on the recipe being prepared.

For fresh salads, oil and vinegar are frequently used, and for cooked green vegetable salads a dressing of oil and lemon is quite popular. Garlic Sauce with fried fish or fried vegetables is a favorite of the Greeks.

EGG AND LEMON SAUCE
Sáltsa Avgolémono

YIELD: 1½ cups
TIME: 15 minutes

If you were to ask whether Greece has a national sauce, the answer would be "Saltsa Avgolemono."

The basic recipe is simple—egg and lemon juice beaten together and flavored with a little liquid from the dish the sauce will be used with. Avgolemono Sauce can be used in soups, stews, fish, vegetable, and even poultry recipes. It is never used, however, in any dish containing tomatoes. The tastes clash.

Some cooks never use egg whites, and so the entire sauce can easily be made in a blender (use 4 egg yolks in place of 3 whole eggs). To those who use egg whites as well as the yolks a whisk or electric beater is recommended.

There are two basic tricks to making this sauce. The first is continuous beating from start to finish of the sauce. The second is to add the liquid very slowly so that you do not curdle the eggs. (This is why all recipes tell you to take out a cup or two of the hot liquid and set aside to cool slightly before starting the sauce.)

If you must reheat any leftovers, do so over extremely low heat, stirring all the while. Never allow food to come to a boil once the Avgolemono Sauce has been added, or you will curdle the eggs.

3 large eggs, separated, at
room temperature
Tiny pinch salt
3 tablespoons lemon juice
1 tablespoon cornstarch
(optional)
1 cup slightly cooled stock or
broth (from accompanying
recipe)

1. Beat egg whites with salt until stiff.
2. Add yolks and continue beating.

3. Slowly, while beating, add lemon juice and, if you want a thicker sauce, the cornstarch.

4. Add stock or broth very slowly and continue beating for 1 minute.

5. Make sure the hot food you are preparing the sauce for is on very low heat; then pour sauce directly into it. Stir quickly several times until spoon is coated and sauce has slightly thickened. Never allow mixture to boil. Remove pot from heat and serve immediately, or, if you must delay, reheat sauce in a double boiler over low heat, stirring.

GARLIC SAUCE
Skorthaliá

YIELD: 2 cups
TIME: 45 minutes

This is the famous Skorthalia as it is made in villages, usually served over fried codfish or fried eggplant slices. It is good and strong—a delight for garlic fanciers.

Skorthalia is always served chilled, even over hot foods. In addition to being used over fried foods, it is good as a dip with an assortment of crisp raw vegetables. With boiled whole artichokes, serve 3 tablespoons alongside each artichoke as a dip.

¼ cup water
4 cloves garlic, crushed
½ teaspoon salt
2 medium potatoes, boiled
and mashed
½ cup finely ground blanched
almonds
¼ cup wine vinegar
1 cup olive oil

1. Put ingredients in order listed into mixer bowl or blender container. Mix or blend at high speed. (If using blender, mixture may be a bit thick. If so, turn off every couple of seconds and mix with a rubber spatula, then turn blender back on again.)

2. When sauce is white and creamy, pour into a bowl, cover, and refrigerate for at least 2 hours.

OIL AND LEMON SAUCE
Latholémono

YIELD: ½ cup
TIME: 5 minutes

This simple Greek sauce is used over grilled or poached fish, shrimp, or lobster as an alternative to mayonnaise. It is also poured over raw salads and cooked green vegetables. It can be used to baste broiling fish to prevent it from drying out. The sauce that is left over can then be put into a sauceboat or poured directly on top of the fish on the serving platter.

½ cup olive oil or light vegetable oil
2 tablespoons lemon juice
1 tablespoon chopped fresh parsley
Pinch salt
Pinch black pepper

Beat all ingredients together thoroughly and serve immediately.

OIL AND VINEGAR DRESSING
Lathóxitho

YIELD: 2 servings
TIME: 5 minutes

Throughout Greece this is the dressing most often used for salads. Most of us know it simply as vinaigrette sauce. On occasion you may add a pinch of dry mustard or a pinch of oregano depending on what the salad will accompany.

1 tablespoon olive oil
2 tablespoons vegetable oil
1 tablespoon wine vinegar
Pinch salt
Pinch black pepper

Shake in a jar or blend well with a fork and pour over salad.

YOGURT ALMOND SAUCE
Skorthaliá Me Yaoúrti

YIELD: 2 cups
TIME: 30 minutes

This mild variation of Skorthalia has a unique flavor and the consistency of sour cream. It should be served cold or at room temperature. Greeks almost always serve it with fried vegetables. It also makes an unusual dip served chilled with lots of crisp raw vegetables.

1 small clove garlic, crushed
8 blanched almonds, finely
  ground
¼ teaspoon almond extract
2 tablespoons olive oil

1½ tablespoons wine vinegar
2 cups plain yogurt
¼ teaspoon salt
¼ cup finely chopped fresh
  parsley

1. Combine garlic, almonds, almond extract, olive oil, and vinegar in a bowl.
2. Discard any excess water from yogurt. Add yogurt, salt, and parsley to bowl, and mix with a whisk until smooth.

WHITE SAUCE WITH CHEESE
Créma

YIELD: 4 cups
TIME: 30 minutes

They say the Greeks invented sauces more than twenty centuries ago. To the unknown chef who created the classic White Sauce so widely used in Greece today, we give our everlasting thanks; it differs from the European one by including a little cheese. It is a crucial ingredient in Moussaka and Pastitsio.

White Sauce is used over pastas, vegetables, fish, or for au gratin dishes. Reheat it when needed (either when frozen or done ahead of time) in top of double boiler over simmering water, stirring occasionally, until hot.

1 quart milk	¼ teaspoon white pepper
¼ pound unsalted butter	¼ teaspoon grated nutmeg
4 tablespoons all-purpose flour	4 tablespoons grated
1 teaspoon salt	Kefalotyri or Parmesan
	cheese

1. Heat milk just to boiling and set aside.

2. Heat butter in a 4-quart heavy-bottomed saucepan over low heat. Gradually stir in flour with wooden spoon until smooth, stirring constantly for 3 to 5 minutes.

3. Add hot milk slowly, stirring vigorously with a wire whisk all the time, and cook over low heat for about 10 minutes, until sauce is smooth and thick, like cream.

4. Remove from heat and stir in salt, pepper, nutmeg, and grated cheese.

FREEZING

Cool the sauce, pack in a covered container, and freeze.

BROWNED BUTTER SAUCE
Kafteró Voútiro

YIELD: 1 cup
TIME: 10 minutes

When you don't feel like making tomato sauce, nothing could be tastier over pasta or rice than simple browned butter with grated cheese. A pepper mill should be on the table for those who prefer the tang of a little freshly ground pepper.

A pound of pasta will serve 6 people; 1½ cups rice will serve 6.

½ pound butter for each pound of pasta,
or 1½ cups rice
Grated Kefalotyri or Parmesan cheese

1. Melt butter over medium heat until butter turns a dark tan, stirring frequently; do not let burn.

2. Immediately pour over cooked hot pasta or rice and toss to coat well. Sprinkle liberally with grated cheese and serve on a heated platter.

CHEESE SALAD DRESSING
Kopanistí Yiá Saláta

YIELD: 1 cup
TIME: 5 minutes

In the Greek cuisine, if a sharp cheese dressing is desired, Kopanisti is used. Kopanisti is imported in jars to this country, but if you cannot obtain it, you may use Roquefort or blue cheese. The dressing won't be the same, of course, but blue-veined cheeses are reasonable substitutes.

This dressing should be added to salad greens just before serving. Toss with only enough dressing to coat the leaves adequately. Since the dressing is sharp, any meats accompanying salad should be only lightly seasoned.

⅔ cup light vegetable or olive oil or equal mixture of both
⅓ cup wine vinegar
¼ teaspoon black pepper
¼ teaspoon sugar
¼ cup crumbled Kopanisti cheese
½ teaspoon Worcestershire sauce
Salt (optional)

Combine all ingredients in a blender or screw-topped jar. Whirl or shake to blend. Taste the dressing. Add a pinch of salt only if required (some cheese batches are saltier than others; but usually you won't need it). Refrigerate.

BOBBY'S YOGURT DRESSING FOR FRUIT
Yaoúrti Me Froúta Tis Várvaras

YIELD: Approximately 2 cups
TIME: 5 minutes

The climate of Greece is similar to that of California, and as a result the assortment of fruit grown in such a small nation boggles the mind. There are oranges, grapes, apples, peaches, pears, nectarines, apricots, melons, figs, cherries, strawberries, watermelons, pomegranates, prickly pears, mulberries, and even bananas.

The Greeks love fresh fruit and often serve it peeled and sliced with either sugar sprinkled over it or chilled plain yogurt.

My friend Bobby once prepared a Greek dinner but was faced with the dilemma of knowing that some of her guests weren't fond of plain yogurt. So she bought some strawberry yogurt and added cream cheese to it. The result was out of this world, and it only took minutes to prepare.

You might arrange watermelon balls, sliced bananas, sliced peaches, orange and grapefruit sections, and honeydew and cantaloupe balls on an iced platter, leaving room in the center for a small bowl containing this dressing. Let the guests help themselves. Greeks serve this fruit salad as often before as after dinner.

3-ounce package cream cheese, at room temperature
2 8-ounce containers strawberry yogurt, well chilled
Ripe fresh fruit in season, chilled

1. Put softened cream cheese and strawberry yogurt into blender. Blend at high speed for a few seconds.

2. Spoon over fruit and serve cold.

SALADS AND VEGETABLE DISHES

Combinations from the Garden

Although I have included the traditional Greek salad, I must point out that to the Greeks a salad does not necessarily mean the raw fresh green variety we have grown accustomed to. The Greeks are also fond of many different types of wild greens, simply boiled, drained, and dressed with a little olive oil and lemon juice. Dandelion leaves and wild chicory head the list. The water from these drained vegetables is saved, refrigerated, and served as a vegetable pick-me-up. I was told as a child that if I wanted to have a beautiful complexion I would have to learn to drink it. I did learn to like it and, as a matter of fact, I didn't suffer the usual trauma of teenage acne.

Any cooked dried beans, mixed with chopped onion, herbs, olive oil, and lemon juice, are considered a salad. The same applies to purées of cooked vegetables.

Summing it up, all vegetables, hot or cold, cooked or un-cooked, are Salatika, which literally means salad vegetables.

GREEK STRING BEAN SALAD
Fasolákia Salátes

YIELD: 6 servings
TIME: 8 to 15 minutes

The most prevalent green vegetable in Greece is the string bean, in many different varieties. Whether green, yellow, mottled, flat, or rounded, the beans you pick should be firm and crisp. Fresh beans are infinitely tastier than frozen beans and well worth the time you spend snipping off the tips.

In Greek cities beans are bought in the vegetable stalls, or stores, but elsewhere women go "out back" and pick what they need just before cooking them. They are a staple of any small garden plot.

2 pounds fresh string beans
1½ teaspoons salt
1 quart water
6 tablespoons olive oil

2 tablespoons lemon juice
Minced onion
Finely chopped parsley

1. Wash beans and trim off ends. Add salt and beans to boiling water, and cook until beans are tender, about 8 to 10 minutes. Drain beans and pour cold water over them to keep them green.

2. Put beans in a bowl, add olive oil and lemon juice, toss well, and refrigerate.

3. About 20 minutes before serving, decorate with onion and parsley. Serve at room temperature.

VARIATIONS

After beans are cooked and drained, add 6 tablespoons olive oil, 2 tablespoons lemon juice, and 1 clove of crushed garlic. Toss all together and serve warm or at room temperature.

After beans are cooked and drained, add 6 tablespoons olive oil, 2 tablespoons wine vinegar, 4 chopped scallions, and a dash of black pepper. Toss and refrigerate. Twenty minutes before serving, sprinkle with finely minced hard-boiled egg.

After beans are cooked and drained, add 6 tablespoons olive oil, 2 tablespoons lemon juice, ⅛ teaspoon black pepper, 1 teaspoon salt, and 1 raw onion, sliced finely. Toss well, and serve hot or at room temperature.

ORANGE AND OLIVE SALAD
Portokália Me Eliés

YIELD: 4 servings
TIME: 20 minutes

This simple and unusual salad is often prepared in Greece, where both oranges and olives flourish. It adds color and zest to any meal.

2 large thick-skinned eating oranges
16 large black Greek olives
1 white onion, sliced thinly and blanched, or 1 sweet red onion, sliced thinly
1 tablespoon olive oil
1 tablespoon lemon juice
Pinch salt
Pinch pepper
Lettuce leaves

1. Peel oranges and slice as thinly as possible, discarding seeds and white membranes.
2. If using olives with pits, remove pits with the kitchen gadget for pitting olives, or do it by hand; if olives look too ragged, dice them.
3. If using white onion, blanch it by placing in a colander and pouring 1 quart boiling water over it. Red onions, being sweeter, don't require blanching.
4. Combine olives, onion, oranges, olive oil, and lemon juice. Add salt and pepper, and toss until well blended.
5. Refrigerate at least 3 hours, then serve on lettuce leaves.

TOMATO SALAD
Domatosaláta

YIELD: 4 servings
TIME: 25 minutes

When tomatoes are in season, the Greeks make this salad almost daily.

5 ripe tomatoes
1 large red onion, very thinly
    sliced
½ tablespoon salt (or to taste)

3 tablespoons olive oil
2 teaspoons oregano
1 teaspoon wine vinegar
    (optional)

1. Peel tomatoes. To remove skin easily, drop tomatoes into boiling water to cover for 10 seconds. Remove at once. When tomatoes are cool enough to handle, cut out stem and peel off skin starting from the stem hole. Refrigerate until cold.
2. Place onion in a shallow salad bowl, sprinkle with salt, and leave for 10 minutes, turning once or twice.
3. Quarter the peeled cold tomatoes and add to the salad bowl.
4. Add olive oil and oregano (at our house we always put in wine vinegar too, but this is a matter of personal taste).
5. Toss salad gently so you do not bruise the tomatoes, but make sure you coat the onions and tomatoes lightly with the oil.

MARINATED PEPPER SALAD
Peperiés Orektiká

YIELD: 4 servings
TIME: 30 minutes

3 large green bell peppers
½ teaspoon salt
¼ teaspoon black pepper
4 large shallots or 1 small onion,
    very finely chopped
½ teaspoon oregano

2 tablespoons olive oil
2 tablespoons light vegetable
    oil
2 tablespoons wine vinegar
Pimiento strips

1. Wash peppers and bake in preheated 450° oven for 20 minutes or until skins blister and peppers become wilted.

2. Remove skins, scoop out seeds, and cut into narrow strips.

3. Sprinkle with salt, pepper, chopped shallots or onion, oregano, oils, and vinegar, and toss lightly. Refrigerate overnight.

4. Serve at room temperature with pimiento for garnish.

GREEK SALAD
Elleniki Saláta

YIELD: 6 to 8 servings
TIME: 20 minutes

The Greek philosopher Aristoxenus is said to have loved lettuce so much that he watered his lettuce garden with the sweet wine from Chios. I've often wondered if he loved the wine more than the lettuce.

Greeks use all kinds of lettuce and salad greens—romaine, hearts of endive, chicory, and escarole. What they can't grow they import. In this salad, however, they prefer to use iceberg lettuce.

Strangely enough, one never sees lettuce torn in a true Greek salad: it is always finely sliced. The success of any salad depends on choosing young garden-fresh greens. Leaves should be separated, washed under cold running water, and drained. They should then be wrapped in a clean bath towel and refrigerated. The towel will absorb the water from the leaves. If the leaves are wet, the dressing won't coat them, thus thinning out the flavor.

In a Greek salad anything can show up, from a few fresh garden peas to finely cut raw string beans along with the other greens. In some parts of Greece you may discover the salad built over a mound of homemade potato salad. The Greek salad, like the Greek personality, is usually full of surprises. So use your own personal preferences and your grocer's supply, but remember that the salad must always be cold, the vegetables fresh, and the pieces small enough to eat easily but large enough to identify. The dressing, of course, is always added just before tossing, at the last possible moment before serving. If using garnishes, quickly place these on top of your salad and bring the bowl to the table.

The amount of salt in the recipe that follows is very low for a salad this size because of the saltiness of the anchovies and the Feta cheese. The dash of Worcestershire sauce is a modern innovation, but it adds to the flavor of the dressing.

1 large head iceberg lettuce or equivalent combination of crisp lettuces and salad greens
6 scallion bulbs or 8 shallots, minced
1 large cucumber, peeled and thinly sliced
2 tablespoons finely cut fresh parsley or watercress
6 radishes, sliced
½ green bell pepper, slivered
¼ cup olive oil

¼ cup corn oil
¼ cup tarragon or wine vinegar
⅛ teaspoon salt (or to taste)
¼ teaspoon black pepper
10 capers
½ teaspoon Worcestershire sauce (optional)
6 to 8 wedges Feta cheese
2 large ripe tomatoes, quartered
6 to 8 large Greek olives
6 to 8 anchovy filets

1. Cut lettuce in half from top to base. Lay flat and with a sharp knife slice thinly, then shred. Place in a large salad bowl and add scallions or shallots, cucumber, parsley or watercress, radishes, and green pepper. Cover and refrigerate until serving.

2. Place oils, vinegar, salt, pepper, capers, and Worcestershire sauce in a jar, seal, and refrigerate.

3. Just before serving, shake dressing well and pour over.the salad and toss thoroughly. Garnish with Feta cheese, tomatoes, olives, and anchovies.

VEGETABLES A LA GRECQUE
Láhana Marináta

YIELD: 6 servings
TIME: 2 hours preparation;
12 hours marinating

"Vegetables à la Grecque" appears throughout the world on menus and is justly famous, but the Greeks simply refer to this manner of preparation as marinated vegetables. The vegetables are simmered in a fragrant broth of water, wine, herbs, oil, and seasonings. They are then removed to a serving platter, where they are tastefully arranged. The marinade, boiled down, is poured over the cooked vegetables, and the entire platter is refrigerated until chilled.

You can prepare 2 pounds of string beans or an assortment of whatever vegetables you have on hand. If cooking an assortment, I would strongly advise cooking each group separately so that you can control the degree of tenderness desired. Assorted vegetables should be arranged creatively with regard to color and texture before being refrigerated. Just before serving, sprinkle them with chopped fresh parsley and garnish with lemon wedges.

1 cup dry white wine	2 stalks fresh fennel or
4 cups water	½ teaspoon fennel seeds
¾ cup olive oil	2 sprigs fresh thyme or
½ cup lemon juice	½ teaspoon dried thyme
3 teaspoons salt	12 peppercorns, cracked
2 cloves garlic, thinly sliced	12 coriander seeds, cracked
10 sprigs parsley	2 pounds vegetables (string
1 large celery stalk with	beans or an assortment)
leaves, washed and peeled	

1. Combine all ingredients except the 2 pounds of vegetables in a 3- or 4-quart pot and bring to a boil. Cover pot, reduce heat, and simmer very slowly for 1 hour.

2. Strain cooked marinade through a fine sieve into a bowl and press down to extract every last bit of taste before discarding vegetables and spices. Pour clear marinade back into the pot.

3. Wash and trim whatever vegetables you're using (see Notes below) and simmer in marinade until tender. Lift out with slotted spoon and arrange tastefully on a platter.

4. Boil marinade down until you have 1 cup marinade left.

5. Pour marinade over vegetables and allow to cool. Cover and refrigerate at least 12 hours.

NOTES

If cooking onions

Use tiny pearl onions or the smallest onions you can get. Peel and make a cross on the bottom of each onion. Drop the onions in the boiling marinade and cover the pot. Turn heat down to simmer and let them cook until they can be pierced easily with the point of a sharp knife but still retain their shape, about 20 minutes. Remove carefully with a slotted spoon to a large shallow platter.

If cooking green and red sweet bell peppers

Cut the peppers lengthwise; then wash them and remove seeds and ribs. Slice or quarter peppers and simmer for 10 minutes in the marinade, covered. Remove with slotted spoon to the serving platter.

If cooking mushrooms

If mushrooms are firm and white, do not peel them; just rub them gently under cold running water. If mushrooms are not looking their best, then and only then, peel them. If very large, cut in half or quarter them. If small, leave whole. Simmer in the marinade for about 15 minutes, covered. Remove with slotted spoon to serving platter.

If cooking zucchini or squash

Wash, scrub, trim ends, and cut into 1-inch lengths. Drop into marinade, cover pot, and simmer until tender, about 8 minutes. Remove with a slotted spoon to serving platter.

If cooking eggplant

Cut eggplant crosswise into slices ½ inch thick. Sprinkle liberally with salt. Place in a colander and weight with a plate and a heavy object. This extracts moisture and rids eggplant of any bitter taste. Allow slices to drain for 1 hour. Rinse off eggplant slices, pat dry, then stack the slices and remove skin. Then cut into 2-inch squares. Simmer the squares, covered, in marinade until tender, about 15 minutes. Lift out with slotted spoon and place on platter.

If cooking artichoke hearts

If using frozen artichoke hearts, defrost until separated, drop into marinade, and simmer covered for about 15 minutes. Lift out with slotted spoon and place on serving platter.

POTATO AND PEPPER OMELET
Omelétta Me Patátes Ke Peperiés

YIELD: 4 servings
TIME: 1 hour

Greeks make tomato omelets, potato omelets, onion omelets, fish, cheese, and sausage omelets. They are all good, and most have fancy names. The following favorite, which you can proudly serve for lunch or dinner, is sometimes called the Gardener's Omelet. As children, my sister Lita and I always put catsup over it. This outraged our mother, who insisted it be served with freshly sliced tomatoes. We think it still tastes great with catsup over it.

6 tablespoons butter
½ small onion or 2 large scallion bulbs, finely chopped
1 green bell pepper, very thinly sliced
1 large raw potato, sliced shoestring style
¼ teaspoon white pepper

1 tablespoon warm water
6 large eggs, at room temperature
Salt
2 tablespoons crumbled Feta or grated Kefalotyri or Parmesan cheese
½ tablespoon chopped fresh parsley

1. Melt 3 tablespoons of the butter in a large skillet, and sauté onions and green pepper until soft. Remove with a slotted spoon and set aside.

2. Add the rest of the butter to the frying pan and fry the potatoes until crisp and brown (about 20 minutes). Remove pan from heat.

3. Add pepper and 1 tablespoon warm water to the eggs. Add ¼ teaspoon salt if using Feta cheese (since it is salty) or 1 teaspoon salt if using other cheese. Whip with a whisk until fluffy.

4. Return sautéed onions and green peppers to the pan and mix with the fried potatoes. Sprinkle with cheese and chopped parsley.

5. Pour egg mixture over the vegetables and cook over medium heat until eggs have set. Do not fold this type of an omelet; just slide it onto a hot serving platter. Or if you are using a decorative frying pan, take it directly to the table.

CAULIFLOWER MACEDONIAN
Kounoupíthi Apó Tin Makethonía

YIELD: 8 to 10 servings
TIME: 45 minutes

The ancient Greeks believed that if you ate cabbages before drinking it would prevent hangovers. I've never tested that theory, but stuffing oneself full of cabbage leaves would certainly dampen any inclination for lots of liquor. No drinking, no hangover—I suppose that's how that theory got started.

An ancient phrase used even today in Greece refers to the common cabbage. When a friend starts to put on airs and you would like him to realize it you say, "Spouthea ta lahana," which means, "How magnificent are the cabbages." This makes him laugh and apologize, for cabbages aren't considered magnificent at all.

Cauliflower and broccoli are the more advanced forms of cabbages. All types of cabbages are among the richest and least expensive sources of vitamin C, so use and enjoy them often.

When preparing cabbages for any recipe, pre-boil them for 5 minutes uncovered; then drain and rinse them with cold water. This step rids all members of the cabbage family of their gassiness. Use a covered pot when you start the actual cooking.

As a side dish, Greeks simply boil the various forms of cabbages in salted water until fairly soft, then drain them and serve with a dressing of olive oil and lemon juice. When used to garnish the Sunday roast, however, they are often cooked as in this recipe.

When shopping for cauliflower remember to buy only a hard, white head. It should not be bruised or discolored, and the outer leaves must be green and crisp.

1 large head cauliflower
1½ teaspoons salt
1 thin slice lemon
1 large egg, at room temperature
⅛ teaspoon white pepper

1 cup milk, at room temperature
1 cup bread crumbs, zwieback crumbs, or Spiced Biscuits crumbs (see recipe)
¼ pound butter or ½ cup light oil

1. Rinse cauliflower and remove all leaves. Cut a deep cross in core of cauliflower but do not separate from head. Place enough water in large, *uncovered* pot to cover entire cauliflower head, add cauliflower, and boil rapidly for 5 minutes. Drain and rinse in cold water.

2. Boil fresh water in a pot and add 1 teaspoon salt, lemon slice (this keeps the cauliflower nice and white), and the head of cauliflower stem downward. The water should be able to reach the flowerets but not quite cover them. Cover pot and cook cauliflower over medium heat until soft but not falling apart (about 20 minutes depending on size). Remove from heat, drain, and set aside to cool.

3. Beat the egg, ½ teaspoon salt, and pepper lightly with a fork in a small bowl and set aside.

4. Cut cauliflower into slices ½ inch thick. Dip them first into egg mixture, then into milk, then into crumbs. Pat well so that crumbs adhere. Fry in hot butter or oil until golden. Drain on paper toweling, and serve immediately.

FRIED EGGPLANT
Melitzána Tiganití

YIELD: 12 slices
TIME: 50 minutes

If the Greeks had to choose one vegetable above all others, I believe the eggplant would easily win. Serve this dish with Garlic Sauce or Yogurt Almond Sauce (see recipes) in a separate bowl. For other eggplant recipes, see the Appetizer and the Meat chapters.

1 large eggplant
Salt
5 tablespoons all-purpose flour
1 cup olive oil

1. Rinse eggplant, and cut it crosswise into ½-inch slices. Pare each slice. Sprinkle lightly with salt, stack in a colander, and

place a plate on top. Weight plate with a heavy object; let stand for at least 30 minutes. (This macerating draws out moisture and eliminates the slight bitterness of eggplant.)

2. Remove eggplant, dry each slice well, and dredge in flour.

3. Heat half the oil in a large frying pan until hot but not smoking. Fry several slices at a time until crisp and golden on both sides; keep your eye on them, since they burn easily. Drain on paper toweling. If oil gets used up, heat remaining oil and fry the rest of the eggplant slices. Serve hot or at room temperature.

VARIATIONS

As a garnish for roasts and poultry: Dip eggplant slices in egg seasoned with salt and pepper, roll in bread crumbs; fry in a combination of hot oil and butter.

To deep-fry eggplant: Cut eggplant slices into strips the size of a finger. Use seasoned egg and bread crumbs as in preceding paragraph, then deep-fry until golden and crisp.

FRIED ZUCCHINI
Tiganitá Kolokithákia

YIELD: Approximately 20 slices
TIME: 30 minutes

Zucchini grows abundantly throughout Greece, and the smaller the zucchini the better the Greeks like it—I've never seen one in the marketplace over 6 inches long.

Serve Fried Zucchini with Garlic Sauce or Yogurt Almond Sauce (see recipes), poured from a sauceboat. Eat hot or at room temperature.

1½ pounds zucchini (3 to 4 squash)
Salt
    4 tablespoons all-purpose flour
    ½ cup olive oil

1. Scrub and rinse the zucchini, slice them lengthwise ¼ inch or less thick, then lay them flat on paper toweling. Sprinkle lightly with salt and allow to sit undisturbed for 15 minutes to exude moisture.

2. Pat each slice completely dry and dredge in flour. Heat oil in a large frying pan until hot but not smoking. Fry zucchini slices, watching them carefully so they won't burn, until crisp and golden brown (about 2 minutes per side). Drain on paper toweling for a few minutes before arranging on a warm platter.

COLD ZUCCHINI SALAD
Saláta Kolokithákia

YIELD: Approximately 20 slices
TIME: 10 minutes

Although the Greeks serve this salad chilled, I find it's every bit as good eaten warm.

1½ pounds zucchini (3 to 4 squash)
1½ teaspoons salt
3 tablespoons olive oil
1 tablespoon wine vinegar
3 tablespoons chopped parsley

1. Scrub, rinse, and boil small whole zucchini in salted water to cover until tender, about 10 minutes. Drain and refrigerate until cold.

2. Before serving, slice zucchini crosswise into ¼-inch slices. Place in a shallow bowl and sprinkle with oil, vinegar, and chopped parsley. Serve with cold roast meats or fried fish.

VARIATION

Plain boiled and chilled zucchini is also very good with a Garlic Sauce or Yogurt Almond Sauce (see recipes).

BAKED VEGETABLE CASSEROLE
Láhana Stó Foúrno

YIELD: 4 to 6 servings as a side dish
TIME: 2 hours

This exceptional dish is prepared as a main course in Greece during religious holidays when meat is forbidden. I prepare it in place of salads as a side dish at least twice a month.

In Turkey it is called toulou tava; in France, ratatouille. Although prepared in somewhat the same manner, this recipe acquires a different taste because of the amount of dill, oil, and tomato used.

If serving as the main course, serve with wedges of rinsed Feta cheese, a crusty bread, and a rosé wine.

This dish is usually served hot in the United States, but in Greece it is always served at room temperature or chilled. Leftovers reheated in the oven or right on top of the stove taste even better the second or third time around.

½ pound fresh string beans, trimmed

½ pound fresh sliced okra, or peeled and cubed eggplant (optional)

1 large potato, peeled and cut into ½-inch slices

2 medium zucchini, cut into ½-inch slices

2 stalks celery, cut into 1-inch pieces

1 large onion, quartered

2 cloves garlic, finely minced

½ cup chopped parsley

1½ tablespoons chopped fresh dill or ½ tablespoon dried dill

2 teaspoons salt (or to taste)

½ teaspoon black pepper (or to taste)

½ pound tomatoes, fresh or canned

Approximately 2 cups boiling water

3½ tablespoons olive oil

1. Place all cut-up vegetables except tomatoes in a large mixing bowl. Add garlic, parsley, dill, salt, and pepper.

2. If using fresh tomatoes, remove skin (dip tomatoes in boiling water for 10 seconds, then peel) and slice. If using canned tomatoes, crush them well. Add tomatoes to the vegetables and toss gently.

3. Arrange vegetables in a 4-quart baking dish or casserole, leaving some room at the top.

4. Pour boiling water slowly over vegetables to *nearly* cover them; then pour the olive oil on top of the vegetables. Cover and bake in preheated 450° oven for 15 minutes, then reduce heat to 350°. Bake for 1½ hours or until vegetables are tender and soft.

BOILED ARTICHOKES
Angináres Vrastés

YIELD: 8 servings
TIME: 30 to 40 minutes

When buying fresh artichokes, choose only those that are heavy and have close green leaves all the way to the tips. The stem should also be green and fresh. Do not buy artichokes that feel hollow or are discolored.

8 medium artichokes
Juice of 1 lemon
Salt

1. Break off small leaves at the base and then break off coarse outer layer of leaves.

2. Scrape off the tough fibers of the stem with a knife. Bend the stem until a part of it snaps off; then trim the crisp remaining end so the artichoke will have a nice solid base to stand on.

3. Lay artichoke on its side and cut 1 inch off the top of the center cone of leaves with a sharp knife.

4. With scissors trim the points off the rest of the leaves, and wash artichokes under cold running water.

5. Rub artichokes with a cut lemon to prevent discoloration and drop them into a bowl of cold water, squeezing into it the juice of 1 lemon.

6. Always cook artichokes in enamel, stainless steel, or Pyrex. Fill a large pot with water and add 1½ teaspoons salt for each quart of water. When it comes to a rapid boil drop in artichokes, cover pot, and cook over medium heat for 30 to 40 minutes, de-

pending on size. Artichokes are cooked when leaves pull out easily and bottoms are tender when pierced with a knife. Remove the artichokes with a slotted spoon and drain upside down in a colander.

7. Removing the choke: Although this is not absolutely necessary, it seems to me that if you are going to go through all the trouble of cleaning the artichoke you might as well go one step further to create perfection. The choke, the purple feathery center of the artichoke, should not be eaten. When artichokes are cool enough to handle, gently spread center leaves apart. Reach into the center and pull out the center cone of tender leaves and set aside. Farther down in the center and covering the heart is the choke. Scrape it out with a teaspoon.

8. Turn the cone of tender leaves upside down and set it back into the hollow of the vegetable.

9. To eat the artichoke, pull off a leaf with your fingers and dip into sauce. Scrape off the tender flesh of the artichoke between your teeth. Set "used-up" leaf aside, and continue until you have gone all through the leaves. When you then come to the heart and stem, use your knife and fork to eat it. (If you are ever served the artichoke and the fuzzy choke still covers the heart, scrape it off with your knife before proceeding to eat the heart.)

SERVING SUGGESTIONS

Artichokes can be served warm or cold. As a sauce for warm ones, set out a small dish of cold Garlic Sauce or Yogurt Almond Sauce (see recipes) or a small dish of hot melted butter with lemon juice squeezed into it. The same cold Garlic Sauce or Yogurt Almond Sauce goes well with cold artichokes, or you can serve them with a bowl of vinaigrette or mayonnaise.

Make sure each artichoke is placed on a plate large enough for all the "used-up" leaves to be pushed to one side while artichoke is being eaten.

I like a white Retsina wine with artichokes, but many wine experts say only water should be served, because the flavor of wine is changed when drunk with this vegetable.

ARTICHOKES PILAF
Anginàres Piláfi

YIELD: 2 to 3 servings as main course;
6 servings as side dish
TIME: 30 minutes

One day my husband, the dogs, and I drove to Loutraki, famous for its mineral waters. It is approximately forty miles from Athens on the way to the Corinth canal. Tourists, Greek as well as foreign, come from miles away to undergo special baths or sip from the Loutraki springs.

During the summer it is a bustling, charming little community, but in the fall and winter the hotels are shuttered, most of the cafés are closed, and the majority of the working people go to the large cities to seek other employment. On the day we arrived, Loutraki looked almost like a ghost town. At the end of the town we found ourselves on a road that seemed to lead in one direction only, straight up. We decided to see where it would lead us. There were large full trees along the road, a rare sight in Greece, where many wars have left vast areas barren. The road, still leading upward, became extremely narrow and increasingly winding.

We'd been on this tortuous track over an hour when we suddenly found ourselves in a lush valley. A valley high in the mountains, with a little village snuggled in the center of it. Men were bent over in the fertile fields, singing as they worked. People smiled and waved at us as we entered the village. Women were sitting in doorways spinning wool on notched sticks.

There were healthy animals everywhere—sheep whose fleece really looked as white as snow, donkeys, goats, and horses—all feeding on the luxuriant grasses. Birds seemed to be on every limb. We felt as though we had found Shangri-la.

The air was crisp, clean, and sunny. Even the people seemed different. Most conspicuous was the slight but definite Oriental aura about their features—slanted eyes and high cheekbones. Their skin, bronzed by the sun, glowed with an incredible rosy hue, and no one seemed tense or nervous. The entire atmosphere had a sense of unreality.

I wish I could tell you that we stopped and had lunch, or

spoke to some of the friendly, smiling people, but we didn't. Although we smiled back, we felt as though we had intruded on their private world, and we became unexpectedly introverted and shy. Another of civilization's imprints upon modern man's personality, I guess.

Later, back at our hotel, we found out that because of the valley's unique location, it gets more rainfall than any other part of Greece. And because it is so inaccessible, conquerors usually left its inhabitants alone. The valley is self-sustaining, and the people rarely leave the village, which we discovered was called Para Hora (City Beyond).

If we had lunched there, I would like to think we would have eaten an artichoke pilaf, an almost utopian dish.

Pilaf is usually made with meat or chicken stock, but it can also be cooked in water. The following recipe is a superb example. Serve it with a hot green vegetable and a dry white wine.

9-ounce package frozen
   artichoke hearts or 8½-
   ounce can artichoke hearts
1 small onion or 4 shallots,
   finely minced
3 tablespoons butter
1 tablespoon tomato paste

1 teaspoon salt
¼ teaspoon white pepper
1 cup long-grain rice
Small dish freshly grated
   Kefalotyri or Parmesan
   cheese or slices of Feta
   cheese, rinsed

1. Cook frozen artichoke hearts for half the time specified on package and drain. If you must use canned ones, rinse them well and drain.

2. In a 2-quart casserole, sauté onion or shallots in butter over low heat until soft and transparent. Add artichoke hearts and sauté over low heat for 3 minutes. Add tomato paste and stir gently to coat artichoke hearts (if using canned ones, only sauté with tomato paste, not separately). Sauté for another 3 minutes and then carefully lift out the artichokes and set aside.

3. Stir into butter and tomato paste exact amount of water for rice as per instructions for brand you are using. Raise heat to high and add salt and pepper. When water comes to a full boil, add rice and stir with a fork only once. Place the artichoke hearts back into casserole but do not stir. Cover pot tightly. Reduce heat to simmer and cook until rice is done (about 25 minutes).

4. A side dish of fresly grated cheese should be on the table for those who wish to sprinkle some over the rice. Or, if preferred, serve a dish of Feta cheese slices.

ARTICHOKES IN ONION SAUCE
Angináres Me Sálsa Kreméthia

YIELD: 8 servings as an appetizer;
4 servings as a vegetable dinner
TIME: 1 hour

A favored dish with Greeks when artichokes are in season. You will see many versions of this recipe in tavernas and hotels as well as in private homes. It is served as a Meze (appetizer) or as a main meal. It is extremely popular during Lent.

8 medium artichokes
½ lemon
3 large onions, finely chopped
½ pound small whole onions, peeled
1 cup olive oil
5 tablespoons lemon juice

2 teaspoons salt
½ teaspoon white pepper
1 tablespoon flour
1 cup water
½ cup finely minced parsley or ¼ cup chopped fresh dill

1. Clean artichokes (see page 65). Cut in half from top through stem. Remove feathery choke with a sharp knife. Rub artichokes with half a lemon to prevent them from darkening.

2. Spread chopped and whole onions in a 3-quart saucepan; then place artichokes, cut side up, in the pan; they will be stacked. Mix together the olive oil, lemon juice, salt, and pepper, and pour this over the artichokes.

3. Mix flour in water until smooth and pour into sides of pan. Sprinkle parsley or dill over the artichokes.

4. Cover with a heavy dinner plate, then cover pan with lid and cook over medium-low heat for about 50 minutes or until tender. Allow to cool in the sauce.

5. Remove artichokes to a platter and surround with the cooked whole onions. Spoon onion sauce over each artichoke and serve at room temperature or chilled.

SWEET AND SOUR GREEN TOMATO PRESERVES
Prásines Domátes (Glykó Toursí)

YIELD: 5 quarts
TIME: 1 hour preparation;
      overnight draining;
      4 hours cooking

If you live near a tomato farm (or have gardener friends who don't know what to do with their tomatoes, particularly in the fall, when a threatened frost may kill the green tomatoes), put up this tangy relish preserve. It's great with boiled, fried, or roasted meats. The Greeks serve this in winter when tomatoes are not available.

15 pounds green tomatoes
5 large green bell peppers
3 pounds onions, peeled
½ cup salt
5 pounds brown sugar

2 quarts cider vinegar
1 box (1¼ ounces) mixed
    pickle spices, tied in
    cheesecloth bag

1. Slice tomatoes, peppers, and onions thinly. Sprinkle with the salt and allow to stand overnight.
2. Drain in the morning and add remaining ingredients. Simmer over very low heat for 4 hours, stirring occasionally to prevent sticking.
3. Discard cheesecloth bag containing spices. Ladle vegetables and liquid into hot sterilized jars and seal at once. Allow sealed jars to remain upright and undisturbed for 14 hours.
4. Label and date jars and place them in a dark cool place.

FAMILY-STYLE TIROPETA
Tirópeta Tou Spetioú

YIELD: 12 to 16 servings
TIME: 2 hours

For family dinners or a hot buffet, an excellent dish to make would be a large baking pan of Tiropeta and Spanokopeta, which can be cut into squares.

Double the cheese mixture for Tiropetes or use the cheese and spinach mixture for Spanokopetes (see recipe). Butter pan (11 by 14 by 2 inches) and line it with about 10 sheets of Phyllo, each individually brushed with warm melted butter. Spread cheese mixture on top. Cover with about 10 more individually buttered Phyllo sheets on top of one another. Roll or push edges of Phyllo down all around the pan to hold in mixture. Brush entire top and edges with warm melted butter. If using homemade Phyllo, place only 2 sheets on bottom and 2 sheets on top of baking pan.

Lightly score Phyllo top into squares with a sharp knife—this is to guide you when you cut and serve it. Sprinkle with about 10 drops of warm water to prevent Phyllo from curling while baking (unnecessary if using homemade Phyllo). Bake in a 350° preheated oven for about 35 minutes or until golden brown. Remove pan from oven and allow to sit for 5 minutes, then cut into squares. Serve warm or hot.

BEAN SALAD
Fasólia Vrastá

YIELD: 6 servings as main course;
10 servings as side dish
TIME: 1 hour preparation;
1¼ hours cooking

This simple but flavorful bean salad shows up on every Greek buffet table both here and abroad. Serve at room temperature or slightly chilled.

1 pound dried beans (navy, white, broad, or lima)	1½ teaspoons salt
	½ teaspoon black pepper
¾ cup olive oil	3 large onions, finely
½ cup lemon juice or wine vinegar	chopped
	½ cup minced parsley

1. Rinse beans, then cover with about 2½ cups water. Bring to a boil, boil 2 minutes, and let stand for 1 hour. Drain.

2. Bring 4 cups water to a boil, add drained beans, cover, and simmer until tender (about 1¼ hours). Drain.

3. Mix oil, lemon juice or vinegar, salt, and pepper with a whisk and pour over beans. Add onions, toss, and refrigerate.

4. Just before serving toss gently once more and scoop into a large decorative bowl or platter. Garnish with minced parsley.

GREEK COUNTRY BEANS
Fasólia Yiahní

YIELD: 6 servings as main course;
10 servings as a side dish
TIME: 1 hour preparation;
1¼ hours cooking

This popular bean dish is cooked at least once a week in Greek villages, as a hot supper in the winter or a cold supper in summer. It is usually accompanied by a few olives.

In the cities it shows up more often as a side-dish salad at room temperature and is served with meat or fish. Humble as it may sound, it is very tasty and a mainstay meal throughout Greece. I personally like a little lemon juice squeezed over it.

1 pound dried beans (navy, white, broad, or lima).
1 cup olive oil
2 large onions, coarsely chopped
2 cloves garlic, crushed
½ cup tomato sauce
2 carrots, diced
2 celery stalks peeled and diced

1½ teaspoons salt
½ teaspoon black pepper
1 teaspoon sugar
½ cup coarsely chopped parsley
1 teaspoon basil or oregano (optional)

1. Soak beans overnight in water to cover (or cover beans with 2½ cups cold water, bring to a boil, boil 2 minutes, let stand 1 hour). Drain.

2. Heat oil in a 3-quart saucepan and sauté onions and garlic for 10 minutes over medium heat until golden. Add remaining ingredients, and sauté for another 10 minutes.

3. Add beans and enough boiling water to just barely cover

(about 1½ cups). Stir once to mix, cover saucepan, and simmer until vegetables and beans are very tender (about 1¼ hours). Allow to cool slightly in the sauce before serving.

SPINACH AND RICE PILAF
Spanakórizo

YIELD: 4 servings as main dish;
        8 to 10 servings as side dish
TIME: 1 hour

Spinach and Rice Pilaf, Spanakorizo, appears as a savory main meal at least once a week in most Greek homes.

No matter how hard Popeye tried to convince us as children that spinach was good for us, my sister Lita and I would eat and enjoy it prepared only in this way.

Garnish this dish with lemon wedges and slices of Feta cheese.

2 pounds fresh spinach or 3 packages (10 ounces each) frozen spinach
¾ cup olive oil
1 large onion, finely chopped
½ cup long-grain rice
1 tablespoon tomato paste
1½ teaspoons salt
¼ teaspoon black pepper
¼ teaspoon dill or mint

1. Wash fresh spinach three times in a pot of running cold water to make sure no grain of sand remains. Tear spinach into small pieces, removing any tough stalks or discolored leaves; drain. If using frozen spinach, partially defrost.

2. Heat oil in a 4-quart saucepan and fry onion over medium heat until slightly golden (about 10 minutes). Add spinach and cover saucepan until spinach wilts (about 5 minutes).

3. Sprinkle rice over spinach. Dilute tomato paste in 1⅓ cups water (if you like moist rice, add ½ cup more water). Add salt, pepper, and dill or mint, and pour over rice. Cover saucepan and reduce heat. Simmer for about 35 minutes or until rice is soft and tender. Keep pot covered until ready to serve. Serve hot or at room temperature.

SEAFOOD

Poseidon's Gifts from Sea and Stream

To the Greeks living along the coast and on the islands, fish has always been a major source of food. The Aegean, the Ionian Sea, and the Mediterranean offer so many different types of fish and shellfish that to this day Greeks enjoy an abundance of seafood.

The Grecian mainland is almost completely surrounded by water, and the countless little islands surrounding Greece are dotted with ports. As a result one finds tiny restaurants offering freshly caught delicacies almost everywhere: cod, porgy, mackerel, skate, red mullet, red snapper, sea bass, halibut, sardines, sole, trout, squid, octopus, swordfish, tunny fish, and many tasty little fish unknown to Americans.

Greeks also enjoy a variety of shellfish, including mussels, scallops, shrimp, oysters, crabs, crawfish, conches, snails, winkles, periwinkles, and—most prized of all—sea urchins.

75

FRIED FISH
Psária Tiganitá

YIELD: 4 servings
TIME: Approximately 35 minutes

Every visitor to Greece comes back with fond memories of succulent dinners eaten in dining rooms perched on the edge of the
sea or at outdoor tables set up by the beach.

Each of these seafood places has a man out front to lure
you in. If you don't understand Greek it doesn't matter—he tells
you of the freshness of the fish, the talents of the chef, the cleanli-
ness of the kitchen, the cheerfulness of the waiters. He goes on
and on until you eventually let him take you across the road to
view the day's catch and see the kitchen. If you see a fish to your
liking, it is weighed and you are told the cost of the fish portion of
your chosen dinner. If the fish is too big or too small for your
party, you go on to the next establishment and undergo a similar
routine. Once you have decided on a fish, you tell how you want
it cooked. Greeks usually like fish pan-fried or charcoal-broiled.

After choosing, you are escorted back to the dining room
across the street, where you may order your apéritif (usually Ouzo
on the rocks) and assorted appetizers to nibble on. You sit back
to listen to romantic ballads played by strolling street musicians
or to *bouzouki* music played on an old phonograph (the *bouzouki*
is a mandolin-like instrument). You gaze at the twinkling lights
from anchored boats on the water—millionaires' yachts, fishing
boats, dinghies, and rowboats, all gently bobbing up and down.

Your reverie is interrupted by the arrival of your dinner. A
pan-fried fish may not sound impressive, but if perfectly cooked
it will be brown and crusty on both sides; as you squeeze a wedge
of fresh lemon juice over it, the aroma is heavenly.

Always try to purchase fresh fish rather than frozen. Bass, trout,
or porgies may be fried whole. Fish roe and filets of any kind may
also be fried successfully. If you are frying a large whole fish,
make a couple of shallow slanting cuts in the fleshy part near the
backbone before you fry it.

If you must use frozen fish (and please, I beg you, only during an emergency or if you live in an area where fresh fish is

unavailable), thaw it slowly in the refrigerator rather than at room temperature. Never refreeze thawed fish.

Remember that fresh lemon juice is to fish what salt is to the egg, and that the oil must be *hot* before frying to ensure a nice crusty brown taste as well as a good appearance.

Serve fish with boiled small potatoes rolled in butter and minced parsley, a crisp salad, and Retsina or a dry white wine. Boiled string beans with a dressing of lemon and oil (see Greek String Bean Salad) would be a good accompanying hot vegetable.

2 pounds cleaned fish	½ cup oil (olive, vegetable, or
½ tablespoon salt	a combination)
¼ teaspoon black pepper	½ tablespoon oregano
½ cup all-purpose flour	1 lemon, cut into wedges

1. Wash fish in cold water and pat dry with paper towels.

2. Sprinkle with salt and pepper, and roll lightly in flour.

3. Heat oil in large frying pan until a few drops of flour dropped into it sizzle and brown almost at once. Do not allow oil to get any hotter, or it will smoke and burn.

4. Fry fish, without crowding, until medium brown and crusty on one side, then turn over with a spatula until second side is also brown and crusty (about 8 minutes on each side for thicker fish, 5 minutes a side for filets or small fish). All fish are done when the flesh flakes easily.

5. Remove carefully to a platter, sprinkle lightly with oregano, and squeeze a wedge of lemon juice over fish. Garnish with remaining lemon wedges.

REMOVING FISH ODOR

To remove fish odor from the house, burn some sugar or lemon peel in a disposable aluminum pan.

To remove fish odor from pans after cooking fish, wash with 1 teaspoon baking soda dissolved in 1 quart water. Rinse with a little vinegar and then wash with sudsy water.

To remove fishy smell from hands, rub with lemon juice and salt or a little vinegar before washing.

FISH MARINATED IN SAVOY SAUCE
Psária Me Sáltsa Savóy

YIELD: 2 servings as a main course;
4 to 6 servings as appetizer
TIME: 45 minutes preparation and cooking;
12 hours marinating

As a child I didn't like fish at all—with one exception, my dad's Fish Savoy. I used to sneak to the refrigerator and dip pieces of bread into the cold marinade or eat a piece of cold Fish Savoy for breakfast.

The rest of my family, being civilized (they ate toast and eggs for breakfast), thought me odd to say the least; and the standing joke was that I had some Russian or Scandinavian conqueror's blood running through my veins.

Putting all this aside, what can I say about this recipe except to ask you to try it. I think you will be pleasantly surprised.

Serve it as a cold appetizer before dinner on lettuce leaves with tiny ripe tomatoes on the side. Serve as a summer luncheon dish with crusty bread, chilled white wine, and a green salad.

1½ pounds cleaned fish
(porgies, bluefish, halibut,
bass, trout, or filets of your
choice)
Salt
Black pepper
Flour

¾ cup olive oil or mixture of
olive oil and corn oil
2 cloves garlic, finely minced
2 bay leaves
½ tablespoon crushed
rosemary
4 tablespoons wine vinegar

1. Rinse fish thoroughly; pat dry with paper towels. Sprinkle with salt and a little pepper. Roll fish lightly in flour.

2. Fry fish in hot oil in large frying pan until crusty and brown on both sides, about 7 minutes per side. Remove fish to a platter or deep bowl. Pour off all but ½ cup of the oil in the frying pan and allow to cool for a few minutes.

3. Add to the remaining oil the garlic, bay leaves, and rosemary, and sauté over low heat until garlic has lightly browned. Remove pan from heat.

4. Mix 2 tablespoons flour into vinegar until smooth, then blend into 1½ cups water. Add to frying pan and scrape bottom and sides of the pan with wooden spoon. Bring mixture to a boil, reduce heat, and simmer over medium-low heat for 20 minutes. Stir occasionally so that the thickening marinade does not stick to the pan. Taste for seasoning, adding salt and pepper only if necessary.

5. Pour marinade over fried fish, cover, and refrigerate. Gently turn fish over once a day so that the marinade will penetrate. Fish prepared in this manner may be kept refrigerated for several weeks, and will improve in flavor with each passing day.

BROILED FISH ANDROS
Psári Tis Scáras Apó Tin Ándro

YIELD: 4 servings
TIME: 25 minutes

My father's best friend, Nick Zagoreos, originally came from the island of Andros. Both men were furriers in New York City for more than forty years. Their only escape from the bustling fur industry was deep-sea fishing on the sweltering hot summer weekends.

On their way back to New York each Sunday evening, they would stop and grill a couple of freshly caught porgies over charcoal. Nick said it was the only thing he'd learned to cook before emigrating to the United States as a boy.

Not having an ocean breeze, salt spray, and a charcoal grill in our city apartment, we broiled the rest of their catch in our oven with results that were almost as good.

At home you could serve this with buttered mashed potatoes, a Greek salad, and a chilled bottle of your favorite white wine. For picnics, you could accompany the fish with sliced tomatoes, cucumbers, freshly made bread, and glasses of cold beer.

2 pounds cleaned porgies or
    other fish
½ tablespoon salt (or to taste)
3 tablespoons olive oil

3 tablespoons lemon juice
2 teaspoons oregano
1 small onion or several
    shallots, minced

1. Rinse fish in cold water, then sprinkle with salt.

2. Beat olive oil, lemon juice, and oregano with a fork until you have a smooth sauce.

3. Grill fish a few inches from heat for about 8 minutes, basting often with the sauce. Turn fish over and cook approximately 8 more minutes, depending on thickness of fish, basting often.

4. Remove fish to platter and pour remaining sauce over it. Sprinkle with minced onion or shallots.

BAKED FISH WITH VEGETABLES
Psári Plakí

YIELD: 6 to 8 servings
TIME: 3 hours marinating;
1¼ hours cooking and baking

If you have never eaten Psari Plaki, you are in for a gastronomical experience. The thin lemon slices baked along with the vegetables are eaten rind and all and are delicious. In Greece the entire fish is baked, making a dramatic presentation. If you don't wish to include the head and tail, have your fishman filet the fish for you. Make sure he gives you the head, however; you can use it to make a fine soup.

Since this dish contains so many vegetables, a salad is rarely served with it. No starchy vegetable is ever served with it, because it also contains potatoes. Chicken Avgolemono Soup (see recipe) could precede this fish dinner nicely. Serve with fresh crusty bread, a dry white wine, and top it off with a sweet Greek dessert and coffee. It is well worth the time and effort.

PREPARING THE FISH

4- to 5-pound ocean fish or 4 to 5 pounds fresh haddock or halibut, cut into serving portions
3 tablespoons lemon juice
1½ teaspoons salt
2 tablespoons olive oil
2 ripe tomatoes, coarsely chopped
1 medium onion, thinly sliced
2 green bell peppers, thinly sliced

Wash fish in cold water and pat dry. Rub lemon juice and salt over fish, rub fish with olive oil, then place it in a large bowl or platter. Put chopped tomatoes, sliced onion, and sliced green peppers inside, on top of, and below the fish. Cover and refrigerate for 3 hours.

PREPARING THE VEGETABLES AND COOKING THE FISH

½ cup olive oil

2 lemons, washed well and sliced as thinly as possible (discard seeds)

3 tablespoons finely chopped parsley

4 ripe tomatoes, chopped coarsely

10-ounce package frozen spinach or 1 pound fresh spinach

2 zucchini, cut into 1-inch pieces

4 medium onions, very thinly sliced

2 stalks celery, peeled and finely chopped

1 cup dry white wine

1 cup tomato purée

2 teaspoons salt

⅛ teaspoon black pepper

3 large potatoes, peeled and sliced ½ inch thick

1. Put olive oil in a large frying pan and heat.
2. Remove fish from refrigerator. Scoop up all the vegetables that have been on and around the fish and put them into the frying pan. Add lemon slices, parsley, tomatoes, spinach, zucchini, onions, and celery, and sauté for 20 minutes, covered.
3. Add wine, tomato purée, salt, and pepper to the pan. Mix gently but well. Simmer for 5 more minutes. Remove pan from heat.
4. Place the fish in the center of a large baking pan (20 by 14 by 2 inches or 15 by 10 by 2 inches), and arrange sautéed vegetables all around it. Decorate fish with some of the sautéed lemon slices. Arrange the sliced potatoes on top of the vegetables.
5. Bake uncovered in preheated 375° oven for 1 hour or until done.

TARAMA CAKES
Taramókeftéthes

YIELD: Approximately 18 patties or 6 servings
TIME: 1½ hours

Your big *glendi* (party) has been over for a couple of months and you suddenly discover a half-used jar of Tarama (salted fish roe) in the back of your refrigerator. A quick and tasty treat can be prepared from it. Either make it into patties and serve with hot buttered beets and a string bean salad; or shape it into small balls, spear each with a tooothpick, squeeze a little lemon juice over them, and serve hot with cocktails. In either case, you can broil or deep-fry them.

2 pounds potatoes
6 to 7 ounces Tarama
Handful fresh parsley, finely
  chopped
8 shallots or 1 small onion,
  minced

¼ cup all-purpose flour
2 cups vegetable oil or
  shortening (if frying)
1 lemon, cut into wedges

1. Boil potatoes in jackets in unsalted water until tender. Drain, peel, and mash.
2. Add Tarama, parsley, and shallots or onion, and mix into a smooth paste.
3. Shape into patties 1½ inches wide. Roll lightly in flour.
4. Broil in an oiled shallow baking pan about 25 minutes or deep-fry in hot oil until browned on all sides, about 2 minutes on each side. Serve hot, garnished with lemon wedges.

SPINACH AND SHRIMP
Garíthes Me Spanáki

YIELD: 6 servings
TIME: 1½ hours

This is a recipe I have never eaten in a Greek restaurant nor have I been able to locate it in any cookbook. None of my Greek friends have ever heard of it.

My grandmother prepared it for my father when he was a

child. I met this grandmother only once, in the village of Cala-
moti, on Chios. I remember being struck by her haunting beauty
and kindness. She was tall and slender and wore black except for
the gold wedding band around her finger. She had been widowed
when my father was only four years old.

Grandmother prepared this dish for us and we liked it so
much she told my mother how to make it. It has remained one of
our favorite family meals throughout the years.

Unusual and delicious, this dish is simple to prepare. The day
before, you can cook and devein the shrimp and prepare the
spinach by washing and refrigerating it in a plastic bag.

Allow at least 4 medium shrimp per portion (depending on
your budget). If using very large shrimp, cut them in half after
they have been cooked and deveined. If using very small shrimp,
allow at least 6 shrimp per portion. Fresh shrimp and spinach are
best, of course, but you can use substitutes in a pinch.

Serve hot with fresh crusty bread, a plate of sliced Feta
cheese, and a white or rosé wine.

2 pounds fresh shrimp in shells	2 medium potatoes, peeled
1 teaspoon salt	and cut into ¼-inch slices
1 stalk celery	½ pound fresh string beans,
1 large lemon	trimmed
5 tablespoons olive oil	¼ teaspoon black pepper
2 pounds fresh spinach	16-ounce can whole peeled
3 large onions, thinly sliced	tomatoes or several large
2 medium carrots, diced	ripe peeled fresh tomatoes,
1 large green bell pepper,	coarsely chopped
thinly sliced	

1. Wash shrimp in cold water and plunge them into boiling
water to just barely cover them. Add salt and celery. When water
comes to a boil again, turn heat down to a bare simmer. Remove
from heat when shrimp have turned bright pink. A general time
guideline is: jumbo shrimp, 12 to 15 minutes; medium shrimp, 6
to 8 minutes; small shrimp, 5 minutes; tiny shrimp, 2 minutes.

2. Discard celery, strain the shrimp broth through a piece of
cheesecloth, and reserve. Put shrimp in a colander or on large
platter to cool.

3. Rinse lemon, grate off most of the rind, then slice as thinly as possible, discarding seeds.

4. Wash lemon, grate off most of the rind, then slice as thinly as possible, discarding seeds.

5. Heat oil in a 3-quart pot. Add spinach, onions, carrots, and green pepper. Sauté over low heat until onions are limp.

6. Add 1 cup of reserved strained shrimp liquid, the potatoes, string beans, lemon slices, pepper, and tomatoes to the pot. Bring to a boil, cover, and reduce heat. Simmer until vegetables are soft and tender (about 40 minutes).

7. While vegetables are simmering, shell and devein the shrimp. Rinse them in cool running water and place in colander to drain.

8. When vegetables are tender and shrimp have all been cleaned, add the shrimp to the pot and simmer for 5 minutes longer. Taste for seasoning. You may want to add a sprinkling of salt. If you do, stir gently after adding.

TO CLEAN COOKED SHRIMP

Remove the shell, tail, and legs with your fingers when shrimp are cool enough to handle. Using a small sharp knife, make a shallow incision down back of each shrimp and remove the vein. Rinse shrimp in cold running water and drain.

SHRIMP AU GRATIN
Garíthes Gratén

YIELD: 4 servings as appetizer;
2 servings for lunch or dinner
TIME: 1¼ hours

In Greece, one frequently sees "Timahia Graten" printed on menus. This means fish filets in a white cheese sauce. Greeks really enjoy their white sauce, or variations of sauce Béchamel, and use it in a great number of recipes. I sometimes substitute shrimp for poached or broiled fish filets.

If baking this in scallop shells as appetizers, serve with crackers or melba toast preceding meat course. If baking as a luncheon dish, serve over buttered toast surrounded with lettuce hearts, quartered hard-boiled eggs, and perhaps a few Greek olives. Top it all off with a bottle of chilled dry white wine.

PREPARING THE SHRIMP

1 pound large fresh shrimp
Pinch thyme or tarragon
1 bay leaf
1 small clove garlic, crushed
2 tablespoons coarsely
chopped fresh parsley
1 tablespoon coarsely
chopped celery leaves
1 scant teaspoon salt
⅛ teaspoon white pepper
or 2 peppercorns
1 cup dry white wine

1. Wash shrimp in cold water; shell and devein. Rinse several times in cold water to rid shrimp of any sand.

2. Put thyme or tarragon, bay leaf, garlic, parsley, celery leaves, salt, pepper or peppercorns and white wine in saucepan and bring to a boil. Add washed shrimp, turn heat down, and simmer for about 10 minutes.

3. Lift shrimp out with a slotted spoon and set aside to cool. Strain wine-mushroom broth through a piece of cheesecloth into a bowl and reserve. Discard spices and vegetables. When shrimp are cool enough to handle, chop coarsely and set aside.

PREPARING THE VEGETABLES

2 tablespoons butter
½ cup chopped fresh
mushrooms or 6 dried
mushrooms, softened over-
night in about 1 cup of
milk and then chopped
6 shallots or scallion bulbs,
finely minced
1 tablespoon finely minced
fresh parsley
1 teaspoon lemon juice
¼ cup water

Melt butter in saucepan, and sauté mushrooms, shallots or scallions, and parsley over low heat until soft but not browned. Add lemon juice and water. (If you have steeped dried mushrooms in milk use ¼ cup of that liquid in place of water.) Bring to a boil, reduce heat, and cover. Simmer for 10 minutes. Strain liquid into reserved wine broth; add mushrooms to chopped shrimp.

PREPARING THE ROUX

4 tablespoons butter
4 tablespoons all-purpose flour
3 egg yolks, at room temperature
½ cup heavy cream or warm milk

1. Melt butter in saucepan over medium heat. Slowly shake in flour, mixing well with a whisk, and cook for about 3 minutes, stirring, being careful not to let it brown. Slowly add reserved wine-mushroom broth, stirring constantly over medium heat until sauce is very thick and smooth. Set aside to cool.

2. Beat egg yolks with heavy cream or warm milk, slowly whip in ½ cup of the cooling sauce, and set aside.

3. Add shrimp, shallots, and mushrooms to the cooling sauce and mix well. Stir in the egg and cream mixture. If you have used milk in place of cream, cook over low heat for 3 minutes, stirring continually until sauce thickens a bit more.

PREPARING THE TOPPING

4 tablespoons unseasoned bread crumbs
4 tablespoons grated Kefalotyri, Kasseri, or Parmesan cheese
2 tablespoons butter

Heap shrimp mixture into buttered scallop shells or a small buttered baking dish. Sprinkle with bread crumbs and grated cheese and dot with butter. Just before serving, place under pre-heated broiler until slightly browned and sizzling. Serve hot.

SHRIMP PILAF
Garíthes Piláfi

YIELD: 4 to 6 servings
TIME: 1¼ hours

A dish of grated Kefalotyri or Parmesan cheese is usually passed around for those who wish to sprinkle some over this pilaf. Feta cheese cut into slices is always on a Greek table. Try a Retsina wine if you are feeling very Greek, or a dry white wine.

3 pounds fresh shrimp in
shells
2 bay leaves
1 stalk celery, peeled
2½ teaspoons salt
3 peppercorns
1 large green bell pepper, cut
into strips ¼ inch wide

1½ tablespoons olive oil
2 cups long-grain converted
rice
1 large onion, finely minced
2 tablespoons tomato paste
2 teaspoons butter
Pimiento strips
Large black Greek olives

1. Wash shrimp several times in cool water to remove any sand. Drain.

2. Place bay leaves, celery, ½ teaspoon salt, and peppercorns in a large saucepan, add 2 cups water, and bring to a boil.

3. Add shrimp to saucepan. Water should barely cover, so add more if necessary. Bring water to a boil, turn heat down, and simmer until shrimp turn bright pink. Remove shrimp with a slotted spoon and set into a colander to cool and drain.

4. Add pepper strips to saucepan, and simmer uncovered for 4 minutes. Remove with slotted spoon and set aside to cool and drain.

5. Strain shrimp broth through a fine cheesecloth into a measuring cup and set aside (remember the level broth comes to). Discard peppercorns, celery, and bay leaves. Shell and devein cooled shrimp.

6. Heat oil in a 3-quart pot, add rice and onion, and sauté over low heat, stirring constantly, until onion is transparent.

7. Dilute tomato paste in shrimp broth and add to rice mixture—be careful, since the combination will spatter for a moment. Add butter, 2 teaspoons salt, and water (figuring in the amount of shrimp broth) required for the 2 cups of rice. I use 2½ cups water per 1 cup raw converted long-grain rice. In this instance, I would be using 5 cups liquid. These measurements give you a moist rice. Bring to a boil. Add pepper strips and stir rice with a fork exactly three times. Put a tight cover on pot and turn heat way down to simmer. I cook converted rice exactly 25 minutes and it's always perfect. Do not lift lid during the simmering.

8. When rice is cooked, add the shrimp and stir once with a fork. Turn heat off and put a small bath towel over the pot. Re-

place cover and allow pot to remain undisturbed for 15 minutes before serving. The towel absorbs excess moisture.

9. If not serving Garithes Pilafi directly from a casserole, put in a large decorative bowl or platter. I have a nice green bowl for just this purpose. Garnish with pimiento and black Greek olives for color.

OCTOPUS AND SQUID
Octapóthia Kai Kalamária

Octopus and squid have something of the flavor of lobster. The octopus, however, can be found in enormous sizes, whereas the largest squid is about 12 inches long.

The octopus has a rounded, saclike body, eight tentacles, each bearing two rows of suckers, a large distinct head, and a strong beaklike mouth. Though a friendly and shy creature by nature, its bizarre appearance has been the basis for many legends, books, and films making it out a monster. The octopus we are used to seeing in American aquariums is not so lucky in Greece. There it is much sought after, not only as a delicacy but almost as a mainstay of the islanders' diet.

Any octopus over 4 pounds must be softened, which the fishermen do by pounding their catch against the rocks for hours before taking it to market. Usually the cook does a little more hammering with a mallet at home or uses a tenderizer in the marinade. The octopus is then cut up in narrow strips and fried in olive oil or simmered in wine, spices, and onions for about four hours, until really tender.

Squid have six arms and two tentacles and can be found in a range of sizes. Greeks adore the tiny ones (bumblebee size) for quick frying in oil as an appetizer. The medium-sized ones are most often stuffed and baked. The larger ones are simmered for hours in a rich wine sauce just as the octopus is.

Both octopus and squid have an ink-expelling mechanism to help them escape their enemies. It is this ink that furnishes the world with the pigment known as sepia. It is also used in recipes just as blood is, to flavor, darken, and thicken sauces.

Greeks often fry it in a little olive oil and serve it spread on small rounds of brown bread as a Meze (canapé). Sprinkle it with a little lemon and eat it while sipping a glass of Ouzo; you will feel like Zorba the Greek.

OCTOPUS IN WINE
Octapóthi Krassáto

YIELD: 4 servings
TIME: Approximately 2 hours

In Greece one finds octopus cooked many ways. It often shows up as a Meze cut into small pieces after being boiled and drained. It is then sprinkled with oil and lemon juice. During Lent, it is boiled, put through a meat grinder, mixed with bread crumbs, and served over pasta. The most traditional method of cooking it, however, is to simmer it slowly in wine until it is very tender. Serve it over rice.

2 pounds octopus (fresh, canned, or dried)
Tenderizer (optional)
¾ cup olive oil
2 large onions, finely chopped
2 stalks celery, peeled and diced

1 bay leaf
2 cups dry red wine
1 tablespoon tomato paste, diluted in 1 cup water
1 teaspoon salt
¼ teaspoon black pepper

1. If buying fresh octopus, have the fishman clean it if not already done. Rinse it in cold water and then either pound it with a mallet about 40 times or sprinkle it with tenderizer. If using canned octopus, drain and rinse it under cold water. If buying dried octopus, soak it for 24 hours in cool water to cover; then drain, rinse, and use the mallet or tenderizer.
2. Cut prepared octopus into bite-sized pieces.
3. Put octopus into a 3-quart saucepan with oil, onion, celery, and bay leaf. Sauté for about 20 minutes over medium heat.
4. Pour wine in very slowly, so it steams as it is added.

5. Add diluted tomato paste, salt, and pepper; cover saucepan, lower heat, and simmer for about 2 hours or until octopus is very tender. Add a little more water during the simmering period only if necessary to prevent scorching. Taste for seasoning, then serve hot.

FRIED BABY SQUID
Kalamarákia Tiganitá

Really small and tender squid are fried whole. Rinse, pat dry, and sprinkle with salt. Dust with flour or dip in egg and bread crumbs and fry in hot oil until brown. Sprinkle with a bit more salt and lemon juice and serve hot as an appetizer. Larger squid are a bit tougher and are better stuffed.

STUFFED SQUID
Kalamária Yemistá

YIELD: 4 to 6 servings
TIME: 1½ hours

12 squid, 4 to 5 inches long
1 cup chopped onion
3 tablespoons chopped fresh parsley
¾ cup olive oil
½ cup cooked rice
2 tablespoons pine nuts or chopped walnuts

1 tablespoon tomato paste
¼ cup currants
1½ teaspoons salt
⅛ teaspoon black pepper
1 cup dry red or white wine
4 tablespoons water

1. Have squid cleaned by the fishman.

2. Simmer onion and parsley in ½ cup olive oil until onion is golden brown. Add chopped squid feelers and simmer until they change color. Mix in rice, nuts, tomato paste, currants, 1 teaspoon salt, and pepper, and cook 5 more minutes. Set aside to cool.

3. Stuff each squid with cooled rice mixture and close openings with toothpicks. Arrange side by side in an oiled baking dish.

4. Combine wine, water, remaining ¼ cup olive oil, and ½ teaspoon salt, and pour over stuffed squid. Bake in preheated 350° oven for 1 hour or until squid are tender and sauce thickens. Serve hot or cold.

SEA URCHINS
Achinoí

Sea urchins, or "pincushions of the sea" as they are sometimes referred to, are little known in the United States. Yet as a child I remember my father buying them in New York. They are clam-like creatures, but dark purple in color, and the shell is covered with tiny sharp spikes. They cling to the rocks along the sea-shore, where the Greeks skillfully pull them off. Only the females are taken, since the roe is considered a delicacy and the males are much smaller.

Sea urchins are pried open just before serving, as one does with oysters or clams, and served on the half shell with a squeeze of lemon juice over each. Sometimes the bright yellow roe is removed and served on crackers or squares of brown bread with a drop of olive oil and lemon juice as a Meze (appetizer).

In Greece, freshly caught sea urchins are sold out of baskets on street corners. Greeks stop, pop one or two into their mouth, and continue down the street.

LAMB AND BEEF
Grills, Roasts, and Ragouts

When one visualizes the barren rocky hills of Greece, the picture that springs to mind is that of a shepherd boy tending his flock of sheep or goats. But these animals are not for eating; they are used for breeding and the making of goods. Beautiful heavy-knit sweaters, blankets, and those fluffy long-haired rugs that have recently been such a rage in the United States are all made of sheep wool. The skins of sheep and goats go into the manufacturing of leather goods.

Unlike other peoples from the Balkans or the Middle East, Greeks find mutton and goat disagreeable. They prefer kid, never more than a year old, or milk-fed lamb, traditional at Easter.

Greeks have also developed a taste for beef. For years they imported what they could from abroad. In the northern part of Greece, where there is some grazing land, the people have recently begun to raise their own cattle.

Pork is not as common, but on occasion in front of a country taverna you might see a suckling pig, its cavity filled with Feta cheese, roasting on a spit over a slow fire.

For the average Greek, meat of any kind has always been expensive because of the lack of good grazing lands. This hard economic fact forced Greeks to use small amounts of meat in their cooking. Instead of this being a deterrent to good cuisine, it became a challenge. Due to the ingenuity of Greek cooks, some famous meat dishes evolved that are now acclaimed worldwide—Moussaka and Pastitsio being just two of them.

Because of religious holidays the Greeks are said to be either fasting or feasting throughout most of the year. It's an interesting fact that most of the important feasting days fall during the time the animals have not yet been turned out to pasture.

ROAST LEG OF LAMB A LA GRECQUE
WITH POTATOES
Arní Bóute Tou Foúrnou Me Patátes

YIELD: 6 servings
TIME: Approximately 4 hours

Some people serve roast lamb while it is still pink in the center. The Greeks do not. For this unusual mouth-watering version, a leg of lamb is roasted very slowly for at least four hours, until it is almost falling off the bone. Only in this way will you achieve a succulent taste with none of the gaminess that often makes people dislike lamb.

Purchase a young leg of lamb, never mutton; it should be fresh, not frozen. Lamb shrinks a great deal during this roasting-braising process, so that a 7-pound roast after cooking will serve only about 6 people. Do not cover roasting pan at any time during the cooking.

Never try to reheat roast lamb. You will find on reheating that too strong a flavor permeates the meat. Cold leftover lamb makes good sandwiches the next day.

Always serve a hot roast and hot potatoes on heated plates (with lamb, this is particularly important). You could substitute Baked Orzo (following recipe) for the potatoes. Serve with Greek salad and rosé wine.

1 leg of lamb, 6 or 7 pounds
2½ tablespoons lemon juice
1½ tablespoons salt
2½ tablespoons oregano
1 large clove garlic
½ teaspoon black pepper,
   preferably freshly ground

1 cup hot water
1 large onion, sliced
1 stalk celery
6 large potatoes or 18
   very small potatoes

1. Wash leg of lamb under hot tap water, pat dry, and put into a large roasting pan.

2. Rub 2 tablespoons lemon juice and 1 tablespoon salt all over lamb. Sprinkle 1½ tablespoons oregano over meat and rub in well. For a strong garlic flavor, sliver garlic, make small deep cuts on both top and bottom of lamb, and insert garlic slivers. For a more delicate taste, crush garlic and rub it evenly over entire surface of meat. Sprinkle ¼ teaspoon black pepper all over meat and rub in well.

3. Insert meat thermometer if you wish to use one, making sure you don't insert against bone, and put roasting pan into preheated oven. Set the thermometer at well done for lamb. Lamb should be placed fat side up in the middle shelf of oven. Bake at 400° for 40 minutes.

4. Add cup of hot water, onion slices, and celery stalk to roasting pan. Turn oven heat down to 325° and continue roasting.

5. Peel large potatoes, cut in quarters, and drop in a large bowl of cold water. If using small potatoes, peel and drop whole in cold water.

6. In about 3½ hours or when meat thermometer reads that lamb is done, remove thermometer. Make 4 deep slashes in the top of the roast to release juices into the pan and turn roast over. Continue roasting.

7. Drain potatoes, and sprinkle them with remaining lemon juice, salt, pepper, and oregano. Lay potatoes around the lamb and continue roasting at the same temperature.

8. When potatoes are half done (about 20 minutes), turn them over so that they will brown on the other side. Turn roast over also, and with a sharp knife make 4 more deep slashes to release more juices into the pan. Continue roasting until potatoes pierce easily with a fork and are nicely browned.

9. Remove pan from oven. Discard celery and onions. Put lamb on a large platter, potatoes into a deep serving dish, and place both in the warm, turned-off oven. Skim fat from pan juices and pour remaining juices into a heated gravy boat.

LAMB WITH BAKED ORZO
Arní Me Kritharáki Giouvétsi

YIELD: 6 to 8 servings
TIME: 2½ hours

Orzo (Manestra or Kritharaki in Greek) is a form of pasta often sold in Italian grocery stores, the macaroni section of supermarkets, or the specialty stores listed in the back of this book. Orzo looks like cantaloupe seeds, and is used in soups and main dishes. It may be cooked in stock (beef, lamb, or chicken), drained, and served with hot Browned Butter Sauce (see recipes) and grated cheese (Kefalotyri or Parmesan).

Orzo is also used very often in place of potatoes when making Greek roasted lamb. The pan juices give the Orzo an unforgettable flavor.

3 pounds lamb (shoulder or leg), cut into large cubes
Juice of 1 lemon
3½ teaspoons salt
½ teaspoon black pepper
1½ tablespoons oregano
1 cup hot water

3 tablespoons tomato paste
5 cups boiling water
1 large onion, minced
1 pound Orzo
Grated cheese
(Kefalotyri or Parmesan)

1. Put cubes of lamb into a roasting pan. Sprinkle cubes with lemon juice, 1½ teaspoons salt, pepper, and oregano. Toss. Bake at 400° for 40 minutes.

2. Add cup of hot water to roasting pan, turn oven heat down to 325°, and roast for 1 more hour. Remove meat and cover to keep warm.

3. Skim excess fat from juices in pan. Dilute tomato paste in boiling water, add 2 teaspoons salt and minced onion, and pour

into pan. Sprinkle in Orzo and bake uncovered in 350° oven for 30 minutes, stirring occasionally, until Orzo is tender and most of the liquid has been absorbed.

4. Place meat in pan on top of Orzo and bake for another 15 minutes until a light crust develops on top of the Orzo.

5. Serve Orzo sprinkled with grated cheese on a heated platter. Roasted meat may be either placed on top of Orzo or served separately on its own heated platter.

NOTE: Because the amount of pan juices varies, you may wish to keep an additional cup of boiling water on hand. If you see Orzo has absorbed all of the liquid long before your 30-minute baking period is up, add a bit more water as needed. If, on the other hand, there is a bit too much liquid, remove pan from oven and cover with a lint-free towel for 15 minutes. This will take up excess moisture.

VARIATION

If you wish to use macaroni in place of Orzo: Cook macaroni until almost tender in a separate pot and drain. Dilute tomato paste in 1 cup boiling water. Skim excess fat from roasting pan and stir in tomato-paste liquid. Add cooked macaroni and meat and bake an additional 15 minutes.

GRILLED MEAT ON SKEWERS
Souvlákia

YIELD: 6 servings
TIME: About 2 hours preparation;
12 to 24 hours marinating;
25 minutes broiling

In different parts of the world skewered meat is called shish kebab or shashlik, but to the Greeks it remains Souvlakia. *Souvla* is the Greek word for skewer or spit. When roasting an entire milk-fed lamb at Easter the *souvla* is a long metal rod. The lamb is then called *arni sti souvla* (lamb on a spit). When lamb, beef, or poultry is cut up and grilled on individual skewers it is called

Souvlakia. Small wooden or bamboo skewers may be used for grilling tiny morsels of marinated meat served as appetizers.

Throughout Greece you can find little covered stalls equipped with small charcoal grills, pots of marinating Souvlakia, and fresh crusty loaves of bread cut into thick slices. The Greeks eat Souvlakia the way Americans consume hot dogs.

The recipe below dates back to before 1000 B.C. In those days lamb was marinated, skewered on a sword, and broiled over a fire. In these days, ordinary skewers and a charcoal grill will do fine. The fragrance of the meat while it is being broiled will drive everyone wild. You can also lay the skewered meat in your broiling pan and broil it in your kitchen, but somehow the true flavor is brought out over a wood or charcoal fire.

A metal skewer about 12 inches long should be allowed for each guest. These may be purchased very inexpensively at most American supermarkets. Souvlakia must be eaten the minute they are ready or the meat will become tough and stringy. Grill over a very hot fire, so that the meat will be well seared on the outside and tender and juicy inside.

Souvlakia can be served on a bed of plain rice or on Pilaf (rice cooked in stock). I have included instructions for making Pilaf (Pilafi to the Greeks) from the lamb bones. Add a nice salad to this meal. Greeks like to drink beer or Retsina with Souvlakia.

THE DAY BEFORE

12 large white mushrooms
2 tablespoons white wine or
  lemon juice
1 cup fine olive oil
⅓ cup lemon juice
½ cup dry red wine
2 cloves garlic, chopped
2 large bay leaves
1 small leg of lamb
  (approximately 3 pounds
  meat)

Salt
½ teaspoon black pepper
  (or to taste)
1½ tablespoons oregano
4 large firm tomatoes or
  18 cherry tomatoes
3 large green bell peppers
2 large onions or
  18 pearl onions

1. Wash mushrooms quickly, sprinkle them with the 2 tablespoons white wine or lemon juice, cover, and refrigerate (this prevents them from turning dark).

2. Combine olive oil, ⅓ cup lemon juice, red wine, garlic, and bay leaves in a large stainless steel pot or glass mixing bowl. Mix well with a fork.

3. Debone lamb and cut it into lean 1-inch cubes, trimming off any bits of fat or sinew. Reserve bones and scraps for stock. Sprinkle lamb cubes with salt, pepper, and oregano, and place into bowl of marinade.

4. Remove the stems of the tomatoes; quarter the large ones and leave cherry tomatoes whole; add to the marinade.

5. Fill a pot with water, add 1 teaspoon salt, and bring to a rapid boil. Wash green peppers and cut into 1-inch squares. Boil peppers for 5 minutes; reserving the water, scoop the peppers into a colander and spray with cold water. Add peppers to the marinade.

6. Peel large onions, quarter them, parboil 5 minutes in pepper cooking water, and spray with cold water. If using tiny pearl onions, parboil them unpeeled, spray with cold water, and you will find the skins will slip off easily. Add onions to the marinade.

7. Take a heavy dinner plate and invert it over the marinade to weight the meat and vegetables. Cover bowl with plastic wrap and refrigerate for 12 to 24 hours. Mix gently once every 6 hours to make sure the marinade covers all ingredients.

8. If you wish to have Souvlakia resting on a bed of Pilaf you must make your stock from the bones of the lamb and any meat scraps the same day you do the marinade.

MAKING THE LAMB STOCK

1 large onion, sliced
2 stalks celery
1 teaspoon salt
5 cups water

Combine ingredients with reserved lamb bones and scraps in a large pot and bring to a boil. Remove foam as it rises to surface. Lower heat and simmer for a few hours. Strain into a bowl, cover, and refrigerate.

ON THE DAY OF YOUR BARBECUE

1. Add mushrooms and their wine or lemon juice to the marinade in the morning.

2. Light the barbecue fire 1 hour before dining. Prepare the skewers, allowing one skewer per guest. Thread a cube of lamb, then pepper, onion, tomato, mushroom cap or stem; repeat. Jam everything tightly, but leave 1½ inches on each end of skewer for easy turning. Be extremely gentle when skewering the tomato wedges; do it lengthwise or from the skin side to prevent them from falling off skewer. As you finish loading up each skewer, set it gently on a large platter or tray.

MAKING THE RICE PILAF

1 tablespoon butter
1 tablespoon olive oil
2 cups long-grain converted rice
2 teaspoons salt
3 pinches saffron (optional)

1. Remove lamb broth from refrigerator and with a spoon remove all the hardened fat on the top. The remaining broth will be jellied. Spoon it into a 2-quart saucepan and melt it. Pour into measuring cup and add water, if necessary, to make 4¼ cups of liquid for converted rice or the amount called for on package of the brand of rice you're using. Pour back into the saucepan and simmer.

2. Combine butter, oil, and rice in a 4-quart pot. Stir over medium heat for 12 minutes, making sure rice starts to brown but doesn't stick or burn. Add salt and saffron (if you want rice to have a golden color) to simmering stock and stir until saffron is dissolved. Pour hot stock quickly into rice, guarding your face, for it will sputter for a minute. Stir exactly 3 times with a fork, cover, and simmer over low heat until rice is done (about 20 to 25 minutes depending on brand of rice you are using). At no time

lift the lid. As soon as you start simmering the rice the charcoal should be ready to cook the Souvlakia. Rice will stay hot off heat for up to 30 minutes, but do not uncover until ready to serve.

BROILING THE SOUVLAKIA

Put skewers at least 2 inches above hot charcoal and broil for 15 minutes on one side; then turn skewers over and broil for another 10 to 15 minutes. Meat is perfect if it is barely pink in center and nice and crusty outside. Holding one end of skewer securely and a fork in your other hand, slide the cubes of meat and vegetables off onto plates for each guest.

BEEF AND SMALL ONIONS IN WINE
Stifátho

YIELD: 4 servings
TIME: Approximately 3 hours

I can remember rushing home from school on cold wintry days and being assailed with the spicy fragrance of Stifatho on the stove. My sister and I would dip a slice of bread into the simmering gravy and proceed to eat while drawing pictures on the steamed-up windows of the kitchen. Thus reinforced, both spiritually and physically, we would bundle up and dash outdoors once more.

Stifatho is a very popular ragout usually made in winter. It smells and tastes a bit like the German sauerbraten, but I like it even better. In Greece, it is made with veal, hare, or beef, and it's always cooked in an earthenware pot. Our mother always made it with beef, used an ordinary saucepan, and achieved crowning results. She always told us, however, that the trick to success was long, slow cooking to bring out the utmost in taste and tenderness—and perseverance in keeping teenaged daughters from sopping up all the gravy before the Stifatho was ready.

If I had to sum it up in a few words, I guess I would say that Stifatho is the kind of dish fond memories are made of. It goes well with rice or mashed potatoes and a green salad.

7 tablespoons butter
1 tablespoon olive oil
1 large onion, chopped
2 cloves garlic, chopped
   very finely
1½ pounds lean stewing beef,
   cut into 1-inch cubes
2 tablespoons tomato paste

1½ cups dry red wine
1 tablespoon wine vinegar
1 large bay leaf
Pinch cumin
Pinch cinnamon
Salt
   ¼ teaspoon black pepper
1½ pounds small white onions

1. Heat 3 tablespoons of the butter and the olive oil over medium heat in a 2- to 3-quart casserole (preferably earthenware). Add the onion, garlic, and meat cubes, and brown the meat on all sides.

2. Add tomato paste; mix for a few minutes, coating meat.

3. Add the wine and enough hot water to just *barely* cover meat cubes.

4. Add vinegar, bay leaf, cumin, cinnamon, 1½ teaspoons salt, and pepper. Stir to mix well, and reduce heat to a simmer. Cover the casserole.

5. Let onions sit in very hot water for a few minutes and then slip the skins off. Boil peeled onions in salted water (1 teaspoon salt to a quart of water) for 3 minutes in a covered pot. Discard the water. Rinse onions with cool water and drain well —this will make them sweeter.

6. Put remaining butter into a frying pan, brown onions over medium heat, then set them aside.

7. Check the meat. It should be just barely simmering. It will take about 2 hours to cook. Test it with a fork. If the meat breaks easily, it is done.

8. When the meat is nice and tender, add the browned onions. They will take about 30 minutes to cook over low heat. Cover and shake the pot a couple of times but do not stir; you will bruise the onions. Continue simmering until the onions are tender; test them with a thin metal skewer or toothpick, which should pierce the center of the largest onion easily.

FREEZING

This dish can be frozen. Put it in plastic containers once it has cooled. You can reheat on top of the stove or in the oven, in a heavy, covered casserole. The heat should be very low, and as mentioned above, shake the pot occasionally; do not uncover and stir.

CORINTHIAN BEEF CASSEROLE
Moscárhi Krassí Tis Kórinthos

YIELD: 4 servings
TIME: 3 hours

Beef and wine, the perfect colleagues, form an alliance with interesting spices to make a rich dark-brown stew elegant enough for a party.

My husband and I dined in a very small seaside restaurant near the Corinth canal one evening and had this earthy stew. The owner-cook and his wife happily told us how it was prepared. If you want to make a larger amount, use two separate casseroles. Somehow doubling this recipe changes the taste.

You could serve mashed potatoes or rice on the side or even some form of buttered pasta. This is a delicious but simple meal to prepare. Accompany it with a crisp green salad and a dry red wine.

¼ cup all-purpose flour
1½ pounds lean stewing beef (chuck), cut into 1-inch cubes
3 strips bacon
1 clove garlic, crushed
½ cup beef consommé
½ cup dry red wine

½ teaspoon salt
1½ cups diced carrots
6 small onions, peeled and sliced thickly or left whole
4 peppercorns
2 whole cloves
2 bay leaves

1. Put the flour into a plastic bag. Add meat cubes a few at a time, and shake bag until meat is lightly coated with flour. Set meat on a large plate.

2. Cook bacon in a deep, heavy frying pan until brown but not crisp; remove from pan, chop into small pieces, and set aside. Add crushed garlic to the hot bacon fat left in the pan.

3. Add half the meat and brown well on all sides. Remove

to clean plate. Add the rest of the meat to the pan and brown it well on all sides.

4. When meat has completely browned, put all the meat together, add the consommé, wine, and salt, and heat to the boiling point.

5. Turn mixture into a 2-quart casserole. Add carrots, onions, peppercorns, cloves, bay leaves, and chopped bacon.

6. Cover casserole and bake in preheated 300° oven for 2 hours. Gently mix once and bake for 30 minutes longer.

FREEZING

Bake for only 2 hours, then freeze. When you wish to use, put casserole in the oven at 325° and bake for about 1¼ hours or until bubbling hot, stirring only once about halfway through the cooking.

BAKED MEAT AND EGGPLANT IN BÉCHAMEL SAUCE
Moussaká

YIELD: 12 servings
TIME: First day: 3 hours;
second day: 50 minutes;
third day: 2 hours

What is Moussaka? It is a layered composition of eggplant, chopped meat, grated cheese, and spices, with Béchamel Sauce poured over the top. It is baked until lightly brown and crusty on the top and then cut into squares or wedges just as you would a piece of cake.

Moussaka takes only an hour of baking time once you get it all put together and into the oven. The preparation time, how-ever, is very lengthy. No matter how I've organized pots, pans, draining, frying, and the baking of this superb dish, I always become exhausted if I do it on the day of the dinner. Therefore I have devised a plan that extends over a three-day period. It will give you the finest-tasting Moussaka and the energy left over to enjoy it.

This is not a recipe you make for the children or for a relative who would be just as happy with a good steak. This is a dish you reserve for friends who really enjoy fine exotic cooking.

Since Moussaka is quite rich, serve small portions. It goes well with a crisp salad with vinegar and oil dressing and perhaps small dinner rolls.

If you bake Moussaka early in the day but plan to serve it in the evening, bake it for 35 minutes only. Allow to cool, cover loosely, and refrigerate the entire pan. One hour before serving, put pan into preheated 350° oven and bake approximately 50 minutes or until crusty and brown. Allow to sit undisturbed for 15 minutes before cutting.

FIRST DAY, FRYING THE EGGPLANT

3 medium-sized eggplants, firm, unwrinkled, and unspotted
Salt
1½ cups all-purpose flour
Approximately 1¼ cups fine olive oil
½ pound butter

1. Rinse eggplants. Cut off stem part of each and slice lengthwise into slices about ¼ inch thick. Do not remove skin. The first and last slice from each eggplant will have more shiny purple skin showing. Keep these together so that you can place them on the bottom of the pan when you put the Moussaka together.

2. Sprinkle slices lightly with salt and put them in colanders to drain. Weight slices with a plate and set a heavy object on top of the plate (or set slices on a baking rack over oven pan; cover slices with a cookie sheet and weight it with a heavy object). Set aside for 2 hours.

3. Rinse drained eggplant slices under cool water. Pat each slice dry and place on a plate. Put flour in another plate and lightly coat the slices.

4. Heat half the oil and half the butter in a large frying pan. When sizzling hot, fry slices, a few at a time, until lightly golden on both sides. Remove carefully and place on paper toweling several layers thick, with a thick section of newspapers underneath the toweling. When you have fried about half the eggplant,

heat remaining oil and butter until it is very hot, and fry the rest of the eggplant slices. Place fried slices in layers with lots of paper toweling between layers. Pick up the entire load of eggplant slices within the layered toweling from the wad of newspapers underneath and refrigerate overnight.

SECOND DAY, PREPARING THE MEAT MIXTURE

¼ pound butter
3 large onions, finely chopped
2½ pounds lean ground beef
  (chuck or round)
¼ cup chopped fresh parsley
3 tablespoons tomato paste

1 cup dry red wine
1 tablespoon salt
¼ teaspoon black pepper
2 dashes ground cinnamon
6 to 8 slices bread
1 cup grated Kefalotyri or
  Parmesan cheese

1. Heat butter in a large frying pan over medium heat, add onions, and sauté for 5 minutes. Add chopped meat, crumbling it with a knife and fork so that it becomes uniform in size as it cooks. Sauté, mixing constantly, for about 15 minutes, until meat is nicely browned.

2. Add parsley. Mix tomato paste into red wine and add to the meat mixture; stir to blend well. Add salt, pepper, and cinnamon, and mix thoroughly. Simmer uncovered until all liquid is absorbed (about 30 minutes). If liquid is absorbed sooner, the heat is too high. If this happens, add ½ cup additional wine or water and continue to simmer until absorbed.

3. Make bread crumbs while meat is cooking. Turn oven to 400°. Place bread in hot oven and bake until dry. Grate in blender or crush with a rolling pin, and measure out a cup of crumbs.

4. Allow cooked meat to cool completely. As it is cooling you will notice excess oil around edges of meat in pan; with a large spoon remove as much as possible.

5. When meat has cooled, mix the grated cheese and 3 tablespoons of bread crumbs into the meat and blend well. Reserve remaining bread crumbs. Put meat into large clean bowl, cover tightly with plastic wrap, and refrigerate.

THIRD DAY, MAKING BÉCHAMEL SAUCE
AND BAKING THE MOUSSAKA

3 cups hot milk
7 tablespoons butter
6 tablespoons all-purpose flour
1 tablespoon salt
¼ teaspoon white pepper
4 dashes nutmeg

4 egg yolks, slightly beaten,
at room temperature (to
freeze egg whites, see end
of recipe)
½ cup grated Kefalotyri or
Parmesan cheese

1. Take eggplant slices and meat mixture out of the refrigerator.

2. Scald milk in a saucepan and remove from heat.

3. Melt 6 tablespoons of the butter over very low heat in a 4-quart saucepan; do not allow to brown. Sift the flour very slowly into the butter, stirring with a wire whisk all the time to blend butter and flour, about 2 to 3 minutes; do not allow roux to brown. Remove from heat and dribble hot milk slowly into the butter and flour mixture, stirring vigorously with wire whisk.

4. Return saucepan to heat and cook over medium heat, beating with whisk until sauce becomes thick and creamy. Add salt, pepper, and nutmeg. Stir to blend well and remove from heat. Allow sauce to cool.

5. Beat egg yolks, then add a little cooled sauce very slowly to them, beating with whisk all the time. Put egg mixture into the pot of cream sauce and place over low heat for about 3 minutes, stirring all the time. Remove from heat.

6. Lightly butter a large baking pan (about 16 by 10 by 2). Scatter about 3 tablespoons bread crumbs over the bottom. Line bottom of pan with eggplant slices, using the thicker end slices first. Arrange them neatly, skin down. Spread a layer of meat mixture over the slices. Add another layer of eggplant slices and then another layer of meat. Finish off with eggplant neatly arranged on top.

7. Pour sauce over the top of last layer of eggplant. Sprinkle with grated cheese and remaining bread crumbs. Dot with remaining tablespoon of butter and bake in a preheated 350° oven for 1 hour or until golden brown and crusty on top.

8. Remove Moussaka from oven and allow to sit undisturbed

for 15 minutes before cutting into squares or wedges—this wait is very important; it allows the mixture to coalesce.

FREEZING EGG WHITES

Making sure no egg yolk gets into the whites or they won't whip properly, drop whites into a little glass jar (baby food jars are good), cover, and label number of whites jar contains. Defrost at room temperature for 2 hours and use as you would fresh egg whites, for soufflés, meringues, frosted grapes, etc.

GRAPE LEAVES STUFFED WITH MEAT
Yaprákia Me Yaoúrti Avgolémono

YIELD: 6 to 8 servings
TIME: 1 hour preparation;
2 hours cooking

Milton Berle once asked me, "Anne, when are you going to make the meatballs with kimonas on?" He was referring, of course, to Yaprakia, the delicious grape leaves filled with rice, meat, and mint.

These little rolls are served hot with Yogurt Avgolemono Sauce. The fragrance of grape leaves cooking makes eating them a sheer delight.

Grape leaves packed in brine and sold in jars can be purchased at many stores listed in the Shopper's Guide (see pages 240–246) or gourmet shops. Lately they have begun to appear on shelves of American supermarkets. They are very easy to work with, being soft and pliable.

The ancient Greeks are said to have used fig leaves, mulberry leaves, and even hazelnut leaves for this recipe. As wars ravaged the Greek countryside, however, grapes grew more quickly than trees in the rocky terrain, and so they were the first to be cultivated.

Stuffed grape leaves are made slightly differently both within Greece and in other Mediterranean countries. Some recipes use tomato sauce, garlic, wine, pine nuts, raisins, and even cinnamon. They are known as Dolmas or Dolmathes in many parts of the Mediterranean. The Spartans have always called them Yaprakia.

As a teenager making this recipe the first time, I thought all the vitamins would be lost if I threw away the liquid packed in the jar with the grape leaves. I didn't know brine meant salt. The Yaprakia never looked more beautiful nor the sauce more elegant. Then the guests tasted them. The entire pot had to be thrown out, and everyone had an omelet that evening instead.

And another time I volunteered to make a huge pot of Yaprakia for a big party my parents were having. Hours later, when I was placing the last little shiny green roll into the pot, I realized that I had forgotten to add the rice. I had to unwrap what must have been over a hundred Yaprakia, add the rice to the meat mixture, rinse all the leaves, and wrap them all up again. Still, it remains my favorite dish.

For a simple accompaniment to Yaprakia, serve a large tray of raw celery stalks, crisp red radishes, and sliced tomatoes. Have a crusty loaf of bread and a dry white wine.

MAKING THE YAPRAKIA

1½ pounds lean ground beef
   or lamb
1 cup long-grain rice
3 large onions, finely chopped
   or grated
1 tablespoon salt

¼ teaspoon black pepper
3 tablespoons olive oil
½ tablespoon finely crumbled
   mint leaves
12-ounce jar grape leaves
¼ pound butter
1 cup beef stock

1. Combine meat, rice, onions, salt, pepper, oil, mint, and 1 cup warm water. Mix well and set aside.

2. Drain brine from grape leaves and discard. Unfold leaves and place them in a pot of cool water. Wash them well by swishing them up and down in the pot, changing water a few times to get rid of any brine clinging to leaves. Place all washed leaves at once in a 4-quart pot of boiling water for 3 minutes and drain. When cool enough to handle, place on a flat surface, dull side up. Snip off all the stems. Oil bottom of the 4-quart pot and spread 4 large coarse or torn leaves on bottom.

3. Place ½ tablespoon filling at base of a leaf. Roll up to cover filling, fold in sides, then roll, not too tightly, toward the point of the leaf (see illustration for Dolmathes, page 15, but do

not make them as small). Each Yapraki should look like a fat, shiny little sausage. Carefully place each roll in the pot so that the tucked-under end of the leaf is on the bottom. Fit rolls snugly together as you place them in the pot so they won't come apart while cooking.

4. When you complete first layer, dot with butter; then make other layers—dotting each layer with butter—until you've used up all the leaves. If you have a bit of meat mixture left over, shape into little meatballs and place in the pot. If you should have a few leaves left (even if torn), place on top of last layer of Yaprakia. Place an inverted dinner plate over the Yaprakia to prevent them from shifting about or opening up as the rice cooks.

5. Slowly pour beef stock over the plate and into the pot. Slowly add enough warm water over the plate to *barely* cover the Yaprakia. Turn on heat until liquid starts to boil, then reduce heat to very low. Cover the pot, simmer for about 2 hours, and remove from heat.

6. Drain remaining liquid from the pot and reserve it for making the sauce. You should have at least 1 cup of liquid left in pot after the cooking is finished. If you don't, add enough hot water to the liquid to make 1 full cup.

7. Carefully lift each of the Yaprakia onto a large serving platter and set in a warm oven while you make the sauce.

MAKING THE YOGURT AVGOLEMONO SAUCE

4 large eggs, at room temperature
1¼ teaspoons cornstarch diluted in 2 tablespoons cold water

5 tablespoons lemon juice
Dash salt
Dash white pepper
½ cup yogurt, at room temperature

1. Beat eggs and diluted cornstarch in a blender for a few seconds (or beat vigorously with whisk or electric beater). While continually beating, add lemon juice, salt, and pepper.

2. Mix yogurt into reserved cup of Yaprakia liquid until smooth, then slowly add it to the egg mixture, blending, whisking, or beating until well mixed.

3. Transfer sauce to a 1-quart pot and stir with a wire whisk over very low heat until sauce thickens. Make sure that as you stir you reach the bottom and sides of the pot to prevent the sauce from lumping, and keep the heat very, very low as you stir, to prevent the eggs from cooking. You should make sauce the consistency of very heavy cream. This should take only a few minutes. Pour the sauce either on top of the Yaprakia or into a separate bowl and spoon about 2 tablespoons over each serving of 5 to 6 Yaprakia.

FREEZING

Pour the cup of Yaprakia cooking liquid into covered container. Place cooked Yaprakia flat with plastic wrap between each layer on a cookie sheet. When frozen, pack into plastic bags or freezer boxes. To reheat, place Yaprakia unthawed in a covered casserole with a few tablespoons of water. Cook in preheated 350° oven until hot. Heat the frozen liquid until it melts, then proceed to make the sauce a few minutes before serving the Yaprakia. The sauce should always be made fresh. If you have used up the stock but have frozen leftover Yaprakia, substitute a cup of homemade beef stock to make the sauce, just before serving.

BAKED MACARONI AND MEAT
Pastítsio

YIELD: 15 servings
TIME: 2½ hours

In the northern parts of Greece there are a few areas of good grazing land; the rest of the country, however, provides poor fodder, so much of the meat has to be imported.

When a Greek cook is confronted with a tough, stringy piece of meat, it is minced, flavored with spices, and simmered in wine.

Pastitsio is a perfect example of what heights a macaroni and meat dish can rise to. You find it frequently served on holidays, at Sunday dinners, or at sophisticated buffet suppers.

Pastitsio is layers of cooked macaroni on the bottom, luscious meat filling in the middle, and more layers of cooked macaroni on top. The entire dish is held together with a white cheese sauce and baked to creamy perfection. Just before serving, Pastitsio is cut into squares and eaten hot. It is sheer ambrosia, and goes beautifully with sliced tomatoes or a Greek salad vinaigrette. Serve Retsina as the wine.

MAKING THE MEAT FILLING

2 large onions, coarsely grated
3 tablespoons butter
2 pounds ground lean beef
4 tablespoons tomato paste
1 cup dry red wine

1 level teaspoon nutmeg
¼ teaspoon black pepper
1 tablespoon salt
½ teaspoon ground
  cinnamon

1. Sauté onions in 3 tablespoons butter over low heat in large frying pan until soft and transparent. Do not let them brown. Add chopped meat slowly and with fork and knife keep crumbling meat over high heat until it is brown and uniform in size.

2. Blend tomato paste into wine and add to meat. Turn heat down to a simmer. Add nutmeg, pepper, salt, and cinnamon, and mix thoroughly. Simmer over very low heat uncovered for 1 hour while you prepare macaroni (following). If before the hour is up it looks as though it is beginning to stick to the pan, add ¼ cup more wine or water and continue to simmer.

MAKING MACARONI AND CREAM SAUCE

1½ teaspoons oil
1 pound macaroni or ziti
6 cups milk

½ pound butter
½ cup sifted all-purpose flour
2 dashes nutmeg

1. Bring a large pot of water to a boil, add oil (to keep pasta from sticking), then cook macaroni or ziti al dente—just until there is a slight resistance to biting. Drain.

2. Scald milk and remove saucepan from heat. Melt the butter in a 4-quart pot over low heat, and sift flour into it slowly. Keep stirring so that you get no lumping. After using up the flour, continue stirring over the low heat for at least 5 minutes so that flour cooks.

3. Add a dash of nutmeg. Start slowly adding hot milk and

beat vigorously with a wire whisk until you have used all the milk. Add another dash of nutmeg. As sauce simmers it will start to thicken. Keep stirring with the whisk so that it will be smooth, but do not let it get too thick. It should have the consistency of heavy cream. Remove from heat and allow to cool.

ASSEMBLING THE PASTITSIO

½ cup unseasoned bread crumbs
3 cups grated Kefalotyri or Parmesan cheese
6 large eggs, at room temperature
About 3 tablespoons butter

1. Mix half the bread crumbs and half the grated cheese into the cooked meat.

2. Butter a large baking pan (about 16 by 10 by 2 inches) on corners, sides, and bottom. Sprinkle with 2 tablespoons bread crumbs. Spread half the cooked pasta evenly in the bottom of baking pan. Sprinkle with ½ cup cheese. Spread all of the meat over pasta as evenly as you can and set aside.

3. Beat eggs well. Whip ½ cup cooled sauce into the eggs, then stir this into the entire pot of sauce. Mix ½ cup grated cheese into the finished sauce. If you follow this procedure the sauce will never curdle.

4. Pour half the sauce over the meat in baking pan. Smooth out with a spatula. Spread rest of the pasta evenly on top of the sauced meat. Sprinkle with 4 tablespoons cheese. Pour remaining sauce over the top. Smooth with a spatula. Sprinkle with remaining bread crumbs and cheese. Dot with the 3 tablespoons butter.

5. Carefully place pan in preheated 350° oven and bake for 50 minutes or until golden and sizzling light brown on top. Remove from oven and allow to sit undisturbed for 15 minutes. Cut into squares and serve.

FREEZING

Pastitsio freezes exceptionally well. Let it cool, then wrap pan in foil and freeze. To reheat, place pan of still-frozen Pastitsio, covered loosely with aluminum foil, in a preheated 350° oven and bake until hot (about 2 hours). Always check the center to make sure it is thoroughly defrosted and hot enough, then let Pastitsio sit undisturbed for 15 minutes before cutting.

SMYRNA SAUSAGES IN TOMATO SAUCE
Souzoukákia Apó Tin Smýrnie

YIELD: 6 servings
TIME: 1½ hours

The people of Smyrna know the magic contained in cumin and have used it to transform ground beef in sauce to an elegant chafing dish recipe that is excellent for parties.

Serve this dish hot with rice or pasta and grated cheese, a crisp salad, and a full-bodied red wine. It can be made two or three days ahead of time. It freezes well, too.

MAKING THE TOMATO SAUCE

1 large can (approximately 2 pounds) peeled whole tomatoes, mashed
6-ounce can tomato paste
1 teaspoon basil

1 clove garlic, very finely minced
1 large bay leaf
½ teaspoon salt
5 peppercorns
1 teaspoon sugar

Combine all ingredients in a 4-quart saucepan. Bring to a boil, lower heat, cover pan, and simmer for 1 hour while you prepare sausages (following).

MAKING THE SAUSAGES

1 pound ground lean beef
½ cup dry unseasoned bread crumbs
1 teaspoon salt

½ teaspoon powdered cumin
1 clove garlic, crushed
Dash cinnamon
¼ pound butter

1. Combine beef, bread crumbs, salt, cumin, garlic, and cinnamon in a large bowl and mix well. (I knead the mixture for about 10 minutes by hand or use the dough hook for 4 minutes.) At the end of that time the mixture is so thoroughly blended it resembles a paste. Shape into small sausages about 5 inches long.

2. Brown sausages well in hot butter in a frying pan. When all have been browned, and tomato sauce has simmered for an hour, put them into the sauce along with any butter and drippings left in frying pan. Continue to simmer sauce and sausages for an additional 30 minutes.

FREEZING

After placing Smyrna Sausages and drippings in tomato sauce, remove from heat and cool. Pour into container and freeze. Reheat in a covered casserole in a preheated 350° oven or in a covered double boiler on top of stove until hot.

LEEK AND MEAT PIE
Prassópeta

YIELD: 8 to 10 servings
TIME: 2½ hours

When Brutus said, "I come to bury Caesar, not to praise him," he was probably waving a leek around in the air—it has been said that ancient orators ate leeks every day because they believed it gave them strong, clear voices. The vegetable we know as the leek goes back a long time. The type we see today is a cultivated variety that seems to be a cross between onions and garlic but has a far more delicate flavor than either.

Throughout most of Europe leeks are so plentiful they are referred to as the "asparagus of the poor." Unfortunately, leeks are rarely seen in the United States and few people know how to cook them. Here are some points to remember about leeks.

To buy leeks: Pick those with firm stalks having a white to pale-green color. The leaves should be crisp.

To wash leeks: Remove the root end and two tough outer layers. Cut off green leafy tops and discard; only the white bulb and part of the pale-green stalks are eaten. Wash well several times to remove any grit between layers.

Greeks enjoy leeks and prepare them in many ways. Their most unusual recipe is Prassopita, a leek and meat pie with a bottom and top crust of layered buttered pastry leaves (Phyllo). It's a bit of work, I admit, but the end result is truly delectable.

As an appetizer, serve Prassopita with sliced tomatoes and make pieces quite small, as this is rich and filling. As an entrée, serve with white wine, a Greek salad, and perhaps buttered green beans. Small dinner rolls would be nice.

4 cups finely chopped leeks, bulbs only (about 2½ pounds whole)
1 pound unsalted butter
1 pound lean ground beef or lamb
¼ cup dry white wine
⅛ teaspoon white pepper
3 dashes nutmeg
Salt

6 medium eggs, at room temperature
1 cup grated Kefalotyri or Parmesan cheese
4 cups White Sauce with Cheese (see recipe), at room temperature
¾ pound Phyllo, at room temperature (see page 9)

1. Slice leeks into ½-inch rounds and rinse these several times in cold water. Use only the white bulbous part of leeks for this recipe; reserve the pale-green stalk parts for other uses, such as making stock. Chop leeks very finely until you have approximately 4 cups.

2. Sauté leeks over low heat in 2 tablespoons of the butter until wilted and golden. Remove from frying pan to a dish and set aside.

3. Add another 2 tablespoons butter to frying pan and sauté meat over high heat, crumbling it with a knife and fork until well browned and uniform in size (about 15 minutes).

4. Add wine to the meat, return the leeks to pan, add pepper, nutmeg, and 1 teaspoon salt, and stir well. Simmer over very low heat for 20 minutes, or until wine has evaporated. Remove pan from heat.

5. Beat eggs well and set aside.

6. Melt remaining butter in a 1-quart saucepan and with a pastry brush use a little to butter a large baking pan (about 20 by 14 by 2 inches), then set butter aside.

7. Add the cheese to White Sauce. Using a wire whisk, beat eggs into the sauce very slowly. Fold the meat and leek mixture into the sauce. Taste for seasoning.

8. Drape a slightly dampened paper towel over half the Phyllo to prevent it from drying out while you work with it, and refrigerate the rest until you are ready to use. Peel off one sheet of Phyllo and lay it flat on bottom of baking pan. Brush with melted butter. Stack 8 to 10 sheets of Phyllo, buttering each layer, to form the bottom crust. If using homemade Phyllo, line pan with only 2 sheets.

9. Preheat oven to 350°.

10. Spread leek mixture evenly over bottom crust. Cover with remaining Phyllo sheets (don't forget that you've refrigerated some), each brushed with butter. You should have at least 10 sheets on top for the top crust (or 2 homemade sheets). Fold in the edges to seal the filling and score top sheets with a sharp knife.

11. Sprinkle with a few drops of warm water and bake for 45 minutes to 1 hour or until pastry leaves are puffed, crisp, and golden. Remove pan from oven and allow to sit undisturbed for 15 minutes. Cut into squares and serve hot.

FREEZING

You can freeze before baking by wrapping pan tightly in plastic and then aluminum foil. When removing from freezer, remove plastic and foil and bake in preheated 350° oven for at least 1½ hours, until hot and crisp. If it starts to brown too quickly, sprinkle with a few drops of warm water and cover loosely with foil.

MEAT TURNOVERS
Kreatópetes

YIELD: 1 dozen 5-inch squares
TIME: 2½ hours

Kreatopetes are simply meat turnovers—a light pastry dough wrapped around a ground-meat filling. They can be shaped as slender rolls or tiny triangles and served as hors d'oeuvres. Or they can be made as large as the familiar turnover and served as a main course with green vegetables and perhaps creamed potatoes. Kreatopetes should be served either hot or warm, never cold. They can be made in advance and frozen.

1 medium onion, finely chopped or grated
2 cloves garlic, crushed
5 tablespoons butter
1 pound ground chuck
1 cup tomato purée
1 cup dry red wine
Salt
1 tablespoon chopped fresh dill

½ teaspoon allspice
2 cups all-purpose flour
2½ teaspoons baking powder
⅓ cup vegetable shortening
About ¾ cup milk, at room temperature
3 hard-boiled eggs, finely chopped
1 egg, beaten

1. Sauté onion and garlic in butter in large heavy frying pan over very low heat until soft and transparent. Add chopped meat slowly and with knife and fork keep crumbling over high heat, mixing the sautéed onion and garlic into it until meat is nicely brown and uniform (about 15 minutes).

2. Add tomato purée, wine, 1 teaspoon salt, dill, and allspice. Blend thoroughly until it comes to a boil, then turn heat down to a bare simmer. Cover pan and simmer for 35 minutes. If you should find liquids being absorbed too fast and mixture beginning to stick to pan, it means heat is too high. Add a few more tablespoons of wine or water and lower the heat.

3. Taste for seasoning; it may need a bit more salt. Remove from heat and allow meat mixture to cool uncovered as you prepare pastry.

4. Combine flour, baking powder, and 1 teaspoon salt in a mixing bowl. Cut in shortening with two knives or a pastry blender. Stir in milk slowly, adding only enough to make dough soft but not sticky. Set dough aside to rest for 5 minutes.

5. Thoroughly mix chopped hard-boiled eggs into cooled meat mixture.

6. Roll out dough thinly on a lightly floured board. Cut into squares: 3-inch ones for appetizers, 5-inch ones for main-course portions. For small squares, place a teaspoon of meat mixture in

h water, fold over to form a triangle,
squares, place a tablespoon of filling
1d fold over to form a triangle. Seal
ng the top edges.

eta top with beaten egg. Cut a very
rnovers only. Place on buttered cookie
s touch one another, and bake in 400°
or until golden brown.

FREEZING

tes flat on plastic- or wax-paper-lined
g them to touch. Place in freezer. When
hem, seal tightly in plastic, and put back
wish to use, remove as many frozen turn-
ace on buttered cookie sheet. Brush with
beaten egg and bake until pastry is golden and toothpick can
easily pierce the filling (about 1 hour); always break one open
to make sure filling is hot before serving. Exact baking time
depends on the size of the Kreatopetes.

OKRA AND LAMB
Arní Me Bámies

YIELD: 4 servings
TIME: ½ hour marinating okra;
1½ hours cooking

Okra can be very, very good, or very, very bad. It all seems to
depend on the okra itself and its preparation prior to cooking.
This particular recipe is out of this world.

Gumbo in the United States means any soup or stew whose
liquid has been thickened by gluey okra sap. In contrast, the
Greeks are determined to avoid having this sap released in their
cooking.

To help you pick okra with this quality in mind, select fresh,
young crisp pods, preferably in season, the smaller the better.
Handle pods tenderly so as not to bruise them, which releases

the sap. Above all, do not omit the step of marinating the okra in vinegar or lemon juice.

1 pound okra, fresh or frozen
¼ cup vinegar or lemon juice
1½ pounds lamb (shoulder or
   leg), cut into 1-inch cubes
6 tablespoons butter

1 medium onion, finely
   chopped
1 tablespoon tomato paste
½ tablespoon salt
¼ teaspoon black pepper

1. Wash fresh okra, cut off stem ends without cutting into flesh, and dry gently with paper toweling. If using frozen okra, defrost thoroughly and pat dry.

2. Place okra in a bowl, sprinkle with vinegar or lemon juice, and set bowl aside for ½ hour, in a sunny spot if possible (customary for Greeks).

3. Rinse lamb cubes and trim off as much fat as possible. Dry thoroughly with paper towels (otherwise it will not brown nicely).

4. Melt 3 tablespoons of the butter in a 3-quart casserole and sauté chopped onion over low heat until limp and transparent; do not let onions brown. Using a slotted spoon, remove them to a plate.

5. Turn heat up to medium and add remaining butter. When butter starts to brown, add lamb cubes and brown well on all sides.

6. Add tomato paste to meat and stir and turn to coat all the cubes.

7. Add enough boiling water to barely cover the meat. Add sautéed onion, salt, and pepper, and mix well. Cover and reduce heat so that the meat will simmer but never boil during cooking. When meat is quite tender and breaks easily with a fork, approximately 1½ hours, turn heat off.

8. Remove meat cubes, place in center of heated platter, and set in a warm oven.

9. Skim off most of the fat from the liquid remaining in the pot, and reheat liquid over low heat.

10. Rinse okra with fresh water several times to remove all the vinegar and then gently add it to the cooking liquid. Simmer

with pot covered until okra is cooked, approximately 20 minutes. Shake pot from time to time, but never stir with a spoon or the delicate okra will be bruised.

11. Arrange cooked okra around the meat like ladyfingers, with all the tips pointing outward. Serve sauce separately or pour over the meat. The Greeks like this sauce on the thin side, but if you wish to make it thicker, mix ¼ teaspoon cornstarch in 1 tablespoon cold water. Add to the sauce and stir continuously over low heat until gravy has thickened to desired consistency.

LITTLE BARRELS IN EGG AND LEMON SAUCE
Youvarlákia

YIELD: 4 to 6 servings
TIME: 1¼ hours

Greek children call this dish "Little Porcupines" because when cooked, the rice sticks out of each meatball like small quills. It's simple, economical, and delicious.

Youvarlakia, "Little Barrels," are traditionally formed into small barrel shapes rather than the conventional round meatballs. However they are shaped, they are very good. Serve them with mashed potatoes and a green vegetable.

1 pound ground lean beef or
    lamb
1 large onion, finely chopped
    or grated
¼ cup long-grain rice
¼ cup olive oil
¾ teaspoon finely crumbled
    mint
Salt
⅛ teaspoon black pepper
1 medium egg

½ cup finely minced fresh
    parsley
½ cup all-purpose flour
2 cups meat stock or 2 cups
    water with 1 beef bouillon
    cube dissolved in it
5 tablespoons butter
3 large eggs, separated, at
    room temperature
2½ tablespoons lemon juice

1. Combine meat, onion, rice, olive oil, mint, 1½ teaspoons salt, pepper, egg, and parsley in a bowl. Knead well for 10 minutes

or until mixture resembles a paste, then form into balls or barrel shapes about the size of a small egg. Roll each lightly in flour.

2. Bring stock or bouillon water to a gentle boil in a 3-quart saucepan. Place meatballs in stock, distribute the butter over them, cover pan, and turn heat down low. Simmer for 45 minutes.

3. Turn heat off, remove 1 cup broth, and set aside.

4. Whip egg whites with a dash of salt in a blender, add yolks, and continue whipping; slowly dribble in lemon juice and the cup of broth, whipping all the time. (This may be done with a wire whisk or electric beater if you lack a blender.) Pour over the little meatballs and shake the pot so that the sauce becomes incorporated into remaining broth and coats all meatballs. Do not cover saucepan once sauce has been added, and do not stir or you will break the meatballs.

REHEATING YOUVARLAKIA

Youvarlakia cannot be reheated once sauce has been added to them *unless* you put them in a double boiler and heat very slowly over extremely low heat, shaking the pot once in a while. Stirring would break the little meatballs. If the heat is high, the eggs in the sauce will cook and make the sauce curdle.

MAKING AHEAD

Cook Youvarlakia for 45 minutes, then drain *all* the liquid and reserve. Refrigerate separately. To serve: Pour liquid into a pot with Youvarlakia and simmer slowly until heated. Just before serving, remove 1 cup of broth and make Egg and Lemon Sauce.

STUFFED PEPPERS AND TOMATOES
Piperiés Ke Domátes Yemistés

YIELD: 4 servings
TIME: 1¼ hours

One of the most frequently made meals in Greek homes, this recipe is easy to prepare. Its ingredients are found in almost every kitchen. If you want a dish that is fragrant, colorful, and succulent, this is for you.

n. 20 years

Out of this world Skillet Moussaka

Serves 4-6

1 med. Eggplant	¼ - ½ tsp. cinnamon
4 T. flour	salt & pepper
1 # ground lamb	
½ c. onion chpd.	2 T butter - 1 c. milk - 1 egg yolk
1 clove garlic, crushed	1 c. grated Kefalotiri cheese
1 (8 oz.) tomato sauce	parmesan or parmesan & swiss
½ tsp. tsp. fresh oregano	GARNISH - 3 tbsp. T. chpd. parsley
1 peel eggplant & cut into ½" pea. - toss w/ 2 T flour - salt
aside [Brown med. heat, sauté lamb - onion & garlic til
lite brown - Drain - 1 Add Eggplant & cook 6-8 min. - til
tender. 1 Stir in tom. sauce, oregano, cinnamon, salt
pepper - 1 Simmer 5 min.
1 Melt butter in pan add 2 T flour, cook, stir, 2 min.

← Add milk - Bring to boil

← Pour a bit into yolk w/ whisk - Return yolk to pan
Combine well -
Cover &
← Pour sauce over meat & top w/ cheese - Cook over med
heat til cheese melts.

2. Garnish w/ rosemary or oregano.

Freeze well - reheat in m/w or oven

I like to bake the tomatoes separately because they are much more delicate than the peppers. If overcooked, tomatoes tend to fall apart as you serve them. This is why it is so important that the rice be almost completely cooked before you stuff the vegetables. Of course the basting makes the rice swell, an important step in baking stuffed vegetables.

Serve one pepper and one tomato to each guest with some of the sauce they were cooked in. Be especially careful removing the tomatoes from the pan to each plate. Any buttered green vegetable is a good accompaniment.

4 large, firm tomatoes
1 teaspoon sugar
4 large, squat green bell peppers
¼ cup long-grain rice
4 tablespoons butter
1 large onion, finely chopped
3 tablespoons finely minced fresh parsley
1 pound ground lean beef or lamb
1 teaspoon salt
⅛ teaspoon black pepper

½ teaspoon crumbled mint
½ cup dry red wine
¼ cup unseasoned bread crumbs
2 tablespoons grated Kefalotyri or Parmesan cheese
2 large potatoes, thinly sliced (optional)
1 large onion, thinly sliced (optional)
1 tablespoon olive oil
8-ounce can tomato sauce

1. Wash tomatoes, cut a thin slice off tops, and save to use as caps later on. Scoop out pulp, chop finely, and set aside to use in stuffing. Sprinkle a little sugar in each tomato and set upside down to drain.

2. Wash peppers, cut off tops (reserve for caps later), and scoop out and discard seeds. Plunge peppers and their caps into 1 quart boiling water and cook over medium heat for 5 minutes. Drain, immediately plunge into cold water, and drain again.

3. Parboil rice in ½ cup water until liquid is absorbed, and set aside.

4. Heat butter in a large frying pan, and sauté onion and parsley until onions are soft.

5. Add ground meat and turn heat up. Mix well with fork

as it cooks so that meat will crumble evenly as it browns. When meat is nicely browned, add reserved tomato pulp, salt, pepper, rice, mint, and wine, and mix well. Turn heat low, cover pan, and simmer for about 20 minutes. Check occasionally to see that mixture doesn't stick to pan. If it needs a little liquid, add a bit of water. Remove pan from stove and allow it to cool slightly.

6. Place pepper shells upright in a cake pan large enough to hold them without touching. Place tomato shells in a similar pan. Use a teaspoon to fill each vegetable with the meat and rice mixture. Sprinkle with bread crumbs and grated cheese and replace caps.

7. Place thinly sliced potatoes and/or onion between peppers if desired. Mix oil with the tomato sauce, and pour three-quarters of it into the pan containing peppers. Pour the remaining sauce into pan containing tomatoes.

8. Place vegetables in preheated 350° oven. Remove caps and baste occasionally with the sauce. Bake tomatoes for 15 minutes, peppers for 35 minutes, or until rice has swelled.

FREEZING

Wrap each stuffed *unbaked* vegetable in aluminum foil and freeze. When you wish to cook, remove foil, place frozen vegetables in pan with tomato sauce, and bake in preheated 350° oven, basting under the caps with the sauce, until the vegetables are tender. Allow at least 1 hour if vegetables are frozen.

GRECIAN MEATBALLS
Keftéthes

YIELD: 50 small egg-sized meatballs
TIME: 1½ hours

Keftethes, featherweight meatballs lightly fried in oil, appear on all festive occasions in Greece, and every Greek seems to have his own treasured recipe. Ideally they should be eaten hot, but I've had them lukewarm at so many picnics I can honestly say they are every bit as good.

For family meals, shape them the size of a small egg; for

cocktail parties, the size of a large marble. Lamb, beef, or veal may be used (the Greeks, of course, prefer lamb). I would suggest you ask the butcher to mince the meat two or three times—mincing and a thorough mixing are what give Keftethes the light, fluffy quality so sought after. If your diet does not permit fried foods, they may be baked, unfloured, in a preheated 350° until well browned on both sides, or broiled, as in the following recipe.

1 large onion, finely minced
1 tablespoon vegetable oil
2 pounds lean ground beef, lamb, or veal
2 cups unseasoned bread crumbs moistened in about ¼ cup warm water
2 eggs, beaten
1½ tablespoons finely crumbled mint
1½ tablespoons finely minced fresh parsley
2½ teaspoons salt
¼ teaspoon black pepper
2 tablespoons Ouzo (optional)
½ cup all-purpose flour
1 cup olive and corn oil, mixed

1. Fry onion with vegetable oil over low heat until golden. Remove to a large mixing bowl.

2. Add ground meat and all other ingredients except flour and 1 cup of oil. Knead for 10 minutes or until mixture is a smooth paste.

3. Shape mixture into balls—egg- or marble-sized depending on how you're serving them.

4. Roll each lightly in the flour.

5. Heat the cup of oil in a large frying pan to the point of fragrance. Fry meatballs in the hot oil until brown on one side; then turn them over carefully with a fork and fry until brown on the other side (approximately 3 minutes on each side if large). Do not crowd them.

6. As they brown, remove with a slotted spoon and place on paper towels to drain.

7. Put drained Keftethes into a covered bowl or casserole and place in a warm oven until serving time. The cover keeps them not only hot but moist as well. Or cover and refrigerate. To reheat, place covered casserole in a 325° oven until heated through.

BROILED GRECIAN HAMBURGERS
Keftéthes Tis Scáras

YIELD: 12 hamburgers
TIME: 30 minutes

For unusual hamburgers, use the preceding recipe for Grecian Meatballs (Keftethes). Form meat mixture into 12 patties instead of meatballs. Do not flour patties. Broil for about 4 minutes on each side and serve on buns with lettuce and sliced tomato; or place each Grecian hamburger on half a bun and place under a hot broiler for 5 minutes. Remove from oven and cover with other half of bun. Carrot sticks and a couple of Kalamata olives on the side would make an interesting accompaniment.

GRECIAN MEATBALLS IN YOGURT GRAVY
Keftéthes Me Yaoúrti

YIELD: Approximately 1½ cups gravy
TIME: 25 minutes

A tart gravy that gives Keftethes (see recipe) a completely different taste and appearance. This is also a great way to heat up leftover meatballs. Serve with hot buttered lima beans and fresh bread so you can savor the gravy and eat up every drop.

1 cup plain yogurt
3 tablespoons flour
Cooked meatballs

1. Blend 2 tablespoons water into yogurt in a saucepan.
2. Mix flour with 1 cup of water, add to yogurt, and stir until it comes to a boil.
3. Add meatballs and simmer over low heat for about 12 minutes. If gravy is not enough to cover meatballs, add a little more water or milk.

GRECIAN MEATBALLS IN TOMATO SAUCE
Keftéthes Me Sálsa Domátes

YIELD: Approximately 1½ cups sauce
TIME: 1½ hours

Cooked Keftethes (see recipe) may also be heated in a simple tomato sauce and served with mashed potatoes, rice, or Orzo and grated Kefalotyri or Parmesan cheese.

1 large onion, finely chopped	1½ teaspoons salt
4 tablespoons butter	¼ teaspoon black pepper
1 cup tomato paste diluted in	⅛ teaspoon sugar
1 cup water	1 bay leaf
1 teaspoon cornstarch mixed	1 or 2 ripe tomatoes,
in 2 tablespoons cold water	skinned (optional)
to make a smooth paste	Cooked meatballs

1. Sauté chopped onion in 3 tablespoons butter in a 3-quart saucepan over low heat until soft and golden, about 10 minutes.

2. Add diluted tomato paste, cornstarch paste, salt, pepper, sugar, and bay leaf, and bring to a boil.

3. Reduce heat, cover saucepan, and simmer gently for 50 minutes. Check from time to time; if you see liquid being reduced too quickly, press fresh tomatoes through a colander and add to sauce.

4. Add meatballs and simmer for 10 to 15 minutes or until they're completely heated through. Just before serving add remaining butter and stir gently.

MEAT AND RICE MOLD
Kréas Me Rízi

YIELD: 6 servings
TIME: 1 hour

I entered and won the Connecticut State championship of the National Beef Cook-Off, which was held in Denver, Colorado, in 1975. This contest is run by the American National CowBelles, the women's auxiliary of the American National Cattlemen's Association.

These contests often remind one of a sorority (even though there are always men to compete with). You make friends with people from all walks of life and professions. The contest was a lot of fun and I discovered for myself that Western hospitality is not just legendary.

This meat and sauce may be prepared in advance and frozen, but the rice should always be freshly cooked.

2 pounds lean chuck, cut into
   1-inch cubes
1½ sticks butter
3 onions, finely chopped
½ cup dry red or white wine
3 tablespoons tomato paste
Beef broth or water
   1 bay leaf

2 teaspoons salt
¼ teaspoon black pepper
1 teaspoon grated orange
   rind
2 cups long-grain rice
Fresh parsley or hot green
   vegetables

1. Brown meat in a 3-quart saucepan with half the butter over medium-high heat. Add onions and stir for 5 minutes. Add wine, tomato paste, 1 cup beef broth or water, bay leaf, salt, pepper, and orange rind, and bring to a boil. Cover the saucepan and simmer over very low heat for 1 hour, or until meat is fork tender.

2. In a 2-quart saucepan boil the rice, following directions on the package and adding remaining butter. (Beef broth may be used instead of water if preferred.)

3. Place all the meat and half the sauce in the bottom of a 9- or 11-inch ring mold. Add the cooked rice and pack tightly. Turn out onto a round heated serving platter (a 10- to 12-inch size will do nicely). The meat will be on top and the sauce will run down the sides of the rice. Serve the rest of the sauce separately. If you want individual molds, even a coffee cup will do. Put some beef and a little sauce into a cup, pack tightly with cooked rice, and invert onto warmed dinner plates. Garnish with parsley or hot green vegetables.

FETA CHEESE SOUFFLÉ WITH HAM
Féta Soufflé Me Hiernó

YIELD: 4 to 6 servings
TIME: 20 minutes preparation;
50 minutes baking

There are few dishes more attractive to bring to the table than a perfect soufflé. There's no trick or magic to making this elegant dish. By following these directions carefully you will create a soufflé that will puff up high above its mold, be crisp on the outside and creamy in the center, and delight your creative soul as well as the appetites of your guests.

A soufflé can be made in any straight-sided ovenproof dish. The straight sides are important to help the soufflé climb upward rather than spreading out.

This soufflé could be served as an appetizer, as a luncheon dish, or for a light dinner. You could accompany it with a salad, hot buttered green vegetables, and a white or rosé wine. I like it best for Sunday brunch, with corn muffins, fresh fruit, steaming pots of coffee, and Grapefruit or Orange Rind Preserves (see recipe).

Remember that guests may wait for a soufflé but a soufflé never waits for guests; it falls as it begins to cool. Even in a turned-off warm oven it will start to fall after about 5 minutes, so as soon as it is baked take it to the table and begin to serve it immediately.

5 tablespoons butter
2 tablespoons grated Kefalotyri, Swiss, or Parmesan Cheese
4 tablespoons flour
1 cup warm milk
1/8 teaspoon white pepper
4 egg yolks, well beaten, at room temperature

2/3 cup (lightly packed) Feta cheese, rinsed, patted dry, and finely crumbled
1 tablespoon minced chives
2/3 cup (lightly packed) finely minced or ground cooked ham
6 egg whites, at room temperature
1/4 teaspoon cream of tartar

1. Butter sides and bottom of a 2-quart soufflé or straight-sided ovenproof dish with 1 tablespoon butter. Sprinkle in 1 tablespoon grated cheese, tipping dish to spread cheese as evenly as possible. This will give bottom and sides of soufflé a lovely brown crust. Though a collar is optional, I advocate making one— I think it gives a soufflé extra height no matter what kind of a mold you happen to be using. Cut a wide piece of aluminum foil or paper long enough to fit around a soufflé dish. Fold in half lengthwise, making a long flat double strip about 2 inches higher than the rim of the dish. Butter one side well and wrap around dish, buttered side toward soufflé. Tie with string or tape to keep it in place to hold the soufflé as it rises (see illustration).

2. Melt remaining 4 tablespoons butter over low heat in a 2- to 3-quart saucepan. Sprinkle in flour and cook, stirring,

over moderate heat for 2 minutes or until mixture is blended and bubbling. Remove from heat and wait for bubbling to stop. Add all of the warm milk at once and beat with wire whisk or wooden spoon until sauce is blended.

3. Stir in pepper, return sauce to moderate heat, and cook for 1 minute, stirring vigorously, until sauce becomes very thick. Remove sauce from heat.

4. Slowly beat the beaten egg yolks into the mixture. Stir in Feta cheese, chives, and ham, and set aside to cool. Heat oven to 350°.

5. Drop egg whites into a large, dry, and perfectly clean mixing bowl. Make sure there isn't even the slightest speck of yolk in any of the egg whites.

6. Add cream of tartar to whites and beat, using large balloon whisk or electric beater, until stiff but not dry. Always begin by beating egg whites slowly until they are foaming, then increase speed to moderate and beat until egg whites are stiff and glossy. Do not overbeat. Egg whites are perfect when they form small points that will stand up without wavering.

7. Stir 3 tablespoons of beaten egg white into the waiting sauce to lighten and thin it.

8. Using a rubber spatula or scraper, gently fold in the rest of the beaten egg whites. Use a cutting and folding motion rather than a stirring motion. Do not incorporate egg whites too thoroughly; you don't want to lose the air beaten into them by too much folding and blending.

9. Gently pour and scrape mixture into prepared soufflé dish. Lightly smooth the top with a spatula. Using spatula, cut a trench about 1 inch deep and 1 inch from the rim all around the dish. This will make a "high hat," or crown, on top of the soufflé.

10. Place soufflé on rack in center of preheated oven and bake for 35 minutes. Open oven door, sprinkle remaining tablespoon of cheese over top of soufflé, and gently but quickly close oven door (remember a draft will make a soufflé fall). Bake an additional 15 minutes. Soufflé is ready when it has puffed up about 2 to 3 inches above the rim of the dish and has browned nicely. Shake the dish gently; if soufflé wobbles, continue to bake for

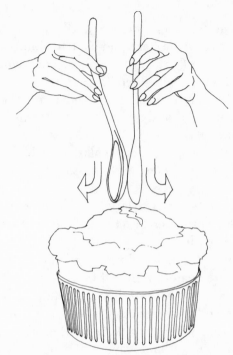

another 6 minutes or until just firm. Carefully remove collar and serve immediately from dish you have baked it in.

11. To serve: Break top of soufflé lightly and spread it apart with two serving spoons held back to back vertically. Make sure each guest gets some of the brown crust from the bottom or sides of the dish plus some of the creamy center and of course some of the golden crown or "top hat" (see illustration).

POULTRY

The Versatile Chicken

The Greeks are enormously fond of chicken and prepare it in many ways. The one important step they insist on prior to cooking chicken in any recipe is that you pour boiling water over the chicken to plump and whiten it and then rub it with half a lemon.

They like chicken simply roasted, with a sprinkling of tarragon and salt; they adore their chicken pilafs, chicken sauced in nutmeats, or chicken wrapped in Phyllo; and, of course, they often cook a chicken stew so delectable that the sauce is poured over pasta (Kapama).

Greeks tend to cook chicken until it is falling off the bone, as they do most of their meats, but this does not mean that you cannot cook chicken to the degree of tenderness you desire in all of the following recipes.

BAKED CHICKEN PILAF
Kóta Piláfi

YIELD: 4 servings
TIME: 1½ hours

Rice, the staple food for the majority of the world's peoples, is said to have originated in India. It was brought to Greece by Alexander the Great, in 300 B.C., from the valleys of the Tigris and Euphrates rivers. The Greeks have been devoted to rice ever since.

The Greeks have as many ways of cooking rice as Americans have of cooking potatoes and they eat it almost daily in one form or another. They do not regard rice as a bland boiled background for gravies and sauces. In fact, a good pilaf, rice cooked in a highly seasoned broth, is often the entire meal.

One of the savory ways to cook rice and chicken is Baked Chicken Pilaf. Converted rice is the easiest to cook, so go get yourself some and make this basic dish. Serve it with slices of Feta cheese, or sprinkle with freshly grated cheese.

1 roasting chicken, 3½ to 4 pounds, cut into serving pieces
1 clove garlic, crushed
1 tablespoon tomato paste
¼ teaspoon white pepper
Salt
¼ pound butter
1 cup long-grain converted rice
2½ cups chicken broth or water

1. Rinse chicken pieces and pat dry. Rub with garlic. Place chicken in an oiled baking pan (approximately 13 by 9 by 2¼ inches) and coat pieces with tomato paste. Sprinkle lightly with pepper and 1 teaspoon salt, and dot with butter.

2. Bake in preheated 350° oven for 40 minutes, turning chicken pieces only once.

3. Parboil rice in 1 cup boiling water for 10 minutes and drain.

4. Bring broth or water to a boil (if using water, add 1 teaspoon salt; most prepared broths already contain salt). Add boiling broth or water and parboiled rice to chicken. Stir care-

fully to ensure that all the rice sinks to the bottom and chicken sits on top of the rice. Cover with foil and bake another 30 minutes.

5. Remove pan from oven and replace foil with a clean fluffy towel. Let it sit undisturbed for 15 minutes (towel will absorb excess moisture) before serving.

PELOPONNESIAN CHICKEN WITH NOODLES
Kotópoulo Helopítes Apó Ta Pelopónisa

YIELD: 6 to 8 servings
TIME: 1¼ hours

As a child visiting Sparta, where my mother's relatives came from, I vicariously relived all the famous battles as I was led from mountain passes to fields and to the warriors' graves.

I especially recall being told about Leonidas and his band of three hundred Spartans holding off an army of ten thousand Persians at the narrow mountain pass. I was told about the spy who showed the Persians the alternate route around the pass, and I was allowed to touch the very boulder on which Leonidas was slain.

My relatives also told me about the austere Spartans eating the same horrible meal once a day, every day. This famous meal, called black soup, was rumored to be made up of bits of pork fat, water, vinegar, and salt. My mouth puckered as I tried to imagine how awful it must have tasted.

As the fame of the Spartan warriors grew (they obviously thrived on black soup or won battles so that they could find better things to eat), kings from other places insisted that their cooks prepare the soup for them so they too could become great warriors. The story was always the same: no one would, or could, eat it. And the reason, I was taught, was that the two most important ingredients had been forgotten—hunger and thirst.

Sparta has changed; its people long ago gave up austerity, and one of their most popular winter dishes is created by this tantalizing way of bringing together chicken, noodles, and grated cheese. A crisp green salad together with a dry white wine would top this off nicely.

2 broiler or fryer chickens, 2 to 2½ pounds each, cut into serving pieces

1½ teaspoons salt (or to taste)

1½ teaspoons white pepper (or to taste)

6 tablespoons butter

2 large onions, finely chopped

2 cloves garlic, crushed

1 cup dry white wine

6 ripe tomatoes, peeled and chopped

1 cup thick tomato purée

2 stalks celery, peeled and finely chopped

¼ cup finely chopped parsley

2 pinches cinnamon

1 pound wide noodles

1 cup grated Kefalotyri or Kasseri cheese (or substitute Parmesan or Romano)

1. Rinse chicken pieces and pat dry. Sprinkle lightly with salt and pepper. Heat butter in a 4-quart pot and brown the chicken pieces. Do not crowd. As pieces brown, remove to a plate.

2. Sauté onions and garlic in the butter chicken was browned in for 10 minutes over low heat. Return all the chicken to the pot and add the wine. Cover and simmer for 15 minutes.

3. Add chopped tomatoes, tomato purée, celery, and parsley, cover pot, and simmer for another 15 minutes. At the end of that time, check the pot; you may have to add up to ½ cup boiling water to prevent sticking. Use as little water as possible so that sauce will be nice and thick.

4. Add cinnamon and continue to simmer with the pot covered until chicken is nice and tender.

5. Cook noodles in another pot according to instructions on package and drain.

6. Remove chicken pieces from the pot. Put drained noodles into the sauce and mix well. Arrange noodles and chicken on a heated platter. Sprinkle with grated cheese and serve.

BRANDIED CHICKEN WITH CREAM
Kóta Methisméni

YIELD: 4 to 8 servings
TIME: 30 minutes

An exquisite dish that raises chicken to undreamed-of gustatory heights. It goes well with garden peas and crusty bread.

If you prefer, you may use a young broiler cut in small serving pieces and baked as they sometimes do in Greece.

You can prepare this recipe a day ahead. Put into a covered casserole and reheat in a very low oven. The brandy has time to permeate the chicken, giving it an unforgettable flavor and gravy.

4 whole broiler or fryer chicken breasts, halved, skinned, and boned	½ teaspoon white pepper
	¼ pound butter
	¼ cup fine Greek brandy
2 tablespoons lemon juice	or Cognac
2 tablespoons salt	½ cup heavy cream

1. Place chicken breasts in a mixing bowl. Sprinkle with lemon juice, salt, and pepper.

2. Heat butter in a large frying pan and sauté breasts over medium heat until golden on both sides (approximately 5 minutes on each side).

3. Lower heat, dribble brandy over the chicken, and simmer (pan still uncovered) until brandy is absorbed—about 5 minutes. Dribble in the cream and stir gently until heated through.

TO BAKE

Place a broiler or fryer chicken cut into serving pieces into a pan (approximately 13 by 9 by 2¼ inches). Sprinkle with lemon juice, salt, pepper, and melted butter. Roast in a preheated 350° oven for 1 hour or until brown and tender, turning over once. Then put pan on top of stove over low heat and proceed with brandy and cream sauce as above.

CHICKEN WITH SPICES
Kapamá

YIELD: 6 servings
TIME: 1½ hours

My favorite family dish is Chicken Kapama. Please don't substitute any of the ingredients, since they all add to the true Balkan flavor of this recipe.

This tastes very good reheated a day or two later, so it can safely be made in advance.

2 teaspoons salt
¼ teaspoon black pepper
½ teaspoon ground cloves
½ teaspoon ground cinnamon
2½ tablespoons lemon juice
3 whole broiler or fryer chicken breasts, halved, skinned, and boned
6 tablespoons butter
1 large onion, finely chopped
1 clove garlic, minced
¾ cup boiling water

¼ cup white wine (optional)
6-ounce can tomato paste
2 cups canned whole tomatoes, crushed
1 teaspoon sugar
1 tablespoon cornstarch, diluted in ¼ cup cold water (optional)
Cooked rice or pasta
Grated Kefalotyri, Parmesan, or Romano cheese

1. Combine salt, pepper, cloves, cinnamon, and lemon juice in a mixing bowl. Stir several times with a fork. Dip chicken breasts into bowl, coating each piece with the marinade.

2. Heat half the butter in a 3-quart pot over low heat. Place half the chicken breasts in and sauté until golden on both sides (no longer than 8 minutes). Remove them to a large plate. Sauté other half of the breasts in remaining butter and remove them to the plate.

3. Using the same pot, sauté onion and garlic for a few seconds; then add water, wine (optional), tomato paste, canned tomatoes, and sugar. Mix and turn heat up until sauce boils.

4. Cover pot, lower heat, and simmer sauce for 1 hour. If you wish sauce thickened, stir in cornstarch mixture after sauce has simmered 40 minutes. Return chicken to the pot and simmer an additional 15 minutes.

5. Serve over rice or pasta, cooked according to directions on the box. Pour sauce from Kapama over it and sprinkle grated cheese over it. Serve chicken breasts on the side.

FREEZING

Remove chicken from heat, and cool. Pour into container and freeze. Heat in covered casserole in a 350° oven or on top of stove in a covered double boiler until heated through.

GREEK CHICKEN PIE
Kotópeta

YIELD: 12 to 15 servings
TIME: First day: 3 hours;
second day: 2 hours

For an unusual way to serve chicken, make a Kotopeta. Layers of buttered Phyllo (pastry leaves) line the bottom of a square baking pan. The filling is made of diced chicken in a sauce. The top is composed of more buttered layers of Phyllo. The Kotopeta is then baked until golden and crisp, cut into squares, and served hot.

I would suggest preparing the chicken on one day (because that part is rather time-consuming) and finishing off the recipe the following day. Lacking Phyllo, you can use puff pastry.

As a main course, serve with cranberry sauce, buttered lima beans, and salad.

FIRST DAY, PREPARING CHICKENS

2 roasting chickens, 3½ to 4 pounds each
½ tablespoon salt
5 medium onions, finely sliced

1. Rinse chickens. Simmer them in water to cover, adding salt. Remove foam as it rises to the surface.
2. When no more foam rises, add sliced onions and continue to simmer, pot now covered, until chickens are very tender (approximately 1½ hours). Lift the chickens from the pot and set them aside to cool.
3. Let broth boil down vigorously until you have only about 3 cups left. Pour through strainer to get onion slices; set them aside. Put broth into refrigerator or freezer. When it becomes very cold, remove the hardened fat from the surface. Add the strained onions to the cold jellied broth, cover, and refrigerate.
4. Carefully bone chickens when they are cool enough to handle. Discard all skin, bones, and fatty parts. Dice chicken, being careful to remove any residual bone, fat, or sinew. Cover loosely and refrigerate.

SECOND DAY, FILLING AND BAKING THE KOTOPETA

1 cup warm milk
Salt (optional)
 1 pound Phyllo, at room
   temperature (see page 9)
¾ pound warm melted butter
 4 tablespoons grated
   Kefalotyri or Parmesan cheese

5 medium eggs, at room
   temperature
¼ teaspoon pepper
¼ teaspoon nutmeg

1. Remove broth and onion mixture from refrigerator, heat over very low heat, and add the diced chicken. When chicken is heated through, add the warm milk and stir until it almost comes to a boil. Remove at once from heat and taste for seasoning. You may want to add a bit of salt.

2. Butter sides, corners, and bottom of a large baking pan (about 16 by 10 by 2 inches). Preheat oven to 350°.

3. Line a baking pan with about 8 sheets of Phyllo, brushing each sheet with warm melted butter as you lay it into the pan. Let Phyllo overlap sides of pan.

4. Add the grated cheese to chicken mixture. Break the eggs directly into the mixture and stir well. Add pepper and nutmeg and, preferably using your hands, mix the spices in very thoroughly.

5. Spread chicken mixture over buttered Phyllo sheets and then cover with remaining sheets of Phyllo, again brushing each one with warm melted butter and letting them overlap sides. When you have used up all the Phyllo, roll edges down all around the pan to hold in the mixture.

6. Brush entire top and rolled-down edges of Kotopeta with warm melted butter. With a sharp knife lightly score Phyllo into squares without cutting through layers—this is to guide you when you cut it to serve later.

7. Sprinkle about 10 drops warm water over the top of Kotopeta to prevent Phyllo from curling while baking. Place pan in oven. Bake for 1 hour or until golden brown and crisp on top. Remove from oven and allow pan to remain undisturbed for 20 minutes. Cut with a very sharp knife into squares and serve hot.

ort shorts

The branches of bridalwreath spirea are now absolutely loaded with pure white flowers. Compare a hedge of this spirea with a planting in which the branches are allowed to naturally arch. To me, the arching branches are much more beautiful. I think this is a perfect example of how the beauty of nature far surpasses our attempts to manipulate it.

The University's recommended pruning procedure: Prune after its blossoms fade. Prune old canes (about 5 years old or older) at ground level. This will stimulate new shoots to develop from the base, giving you a full-looking shrub. Avoid trimming branches to artificially shapen bridalwreath spirea, since this will destroy its natural, arching habit.

Tom Kalb, is Kenosha County UW-Extension horticultural agent.

nic."

**Michelle Kohel
Kenosha**

"I'm going to a basket-
ball tournament with my
daughter in Kenosha."

**Diane Sterba
Kenosha**

Video helps

TO FREEZE

Seal unbaked Kotopeta in pan with foil and freeze. Bake frozen in preheated 350° oven for about 1¾ hours or until very hot and brown and crisp on top. If it's browning too fast, cover lightly with foil during the last 20 minutes of baking. Always make sure the center is hot.

GRECIAN CHICKEN
Ellenikí Kóta

YIELD: 4 servings
TIME: 1½ hours

One day I bought a bottle of Mazola oil and noticed a tag hanging from it. It was an entry form for "The National Chicken Cooking Contest." The rules were simple: You had to use 1 broiler or fryer chicken (2 to 3½ pounds), whole or any part or parts. The recipe had to include at least 1 teaspoon of Ac'cent flavor enhancer and at least ¼ cup Mazola corn oil.

It sounded like a challenge, so I sat down and created the following recipe. I won an all-expense-paid trip to North Carolina four months later for the National Cook-Off. There, after cooking this recipe twice (once for the judges and once for the big banquet), I won a silver medal, an engraved silver trophy, a cash prize, and all kinds of pots, pans, and knives plus a year's supply of oil and flavor enhancer.

It was such fun that I heartily recommend it to everyone who likes to cook chicken. Serve with Rice Pilaf and a green salad.

1 broiler or fryer chicken (2 to 3½ pounds), cut into serving pieces
½ cup Mazola corn oil
2 tablespoons lemon juice
1½ teaspoons Ac'cent
1½ tablespoons oregano
1 teaspoon salt
⅛ teaspoon freshly ground black pepper

1. Rinse chicken pieces in cool water and pat dry.
2. Heat oil in a 10-inch frying pan over medium-high heat. When hot, but not smoking, add chicken parts. Cook until lightly

browned on all sides, about 8 minutes. Remove chicken with a slotted spoon and set aside.

3. In a large bowl, mix remaining ingredients. Add browned chicken and toss gently to coat pieces well. Preheat oven to 350°.

4. Place chicken pieces in baking pan (approximately 13 by 9 by 2 inches) and bake for 45 minutes, or until done, turning over once during baking.

RICE PILAF

3 tablespoons butter
1 cup long-grain rice
1 small onion, finely minced
2½ cups chicken stock, degreased
1 teaspoon salt

1. Melt butter over low heat in a 2-quart saucepan. Add rice and onion, and sauté, stirring over medium heat for 4 minutes.

2. Add stock and salt, and bring to a boil. Stir twice with a fork. Cover and simmer undisturbed over low heat for 25 minutes.

CHESTNUT SAUCE FOR COOKED POULTRY
Sáltsa Kástana Yiá Kóta

YIELD: Approximately 2 cups sauce; 4 servings
TIME: After preparation of chestnuts, 20 minutes

The Greek version of chicken à la king is this marvelous chestnut sauce. Serve it with buttered beans and cranberry sauce. The Greeks usually serve this with Grapefruit or Orange Rind Preserves (see recipe).

12 chestnuts, fresh or dried
1 tablespoon butter
1 tablespoon all-purpose flour
1 cup warm milk
½ cup heavy cream, scalded
2 tablespoons sherry

2 dashes grated nutmeg
  or mace
½ teaspoon salt
⅛ teaspoon white pepper
2 cups diced cooked chicken
  or turkey
6 slices buttered toast

1. Cut an X in the flat side of each chestnut shell with a small, sharp knife. Cover the nuts with water, bring to a boil, and simmer 45 minutes to 1 hour, covered. Drain and, while still hot, peel them. If you use the dried shelled chestnuts available at foreign grocery stores, you must soak them in warm water for 1 to 2 days before simmering them as above. Coarsely chop and then rub chestnuts through a sieve.

2. Melt butter over low heat in a 2-quart saucepan. Add flour and let the roux bubble while you stir for about 1 minute. Add warm milk, stirring with a whisk all the time, until thickened slightly. Remove from heat.

3. Add sieved chestnuts, scalded cream, sherry, nutmeg or mace, salt, and pepper. Add diced chicken or turkey and mix.

4. Slice buttered toast diagonally, divide pieces among serving plates, and pour hot sauce over them. Serve immediately.

FATHER'S TURKEY WITH CHESTNUT STUFFING
Parayémisi Meh Kástana Tou Patéra

YIELD: Stuffing for a 20-pound turkey
TIME: 2 hours, after preparation of potatoes
and chestnuts

Turkey is very popular in Greece and is traditionally served on Christmas or New Year's Day. From November onward, one can see hundreds of freshly killed turkeys hanging in butcher shops.

They are much smaller than the ones in the United States. A ten-pound bird is considered large, and as a Greek friend wistfully pointed out to me, "Everything seems to grow bigger in America." Athough roasting a turkey is pretty much the same everywhere, the Greeks have many interesting stuffings to offer the culinary world.

They often use a rice stuffing, which is very good. The rice is sautéed in butter and onions and blended with herbs, raisins, chopped almonds, and crumbled Feta cheese. An egg binds it all together.

Another savory stuffing is made with roasted chestnuts, raisins, minced turkey liver, black olives, and bread crumbs, all soaked in turkey broth.

I watched a native from the island of Andros use ground lamb, pine nuts, herbs, chopped apples, and white wine. The result was mouth-watering indeed.

Of one thing we can be certain. Greeks love stuffing and always have some left over after sewing up the cavity. This extra stuffing may be wrapped in foil and roasted along with the bird. It is good served with a bit of gravy over it after all the regular stuffing has been consumed. Some cooks shape cooked stuffing into "meatballs" that are dipped into beaten egg and bread crumbs and lightly sautéed in butter. They are then served as a garnish with vegetable dishes.

I've eaten chestnut stuffing in many homes, hotels, and famous restaurants throughout the world, but never has it come close to the one my father used to make for our Thanksgiving bird.

2 pounds chestnuts	¼ pound butter
3 large baked sweet potatoes or yams	1½ pounds lean ground beef
	½ pound lean ground pork
2 large onions, finely chopped	1 cup dry red wine
4 stalks celery, peeled and coarsely chopped	Nutmeg
	Salt
½ cup finely minced fresh parsley	¼ teaspoon black pepper
	1 large egg, lightly beaten
¼ cup pine nuts (optional)	Lemon juice

1. Preparing the chestnuts and potatoes is time-consuming, so two days before you are going to stuff a big turkey, boil the chestnuts and peel them (see page 143). Crumble them coarsely into a clean bowl, cover, and refrigerate.

2. Rinse and prick sweet potatoes with a knife and bake at 350° for 1 hour or until soft. Allow them to cool unpeeled, then cover and refrigerate.

3. The night before roasting the turkey, prepare the stuffing by sautéing the onions, celery, parsley, and pine nuts (if you wish to add them) in butter over low heat in a large frying pan. Sauté until vegetables are soft but not brown (about 20 minutes).

4. Turn heat up to medium and add ground meat slowly, cutting with a knife and fork until meat is crumbly and uniform

in size. Cook, stirring occasionally, until meat is nicely browned, approximately another 20 minutes.

5. Add wine, 1 teaspoon nutmeg, 2 teaspoons salt, and pepper, and mix well. Turn heat down low and simmer uncovered for 1 hour. Stir from time to time to prevent sticking. If you find you need a bit more liquid, add a little more wine if you have it, or water.

6. While meat is simmering, remove sweet potatoes and chestnuts from the refrigerator. Peel and then mash the potatoes and place in a large mixing bowl. Add crumbled chestnuts and set mixture aside.

7. When meat has finished simmering, allow it to cool, then mix in the lightly beaten egg. Add meat to the potatoes and chestnuts and stir entire mixture for 10 minutes or until thoroughly blended.

8. Taste for seasoning. You may wish to add ½ teaspoon more salt and ¼ teaspoon more nutmeg. If you do, mix into stuffing thoroughly. Cover and refrigerate.

9. On the morning you are going to roast the turkey, rub cavity of rinsed bird well with lemon juice and a sprinkling of salt. Stuff the bird in large cavity and at the neck; close openings. Any leftover stuffing can be baked in a separate small covered casserole or frozen for later use.

FREEZING

Never freeze either an uncooked or cooked turkey *with* the stuffing in it. And if freezing a cooked bird, you must also bone it. Both are precautions against the growth of bacteria. Save turkey bones to make stock for soup or a pilaf. To reheat frozen cooked turkey or stuffing, defrost in refrigerator overnight. The next day, heat in 325° oven until warm.

Frozen turkeys, when of the highest quality, are almost as good as fresh turkeys in the United States. Make sure all poultry is thoroughly defrosted in accordance with directions on package before cooking in any way, or flesh will be stringy and dry.

NOTES: I don't recommend "self-basting" varieties of turkey because the bird is saturated with oils that affect its texture and taste.

A piece of clean cheesecloth dipped in melted butter and placed over the bird and kept moist from time to time with the drippings from the pan (use a bulb baster) provides a much more succulent turkey, and it is really worth that little bit of extra effort.

Try unwaxed dental floss instead of thread to sew up a stuffed bird; it's much stronger.

SESAME CHICKEN
Kóta Susáme

YIELD: 8 servings

TIME: Approximately 30 minutes

The Greeks use sesame seeds every chance they get, particularly in breads. In this recipe sesame seeds combine with chicken to create a marvelous flavor. You can prepare and coat it ahead of time. Refrigerate it, and fry just before serving.

1 egg, slightly beaten
½ cup all-purpose flour
1 teaspoon sugar
1 teaspoon almond extract
1 teaspoon salt
¼ teaspoon black pepper
¼ teaspoon baking powder

4 whole broiler or fryer chicken breasts, halved, skinned, and boned
1 cup sesame seeds
Approximately 4 cups corn oil
Watercress or parsley sprigs

1. With a whisk, mix together the egg, 1 tablespoon of the flour, sugar, almond extract, salt, pepper, and baking powder to make a batter.

2. Dip chicken pieces in batter; place on waxed paper. Sprinkle both sides with sesame seeds. Coat with remaining flour.

3. Heat oil in a deep fryer or frying pan, over medium heat, until it reaches 375°.

4. Carefully place the coated chicken pieces, a few at a time, into the hot oil. Cook 5 minutes, or until golden brown and chicken is done; drain on paper towels. Serve immediately, garnished with watercress or parsley.

BREADS

The Sustaining Loaves

The value of cereal grains has always been understood by man, from the time he chewed the seeds of wild grasses until he started to pound the seeds with a rock to make a coarse type of flour. It is generally believed by archaeologists that many of the interesting forms of bread started from ancient religious pagan rites. For example, it would have been easier to offer a daily sacrifice of a loaf of bread rather than one of the livestock, and so bread was made round in the shape of the sun, or crescent-shaped to represent the moon, and it has even been suggested that plaited loaves may have been a substitute offering of cut braided hair by the women.

The importance of bread is stressed over and over again throughout history. In Rome, bread was distributed free to the poor in times of famine. The English formed the phrase, "Bread is the staff of life." In the Old Testament: "Man does not live by bread alone," and in the New Testament, "Give us this day our daily bread."

Today's Greeks love bread and eat it at every meal. Whether it is a country bread or a sweet decorated holiday loaf, bread is always present on the Greek table. The only requirement is that the bread be freshly baked.

EASTER BREAD
Lambrópsomo

YIELD: 2 large snowballs or twists
TIME: 1½ hours preparation;
6½ hours rising;
30 minutes baking

I flew to Ohio to obtain this recipe from Coula Maistros, my cousin and a magnificent baker. She started out in the morning, and by the end of the day had baked nine exquisite loaves that were not only mouth-watering but also a sheer delight to look at. She braided some into circles, formed some into Byzantine crosses, made snowball designs of others. She decorated many with deep-red Easter eggs. She explained every step thoroughly and patiently.

That evening on the flight home, I came to the conclusion that Coula has more energy than most people. I also noted that she worked with three ovens, whereas most of us have only one. Therefore I have cut the recipe down to yield two loaves of Lambropsomo.

The Greek word for Easter is *lambri,* and the word for bread is *psomi.* This traditional holiday bread is called Lambropsomo, a combination of both words.

MAKING THE SPICE LIQUID

1 tablespoon whole cloves
3 large bay leaves
1 large cinnamon stick
¾ cup water

Bring all ingredients to a boil in a small pot and reduce heat. Simmer gently with the pot covered for 30 minutes. Remove from heat and set aside to cool.

PREPARING THE YEAST

3 packages (¼ ounce each) fresh cake yeast
or active dry yeast, at room temperature
½ tablespoon sugar
½ cup warm water

Crumble or sprinkle yeast into a small warmed bowl. Sprinkle the sugar over it and dribble the warm water over it. Cover with a warm plate and set aside.

PREPARING THE DOUGH

½ cup milk
¼ pound butter
2 large eggs, at room
temperature
¾ cup sugar

½ teaspoon salt
1 teaspoon vanilla extract
6 cups unsifted all-purpose
flour
1 tablespoon vegetable oil
(optional)

1. Scald milk and set aside. Melt butter and set aside.
2. Place eggs in small bowl of electric mixer and beat for exactly 6 minutes at medium speed. This will make them thick and creamy rather than frothy. Increase beaters to high speed and add sugar very slowly. Use your spatula to make sure all the sugar has dissolved. With beaters still on high speed, slowly add melted butter to mixture. Beat for another 4 minutes.
3. Pour mixture into a huge mixing bowl or large pot. Add lukewarm milk, salt, and vanilla; stir with a spoon.
4. Strain the lukewarm spice liquid and measure ½ cup into mixture, stirring to mix.
5. Add the yeast mixture prepared earlier, and mix well with a spoon.
6. Start adding flour, 1 cup at a time. Using your hand, keep mixing the flour into the mixture. Add at least three-fourths of the flour in this fashion. Dough should now be getting spongy and springy, but still sticking to the sides of the bowl.
7. Continue adding flour, but now much more slowly. Knead the dough by punching it repeatedly and sprinkling the remaining flour slowly *underneath* the dough, each time you turn it. Do this

until dough leaves the sides of the bowl. When that happens, use no more flour and use dough hook for 5 minutes; or if kneading manually, place dough on lightly floured board and use a bit of salad oil on your hands from time to time, to help the dough and prevent hands from sticking.

8. If kneading manually, knead dough for 15 minutes *after* putting in the last drop of flour; punch it like a prizefighter, with slow steady jabs. Turn dough over, using thumbs, punch again, turn, punch.

9. Set bowl in a warm corner, out of drafts. Cover with a large clean cloth and then wrap several blankets or towels loosely around the bowl. (I have seen handwoven wool rugs put around the bowl in villages in Greece.) Allow dough to rise for 3 hours or until doubled in size.

10. When dough has risen, punch down and knead vigorously in the bowl for a minute. Cover and allow to rise for 2 more hours in a warm place, or until doubled in size.

11. When dough has doubled in size, you are ready to shape loaves into one of the following designs.

FORMING THE DOUGH

TO MAKE A SNOWBALL DESIGN

Line two round 10-inch cake pans with foil. Using a sharp knife, cut off a piece of dough the size of a large apple and place on a clean surface. Knead dough for a minute with hands dipped in oil, then roll it into a smooth snowball. Place in center of cake pan. Make 5 more balls, a bit smaller than the one in the center. Place around the center one, touching (see illustration). Repeat with second pan. Lay clean dish towel lightly over pans and place in a warm corner out of drafts. Allow dough to rise for 1½ hours or until doubled in size.

TO MAKE BRAIDED WREATHS

5 deep-red-dyed hard-boiled eggs (see page 211)

Cut dough in half. Cut each half into three equal portions each the size of an orange. Oil hands. Take one portion and roll into

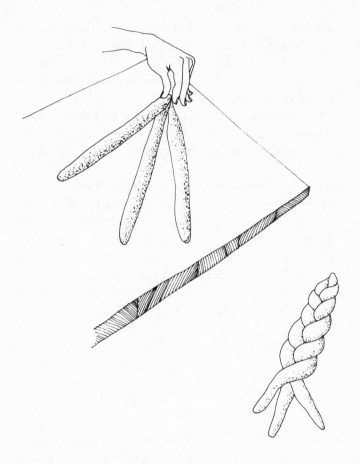

a long smooth rope about 12 inches long. Do this with the other two portions of dough. Press the three dough ropes together at one end and then braid them. Finish by pressing ends together at other end. Place braided dough in a round 10-inch foil-lined cake pan, forming a circle. Deeply push 4 dyed hard-boiled Easter eggs upright into joints of braided dough and 1 in the center hole. Repeat with remaining dough. Cover pans with clean dish towels and place in a warm corner out of drafts for final rising of 1½ hours. As dough rises it will push eggs up higher and close in around the one placed in the middle. When baked, the eggs will be sealed in place (see illustration).

TO FORM LONG BRAIDED TSOUREKIA

2 deep-red-dyed hard-boiled eggs (see page 211)

The Greeks traditionally make at least one large braided bread for
Easter, and it is always decorated with red hard-boiled eggs. This
is called a Tsoureki. It may be round, as described above, or
long. If making a long braid, make three ropes, as described,
in preceding directions for braided wreath, but roll each slightly
thicker in the center so the braid will taper nicely. *Starting in the
middle*, braid first one half, twist the ends together, and tuck
under. Then braid the other half, twist ends, and tuck ends under.

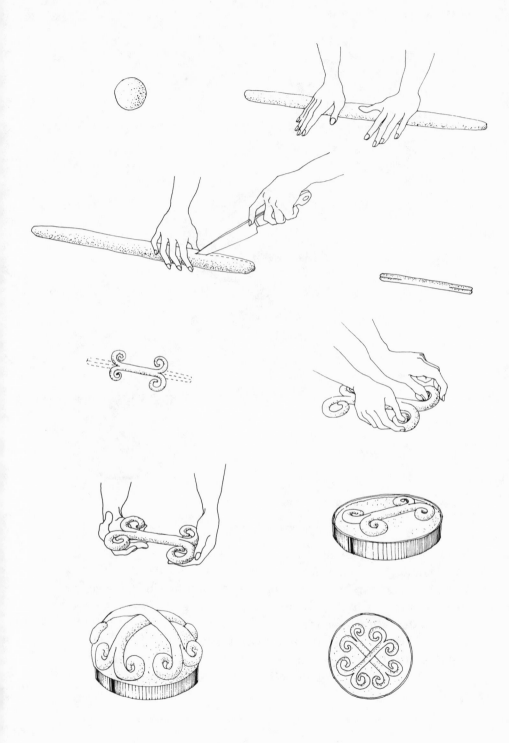

Lay flat on a foil-lined cookie sheet and push a hard-boiled red egg deeply into center of the braid. Repeat with remaining dough. Cover with clean dish towels. Place in a warm corner out of drafts for final rising of 1½ hours.

TO FORM A BYZANTINE CROSS

Walnut halves (optional)

This interesting design is often seen in Greece during Easter and Christmas. Cut off two pieces of dough each the size of a lemon and set aside. Shape remaining dough into a round loaf and place in a 10-inch greased cake pan. Roll each small dough ball into a rope 12 to 16 inches long. Slice from each end vertically 5 inches down the rope. Cross the two slashed ropes on top of loaf. Do not press flat. Curl the slashed parts in opposite directions (see illustration). Decorate here and there with about 10 walnut halves (optional), cover with clean dish towel, and place out of drafts for final rising for 1½ hours.

GLAZING AND BAKING THE BREAD

2 egg yolks, at room temperature
3 tablespoons warm milk
Sesame seeds

1. Preheat oven to 350°. With fork, beat egg yolks and milk.
2. When the 1½ hours for the last rising are up, take pans and paint surfaces of loaves with egg-milk glaze. Do not glaze the hard-boiled red eggs. Sprinkle loaves with sesame seeds.
3. Bake loaves for approximately 30 minutes. Exact time depends on shapes formed. Bread is ready when it is golden brown and has shrunk from sides of the pan slightly. Another test is to tap the bottom of the loaf and, if it sounds hollow, the bread is done. Let cool for 30 minutes before removing from pan. Allow loaves to cool for at least 6 hours before cutting.

FREEZING BREAD

To freeze, allow loaves to cool completely, slip into plastic bags, and seal. When you wish to use, place frozen bread into preheated 325° oven until completely thawed.

CHRISTMAS BREAD
Christópsomo

YIELD: 1 round loaf
TIME: 1½ hours preparation;
6½ hours rising;
50 minutes baking

Christ's Bread, called Christopsomo, is made at Christmas and decorated with a Byzantine cross made of dough. Make exactly as you would Easter Bread (preceding recipe), but substitute these spices when making the spice liquid. Use walnut halves as a decorative touch if you want to.

½ teaspoon cinnamon
½ teaspoon grated orange
  peel
2 bay leaves
½ teaspoon unground Mahlepi
  (or 2 teaspoons vanilla)

5 pieces washed unground
  Mastiha (see page 41)
¼ cup Ouzo or brandy
¾ cup water

For final rising of dough, cut two balls of dough each the size of a lemon and set aside. Shape remaining dough into a round loaf and place in a 10-inch round greased cake pan. Make Byzantine cross on top of loaf as described for Easter Bread (see illustration on page 154). Place walnut halves on top and around sides of the bread. Cover and set aside for final rising. Paint surfaces of bread with the egg-milk glaze just before baking. You don't have red eggs to worry about, so you can glaze the entire bread freely. Bake about 50 minutes or until bread is golden brown, sounds hollow when thumped, and inserted tester comes out clean.

NEW YEAR'S BREAD
Vasilópita

YIELD: Three 9-inch cakes or 1 large one
TIME: 1 hour preparation;
4 hours rising;
45 minutes baking

The Vasilopita is a large cakelike bread, customarily baked with a gold or silver coin in it. It is the centerpiece of the dining table on New Year's Eve and is cut precisely at midnight. This ceremony goes back to the days of Byzantium.

On New Year's Eve in Greece, young men go from house to house singing the songs of St. Basil (Agios Vasilios), the patron saint of the Greek New Year. Relatives and friends gather together early to drink, eat, and play baccarat or roulette. For that evening, Greece becomes one big Monte Carlo, as the Greeks try to see what their luck will be in the coming year.

Just before midnight, the gambling stops and the huge Vasilopita with its lucky coin is brought in. Amid darkness and noisemakers everyone hugs, kisses, and says, "Hronia polla," which literally means: Many happy years. The lights are turned back on, and the head of the household makes the sign of the cross over the cake and cuts the first slice. This is set aside as an offering to the *Panayia* (the Holy Mother). Slices are then cut for the family in order of age and then for the relatives and friends present.

If the gold or silver coin should be in the slice offered to the Holy Mother, it is donated to the poor at the local church. After each person is handed his slice, he searches for the coin. If he says, "No coin," everyone yells, "Poor loser!" The finder of the coin is loudly cheered, for this means he will have good luck and fortune in the new year.

Champagne is served, the Vasilopita is eaten, and the gambling is resumed until dawn. The dawn on New Year's Day is greeted with a twenty-one-gun salute from Mount Lycabettus.

Greek-Americans usually bake several small Vasilopites, each one with a coin inserted into it. If planning a big New Year's Eve celebration with lots of guests, then of course a big Vasilopita should be baked.

This bread is somewhat like a coffee cake in texture and is wonderful with coffee or with meals. Children love to eat it all through the year, spread with butter or jam. It freezes beautifully, so please don't wait for New Year's Eve to try it.

1 cup sugar
1 teaspoon salt
11 tablespoons unsalted butter,
   melted and cooled
½ cup scalded milk
½ cup lukewarm water
   3 packages (¼ ounce each)
   active dry yeast
   3 medium eggs, well beaten,
   at room temperature

Approximately 6 cups sifted
   all-purpose flour
1 tablespoon ground Mahlepi
   (or 2 tablespoons substitute, see page 159)
¼ cup whole blanched
   almonds (see page 175
   for blanching)
1 small egg, beaten, at room
   temperature
Sesame seeds

1. Stir ¾ cup sugar, salt, and 10 tablespoons of the melted butter into scalded milk and allow to cool to lukewarm.

2. Rinse large mixing bowl with hot water and pour ½ cup lukewarm water into bowl. Add remaining sugar, and sprinkle in the yeast. Cover with clean towel and set aside for 15 minutes.

3. Stir lukewarm milk mixture and the 3 well-beaten eggs into yeast mixture. Slowly add 3 cups of the flour and the Mahlepi, and beat with a large spoon until smooth.

4. Work the 3 cups of remaining flour in very slowly until dough starts leaving sides of bowl. When this happens, do not add more flour. If you have added all the flour and dough is still sticky, add a bit more, a little at a time, until dough leaves sides of bowl. Put dough on lightly floured board and knead for 15 minutes or until smooth (5 minutes if using a dough hook).

5. Put dough in lightly greased bowl and brush top with remaining tablespoon of melted butter to prevent it from forming a crust while rising. Place in a warm area out of drafts. Cover with a clean dish towel and wrap a bath towel loosely around bowl. Allow 2 hours for rising.

6. When dough has doubled in bulk, punch down and knead lightly for 2 minutes in bowl or on clean board.

7. Either shape dough into three round cakes and place in greased and lightly floured 10-inch cake pans, or form into one round cake and place in a large 13-inch shallow cake pan. (Always make cakes 1 inch smaller than pan you are to bake them in to allow for last-rising expansion.) Wrap a clean silver coin in

foil and push up into dough from the bottom of each cake. To avoid accidental swallowing, always use a quarter or fifty-cent piece, never anything smaller in size. Lightly cover cakes with a clean dish towel, wrap a bath towel around the pan, and let cakes rise in warm area free from drafts until dough has doubled (about 2 hours).

8. When cakes have risen, decorate with almonds: for instance, it is traditional to make the number of the New Year on top of the cake and/or simple flower and leaf patterns. Place almonds on sides very low, since as cake rises so will the almonds. Brush cake and almonds with beaten egg. Preheat oven to 350° and sprinkle cakes with sesame seeds.

9. Bake in preheated oven for 45 minutes or until Vasilopita is a deep shiny brown. Tester inserted in center should come out perfectly clean and cake should sound hollow when thumped. Remove from oven and allow to cool for 30 minutes before removing cakes from pans.

10. Place cakes on rack until cool. For perfect texture, always allow at least 6 hours before cutting. If storing, wrap tightly in plastic wrap when cool and store or freeze exactly as you would bread.

SUBSTITUTE LIQUID FOR MAHLEPI

Simmer, covered, over low heat for about 20 minutes: 3 cloves, 1 bay leaf, ½ stick cinnamon, and ¾ cup water. Strain and use, substituting approximately 2 tablespoons of the liquid for 1 tablespoon ground Mahlepi.

BRAIDED DINNER ROLLS
Tsourekákia

YIELD: 1 dozen rolls
TIME: 1 hour preparation;
1¾ hours rising;
30 minutes baking

The French have their croissants and the Greeks their Tsourekakia. Tiny tables and chairs, some sheltered from the sun by huge gaily colored umbrellas, line most of the sidewalks of

Greece. People are constantly stopping for a sip of coffee. When the young boy from the coffeehouse comes out to your sidewalk table to take your order he always asks, "And a freshly baked Tsourekaki perhaps?" By this time, of course, your nostrils, first having been tantalized by the freshly ground coffee, are very much aware of the fragrance of sweet baking rolls. Who can resist?

So you give the coffee boy a few drachmas and he runs into the bakery (always conveniently very close to the coffeehouse) and buys you a couple of Tsourekakia fresh out of the oven.

As you sip your coffee in the Greek morning sun and munch on a Tsourekaki, you begin to forget the world's problems, your age, and your waistline; for a little while you truly feel almost immortal.

Now to come back down to earth. Next time you decide to do some baking, why not make these delightful little braided rolls and freeze them? When your spirits need a lift, pop a couple into the oven, make yourself a cup of fresh coffee, bring out some butter or marmalade, and sit in the sunshine—inside or out. Relax and enjoy.

¼ cup warm water (between 110° and 115°)
1 package (¼ ounce) active dry yeast
3 tablespoons sugar
2 teaspoons salt
¼ cup melted butter
¾ cup warm milk
1 large egg, at room temperature

3½ cups sifted all-purpose flour
¼ teaspoon ground Mahlepi (or 1 teaspoon substitute, see page 159)
1 teaspoon melted butter
1 egg yolk, lightly beaten with fork
Sesame or poppy seeds

1. Rinse a large mixing bowl in warm water. Pour the ¼ cup warm water into bowl and sprinkle on the yeast. Cover with a warm plate and set aside for 15 minutes.

2. Add sugar, salt, ¼ cup melted butter, and warm milk to the yeast and cover. Beat the egg and add to yeast mixture.

3. Sift flour and Mahlepi slowly into the yeast mixture, stirring until a soft dough is formed. Knead for 15 minutes, with

5-minute rest intervals between each 5 minutes of kneading. Put dough back into bowl and brush lightly with about a teaspoon of melted butter. Cover with a clean dish towel and wrap a bath towel loosely around the bowl. Let dough rise for 1 hour or until double in bulk, in a warm place, out of drafts.

4. Divide dough in half. Cut each half into six balls. Roll each ball out onto a floured board into a rectangle about ¼ inch thick. Cut into three strips each about 3½ inches long and ½ inch wide. Take the three strips, press together at one end, and braid them. Finish by pressing braids together at other end. (You can also shape dough into miniature versions of snowball design described on page 151.)

5. Place in buttered cookie sheets, leaving at least 1½ inches around each roll for rising. Brush with egg yolk and sprinkle with sesame or poppy seeds.

6. Cover cookie sheets with a clean dish towel. Let rolls rise in a warm place for about 45 minutes or until double in bulk.

7. Bake in a preheated 350° oven for 30 minutes or until a deep golden color. They should be shiny and the color of tea when removed from the oven.

COUNTRY BREAD
Horyátiko Psomí

YIELD: 2 loaves
TIME: 1 hour preparation;
4 hours rising;
45 minutes baking

Not too long ago, the outdoor communal oven was a center of activity throughout Greece. People would prepare their foods, pastries, or bread at home and take them to the *fourno*, an oven shaped like a giant beehive and heated with wood or charcoal. For a small fee, the baker tended the fire and saw to it that everything was baked to perfection. Greeks insist that food tasted much better made in the *fourno* than in today's kitchens. Since the end of World War II most Greek homes have acquired their own kitchen ovens.

Although *fournos* still exist in the cities, they are used only around holidays, when a lot of baking in large pans is done. In tiny villages and towns the stone *fournos* are still very much in use; fresh country bread is made in them daily.

This bread has a firm heavy texture and a nice thick crust.

1 cup scalded milk
¼ cup vegetable shortening
1 teaspoon salt
2 tablespoons sugar
1 package (¼ ounce) active
   dry yeast
¼ cup warm water (between
   110° and 115°)

4 cups sifted all-purpose flour
2 tablespoons warm
   melted butter
2 tablespoons warm milk
1 egg white, beaten with 1
   tablespoon cold water
   (optional)
Poppy seeds (optional)

1. Heat milk; stir in shortening, salt, and sugar.

2. Sprinkle yeast into ¼ cup warm water, cover with a warm plate, and set aside for 15 minutes.

3. Sift flour into a large bowl. Make a well in the flour and pour in the yeast liquid. Gradually stir in warm milk mixture to make a firm dough.

4. Knead on a lightly floured board for 15 minutes, with 5-minute rest intervals between each 5 minutes of kneading.

5. Place smooth dough into lightly greased large mixing bowl and cover with a clean dish towel. Wrap a bath towel loosely around bowl. Allow to rise in a warm place out of drafts for 1½ hours or until double in bulk.

6. Punch down dough and knead in bowl for 5 minutes; cover and allow it to rise for another 1½ hours.

7. Knead dough briefly and form into two loaves, either oblong for pans or round to make country-style loaves. **Place oblong loaves in greased, floured bread pans (about 8½ by 4½ inches). For country style, place round loaves on a greased, floured baking sheet. Brush tops of loaves with half the melted butter. Cover with clean dish towel, and allow to rise for about 1 hour or until double in bulk.**

8. Preheat oven to 375°. Brush tops of loaves with warm milk and bake until golden brown (about 45 minutes). **If you**

prefer a hard crust, 5 minutes before removing loaves from oven, brush with glaze of egg white and water. Scatter some poppy seeds over the tops if you wish. For a soft crust, brush with remaining butter upon removal from the oven.

KOULOURA RING
Kouloúra

YIELD: 2 large loaves
TIME: 15 minutes preparation;
      4 hours rising;
      45 minutes baking

This is a plain but tasty bread. If you have tube pans, use these to make the loaves; otherwise, two large round cake pans will do.

If you wish to form the dough into ropes and then braid them Tsoureki-style (see page 153), this dough also lends itself to that quite nicely.

½ cup warm water (between 110° and 115°)
2 packages (¼ ounce each) active dry yeast, at room temperature
Salt
Sugar
2 cups milk
3 tablespoons butter
7 cups all-purpose flour
1 egg, at room temperature
1 egg yolk, lightly beaten
3 tablespoons sesame or poppy seeds

1. Rinse a small bowl with hot water. Pour in the warm water, sprinkle in the yeast, and stir with your fingers to dissolve it. Add a pinch of salt and a pinch of sugar and cover with a warm dish for about 15 minutes.

2. Scald milk and remove from heat. Add butter, 3 tablespoons sugar, and 1¼ teaspoons salt. Stir well and allow to cool slightly while yeast is rising.

3. Put unsifted flour in a large bowl and make a hole in the center. Into this pour the lukewarm milk mixture, then the yeast mixture. Add the egg. Using a wooden spoon, push flour from all sides toward the center until all the flour is absorbed.

4. Knead dough in bowl for 5 minutes, transfer to a floured

surface, and knead until smooth. This usually takes about 15 minutes. If you have a mixer with a dough hook attachment, let the dough hook do all the kneading until dough is smooth and elastic.

5. Place dough in a large greased bowl or pot and cover with a hot damp dish towel. Wrap a bath towel around bowl and set aside in a warm place out of drafts until dough has doubled in size. This usually takes about 2 hours.

6. Punch down dough and knead in bowl for 2 minutes, then divide into two and roll into two thick ropes. Place each dough rope in a greased tube pan or a round cake pan. You may have to stretch it to make the ends meet. Use egg yolk to stick ends together. Cover well as before and allow dough to rise for 2 more hours or until doubled in bulk.

7. Preheat oven to 375°. Glaze bread tops with egg yolk, sprinkle with sesame or poppy seeds, and bake for 45 minutes. For a crustier ring, place a large flat pan filled with boiling water on the bottom of the oven throughout the baking time.

8. Allow bread to cool in pans at least 15 minutes after removal from oven.

GREEK GARLIC CHEESE BREAD
Psomí Me Skórtho Ke Tyrí

YIELD: 4 to 6 servings
TIME: 30 minutes

This recipe uses the popular long narrow loaves made of yeast, flour, water, and salt, with a crisp hard crust dotted with sesame seeds and a firm, chewy interior. In Greece this type of bread is usually made by commercial bakers, who use ovens with brick floors and steam injection systems.

These toasted slices are marvelous with lentil soup or pasta of any kind.

1 long crusty loaf of bread (Greek, French, or Italian style), cut into 1-inch slices
1½ cloves garlic, crushed
¼ pound softened butter
½ cup grated Kefalotyri or Parmesan cheese

1. Line a cookie sheet with foil and lay the bread on it.

2. Mix the crushed garlic into the butter, and spread half the mixture on the bread slices. Sprinkle with half the cheese.

3. Turn pieces over and repeat, using remaining garlic butter and cheese. Put into preheated 350° oven for 15 minutes. Set aside.

4. Just before serving, put cookie sheet under broiler until bread is toasted and sizzling. Turn pieces over and repeat. Serve hot.

FETA BISCUITS
Biscotákia Me Féta

YIELD: 16 two-inch biscuits
TIME: Approximately 30 minutes

These are eaten by the Greeks the way croissants are by the French, with one important difference—they are so simple to make. Some cooks add only 3 tablespoons of Feta cheese, in which case you know the biscuit is distinctive but you can't define what makes it so. If you prefer a definite taste of cheese, you can safely use up to ½ cup of crumbled Feta. You can also substitute Kopanisti or Roquefort cheese for the Feta.

Biscotakia Me Feta can make an incomparable addition to any simple meal.

2 cups all-purpose flour
½ teaspoon salt
3 teaspoons baking powder
1 tablespoon sugar
6 tablespoons butter
¾ cup milk

3 tablespoons to ½ cup Feta
   cheese, rinsed and
   crumbled
1 small egg yolk, beaten with
   1 tablespoon water

1. Sift the flour, salt, baking powder, and sugar into a large bowl.

2. Quickly cut butter into the mixture with two knives or a pastry blender until mixture resembles coarse oatmeal. Pour in

the milk, add cheese, and stir to make a soft dough (about 30 seconds).

3. Knead it quickly and gently for another 30 seconds on a lightly floured board, making about 8 to 10 folds. Roll out with floured rolling pin to about ½ inch thick.

4. Cut dough into rounds 2 inches wide with a floured biscuit cutter. Brush tops with egg-yolk mixture.

5. Place biscuits on ungreased cookie sheet. If you like them neat, trim, and browned all over, don't place them close together when baking. If you like them rather high, soft, and golden in color, place them touching one another. Bake in preheated 425° oven for 15 minutes or until lightly browned. Serve hot.

FREEZING

Allow biscuits to cool completely before sealing in a plastic bag and freezing. To defrost, place biscuits in a brown paper bag and heat in a 300° oven for 10 minutes or until heated through.

PASTRIES
AND DESSERTS

Sweet Treasures

Although fresh fruit is always served after a Greek meal, a sweet dessert follows an hour or two later. There is no doubt that Greeks have a sweet tooth.

Greeks love going out and very often will meet their friends during the day or in the evenings at the neighborhood pastry shop for a cup of coffee. Coffee alone seems incomplete, however, unless accompanied by a sweet dessert. You can buy sweets to take home, to eat on the spot at the counter inside, or to eat at one of the tiny tables and chairs set out in front of the shop. The Greeks prefer this last over all others—they sip their Greek coffee, nibble at sweets, converse with friends, and people-watch.

There are countless pastry shops throughout Greece and the windows are arranged as though in tribute to temptation. There are sculptured tiers of glacéed petits fours, cheesecakes, creamed cakes, chocolate cakes, glistening fruit tarts, cream puffs, tortes of every description, and, of course, the traditional ancient desserts. The Greeks love them all.

It is these traditional desserts, popular since antiquity, that this chapter is dedicated to. They are not difficult to prepare; they are wholesome and luscious; and each one has its own unique taste and texture.

NUT-FILLED PASTRY BATHED IN FRAGRANT SYRUP
Baklavá

YIELD: 34 triangles
TIME: Approximately 2½ hours preparation and baking;
4 hours or overnight for resting time

Baklava, the most celebrated of all Greek desserts, is served throughout the Near East, with all countries claiming it for their own. It is easily recognized by its layers of a sweet nut filling and the many sheets of thin pastry leaves—a wonderfully rich and sticky dessert.

Baklava can be made a day or two before it is required.

The recipe that follows is made with walnuts and a syrup flavored with clove and lemon. If you wish to substitute chopped almonds or pecans, flavor the syrup with 2 teaspoons rosewater and 2 tablespoons brandy or 2 cinnamon sticks and 2 pieces orange rind.

I have often had Baklava that almost choked me with its sweetness. In the following recipe I have included the juice of an entire lemon as well as a slice of lemon with rind. This seems to eliminate that cloying sweetness many people find objectionable. If you wish to cut the sweetness down even further, leave out the honey altogether and add an additonal ½ cup of water when making the syrup.

Although Greeks nibble on sweets almost constantly, they prefer fresh fruit after a hearty meal. Therefore Baklava or any honey-drenched Greek pastry is eaten in the middle of the afternoon, as a late-night snack, or on special occasions. Greek desserts are always accompanied by a glass of cold water, even if coffee or tea is being served.

4 pounds shelled walnuts, finely
    chopped or coarsely ground
1 teaspoon ground cinnamon
1/4 teaspoon ground cloves
5 cups sugar
1 pound unsalted butter,
    melted and kept warm

1 1/2 pounds Phyllo, at room
    temperature (see page 9)
2 cups water
1 thin lemon slice with rind
2 tablespoons lemon juice
2 whole cloves
1/2 cup honey

1. Place the chopped or ground walnuts in a large mixing bowl. Add the cinnamon, ground cloves, and 1 cup sugar. Mix well with hands, and set aside.

2. Brush melted butter over sides, corners, and bottom of a large rectangular baking pan (20 by 14 by 2 inches or 15 by 10 by 2 inches).

3. Drape a slightly dampened paper towel over a portion of Phyllo to prevent it from drying out while you work with it. Refrigerate the rest until ready to use. Peel off 1 sheet and lay it flat on the bottom of pan. Brush with melted butter. When you have stacked 10 sheets of buttered Phyllo on top of one another, you have the bottom crust for the Baklava.

4. Sprinkle tenth sheet lightly with some of the nut mixture and place 2 buttered Phyllo sheets on top. Sprinkle with nut mixture. Continue adding buttered Phyllo sheets; sprinkle every second sheet with nut mixture until all used up.

5. Preheat oven to 325°. Make top crust of Baklava with remaining sheets of individually buttered Phyllo, including those you've refrigerated. When you finish, roll down any buttered edges and tuck them inside the pan.

6. Brush top of the Baklava liberally with warm melted butter and sprinkle with about 10 drops cold water. This prevents Phyllo from curling up during baking. Using a sharp pointed knife, cut only top layers of Phyllo into diamond- or triangle-shaped pieces (see illustrations on page 170). Bake for 1 1/2 hours, or until golden brown.

7. Make the syrup while Baklava is baking. Combine remaining 4 cups sugar, water, lemon slice, lemon juice, and whole cloves in a saucepan and bring to a fast boil. Reduce heat and boil gently for 20 minutes. Remove saucepan from heat and

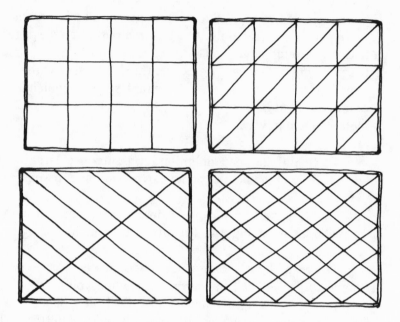

discard lemon slice and cloves. Stir in honey and set syrup aside to cool.

8. When Baklava is done and out of the oven, pour half the syrup slowly all over it. Twenty minutes later slowly dribble the rest of the syrup all over the dessert. Allow pastry to rest in pan for 4 hours or overnight before cutting and serving. Do not refrigerate.

9. When ready to remove pieces from pan, remember you cut through only the top layers of pastry before baking. You must now cut through the entire pastry, including the bottom crust. Using a sharp knife, cut deeply and at least twice, so that pieces come out cleanly and easily.

FREEZING

Pieces of baked Baklava can be frozen; thaw at room temperature before serving. To freeze in advance, prepare Baklava but do not bake. Wrap well and freeze. Bake frozen Baklava in a 350° oven for 1½ hours, then at 325° for 1 more hour or until golden brown. Prepare the syrup and pour over the pastry.

CUSTARD ROLLS
Créma Me Phýllo

YIELD: 30 rolls
TIME: Approximately 2½ hours

This marvelous dessert should be eaten at once or refrigerated once cooled. These pastries are formed into individual rolls each about 6 inches long and 3 inches wide with a custard filling and a sprinkling of syrup on top. Pieces will keep for several days in your refrigerator. Never stack them, and always keep them on a flat surface. Any leftover custard can be mixed with a little liqueur for an elegant cold dessert.

5 cups sugar
2 cups water
2 tablespoons lemon juice
6 cups milk
6 medium egg yolks, at
    room temperature

1 cup uncooked regular (not
    instant) farina or cream
    of wheat
1 teaspoon vanilla or orange
    extract
¾ pound unsalted butter
1 pound Phyllo, at room
    temperature (see page 9)

1. Make the syrup first: Combine 4 cups sugar, water, and lemon juice, bring to a boil, and cook gently over medium heat for 15 minutes. Set aside to cool.

2. Scald milk and keep warm.

3. Combine egg yolks and remaining cup of sugar in large bowl and beat vigorously for 6 minutes with electric beater or whisk. Add farina or cream of wheat and mix well with a wooden spoon.

4. Transfer to a large pot and add vanilla or orange extract. Cook over very low heat, stirring constantly, to prevent lumping. Cook for about 12 to 15 minutes until mixture is smooth, thick, and creamy. Refrigerate.

5. Melt butter in a small saucepan over very low heat (do not let it brown).

6. Butter a large baking pan or cookie sheet and place within easy reach.

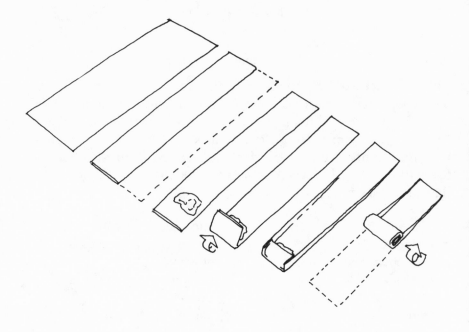

7. Cut entire stack of Phyllo sheets in half, lengthwise, using scissors. Keep pastry not in use covered with a slightly damp paper towel. Take 1 cut sheet of Phyllo, place it in front of you lengthwise, and brush with warm melted butter. Fold in half lengthwise and butter again.

8. Take the slightly cooled custard out of the refrigerator and stir it well to make sure you don't have any lumps in it (if you should find any, remove them).

9. Place 1 tablespoon custard at the base of the buttered Phyllo, and fold in the two long sides over the custard, buttering the folded-in sides with your pastry brush so they will seal better. Roll the little package up. Don't roll too lightly or the custard will ooze out (see illustration). Remember that you want the wrappings of each roll to puff up and crisp while baking.

10. Carefully place each custard roll as you make it into the

buttered baking pan. Allow at least ½-inch space around each roll. Preheat oven to 350°.

11. When you have filled a baking pan, brush tops of rolls with melted butter and place on middle shelf of oven. Bake for 30 to 35 minutes or until golden brown. Do not turn them over. While this batch is baking, continue making rolls on another buttered baking sheet until you have no more Phyllo left.

12. As each batch of rolls is baked, remove carefully to a large platter and prick each roll in 3 places with a fork or a sharp pointed knife. Dribble cooled syrup carefully over each piece. Do not attempt to cover custard rolls until they have completely cooled, or the Phyllo pastry will become soggy.

FREEZING

Place unbaked buttered Custard Rolls flat on baking sheets lined with plastic wrap and place in freezer. When frozen, stack in a container and cover tightly. To bake: Place frozen rolls on un-buttered baking sheets and bake 30 minutes at 425° or until puffed and golden. Do not turn rolls over while baking. Syrup can be made, cooled, and refrigerated in a covered glass jar. Reheat only slightly before dribbling over hot rolls.

CUSTARD PIE
Galatoboúreko

YIELD: 24 two-inch squares;
12 three-inch squares
TIME: 1¾ hours

If you don't want to make individual Custard Rolls, you can make a large pastry in a baking pan and cut into squares to serve. The dessert is then called Galatoboureko and is equally good. I like pieces 3 by 3 inches, but at buffets, where there are many desserts, people seem to want to try one of everything, so the 2-by-2 size is the one to use.

1. Follow steps 1 to 5 in preceding recipe, preparing syrup, custard, and butter.

2. Butter a baking pan (13 by 9 by 2 inches) and lay 8 to 10 entire sheets of Phyllo on the bottom, brushing each with warm

melted butter; these form the bottom crust. Spread over it all of the cooled custard.

3. Lay another 8 to 10 sheets of pastry leaves on top of the custard, brushing each with warm melted butter as you layer it; these form the top crust. Sprinkle with a few drops of water to prevent pastry from curling while baking. Cut through only the top layers of Phyllo, making 2-inch or 3-inch squares.

4. Bake in a preheated 350° oven until golden brown and crisp, 45 minutes to 1 hour.

5. As soon as you remove pastry from the oven, pour cooled syrup over it, very slowly, a cup at a time. Give pastry ample time to absorb each cupful.

6. Allow pastry to cool in pan for at least 4 hours before cutting. Do not cover during this period or your pastry will become soggy. Cut pastry while still in pan. Use a sharp knife and cut cleanly through the custard filling and layers of pastry forming the bottom crust.

ALTERNATE TOPPING

If you would prefer not to serve syrup over the pastry, sift 1½ cups confectioner's sugar over the entire pastry when it comes out of the oven, then sprinkle heavily with powdered cinnamon. Allow to cool for 4 hours uncovered. Cut and serve or refrigerate.

KATAIFI PASTRY ROLLS
Kataífi

YIELD: 1 dozen rolls
TIME: 2 hours

Kataifi pastry is almost as popular as Baklava among Greek people both here and abroad. Kataifi batter is made of flour and water and is poured into a huge funnel. It is then fed in a very fine stream onto a hot rotating turntable in ever-widening circles. The pastry chef scoops up loops of the threadlike dough at precisely the right moment, before it becomes dry and brittle. It is then put into plastic bags and usually frozen. Kataifi dough must be treated like Phyllo; it dries out quickly.

Kataifi can be purchased by the pound in many of the same

stores that sell Phyllo. If frozen, allow it to thaw at room temperature for 2 hours and you are ready to work with it. Unbaked Kataifi is white, soft, and resembles shredded coconut. Once baked, however, it is crisp and golden on the outside and moist and chewy on the inside. A filling of chopped nuts is sprinkled on Kataifi and then it can be formed in many shapes. It can be made like a jelly roll with Phyllo dough on the outside, sliced and then baked, or formed into the popular individual oblong rolls or into squares. Either way, it's the kind of dessert most people love.

The Turkish version, called Kadaife Ekmek, is also very good. Heavy cream is used in place of the nuts, and the end result is rather like a baked custard enveloped within the shredded Kataifi dough. It is then sweetened with syrup poured over it after baking. Ah, if we didn't have to think about calories, what a wonderful world this could be.

2 pounds Kataifi dough	1 pound unsalted butter
1 cup blanched, toasted almonds, coarsely chopped	2½ cups water
	5 whole cloves
1 cup coarsely chopped walnuts	1 thick slice orange with peel
3½ cups sugar	1 tablespoon lemon juice
1 medium egg	¼ cup honey (optional)
1 teaspoon cinnamon	

1. If Kataifi dough is frozen, defrost until it comes to room temperature (about 2 hours).

2. If almonds still have skin on, blanch them: drop them in boiling water and turn off the heat. Let stand exactly 3 minutes, then drain, slip skins off, and dry in a clean dish towel. Then toast them: place nuts on a buttered cookie sheet and roast in a preheated 325° oven until slightly golden and fragrant; toss them occasionally. Then chop them—you should have a cup of chopped almonds.

3. Combine almonds and walnuts, ½ cup sugar, egg, and cinnamon in a large bowl. Mix well for 5 minutes with a wooden spoon or dough hook.

4. Take a fistful of shredded Kataifi dough and spread it at least ½ inch thick on the palm and fingers of your left hand to make a 3-by-4-inch piece. Pat it down firmly and sprinkle with a tablespoon of nut mixture. Fold two outside edges inward so that nuts don't fall out the sides, then roll into an oblong roll. (It will look like an uncooked shredded wheat roll and about the same size.) Place the rolls as you make them ½ inch apart in a buttered baking pan (13 by 9 by 2 inches or 9 by 9 by 2 inches). Preheat oven to 350°.

5. Melt butter over very low heat, and dribble it slowly and carefully over all the rolls. Bake, uncovered, for 45 minutes or until tops and sides are crisp and medium brown in color. While Kataifi are baking, prepare the syrup.

6. Combine remaining 3 cups sugar, water, cloves, orange slice, and lemon juice in a saucepan and bring to a boil. Boil gently for 15 minutes, remove from heat, and stir in honey if you like.

7. As soon as Kataifi are out of the oven, reheat syrup and slowly and evenly pour it over the rolls. The pouring of the syrup can take as long as 20 minutes. Pour a little over each roll, then let it be absorbed; pour a little more and repeat until syrup has been used up. Cover entire pan with a linen napkin and a clean bath towel for 2 hours. This allows the steam to soften the tops of the rolls and gives the pastries time to absorb the syrup. At the end of that time, remove towels and serve. These rolls may be refrigerated but should always be allowed to come to room temperature before serving.

FREEZING

If you wish to freeze unbaked Kataifi Rolls, you must do it before pouring on the syrup. Place the rolls next to one another on a plastic-lined cookie sheet and freeze. Remove frozen rolls from sheet and pack into containers or plastic bags. Seal and return to freezer. When you wish to use, take out as many as required and bake at 350° for about 1½ hours. Proceed with syrup.

Syrup may be made ahead and refrigerated in a covered jar. Reheat as much as you will need before using over pastry.

A simpler version would be to place half of the Kataifi pastry in a buttered baking pan and press down gently. Sprinkle nut mixture over it and dribble with half the melted butter. Top with remaining Kataifi dough; dribble with rest of the butter. Bake uncovered for 45 minutes or until browned and crisp on top. Pour hot syrup over the pan as soon as it comes out of the oven. Cover with towels for 2 hours, then cut into squares and serve.

FRITTER PUFFS
Tiganítes

YIELD: About 3 dozen puffs
TIME: 1 hour

Simple to make and luscious, these browned little puffs sprinkled with confectioner's sugar will delight you.

1 cup water
¼ pound unsalted butter
½ teaspoon salt
1 teaspoon granulated sugar
1 cup all-purpose flour
½ teaspoon baking soda
4 medium eggs, at room temperature

2 tablespoons rum or 1 tablespoon orange flavoring
At least 3 cups light vegetable oil
1½ cups confectioner's sugar

1. Combine water, butter, salt, and granulated sugar in a small pan and bring to a boil, stirring. When butter has melted, add flour and baking soda all at once. Cook, stirring vigorously, until mixture leaves sides of pan.

2. Put batter into large bowl of an electric mixer and add 1 egg at a time, beating well after each addition. Add rum or orange flavoring, and beat for 4 minutes at high speed.

3. Heat oil in wide, deep, heavy pot. When it is very hot but not smoking (about 370°), take a teaspoon of batter and, using another teaspoon, push it off into the oil. Puffs will turn over of their own accord when one side is golden. Do not crowd them. Cook until they are well browned on all sides (the color of

crullers). Remove with a slotted spoon and drain on paper towels. Break one open to make sure it's cooked through. When you have cooked them all, transfer to a serving platter and sift confectioner's sugar over them. Serve at room temperature.

SOUFFLÉED FRITTER PUFFS
Loukoumáthes

YIELD: 3 dozen puffs
TIME: 2 to 3 hours for yeast;
30 minutes frying

This working man's dessert is sold in every coffeehouse throughout Greece, always accompanied with a glass of cold water or a bottle of Negrita (a mineral water) and a small cup of thick Greek coffee.

There is no one true recipe. Some cooks use yogurt in place of water to make the batter, some use yeast, some use baking powder, and some add grated orange rind. No matter how you make them always remember to fry them in fresh hot oil. They should be as light as a feather.

1 package (¼ ounce) active dry yeast
2¼ cups warm water
2 cups all-purpose flour
¼ teaspoon salt

Approximately 4 cups corn oil
2 cups honey
1 cup water
Cinnamon

1. Dissolve the yeast in ¼ cup warm water.
2. Sift the flour and salt into a large bowl. Add remaining 2 cups warm water and yeast mixture and mix well with a spoon to make a sticky batter. Batter will be just right when you can pull some of it up between your fingers and it will hold together without breaking off. Beat with a whisk for 2 minutes, cover with a dish towel, and set aside to rise in a warm place for 2 to 3 hours. (The batter is ready to use when it bubbles and blisters.)
3. Heat oil in a deep frying pan or a pot to 375°. Drop a teaspoon of batter into the hot oil, using another teaspoon to help push off the dough. The real professionals wet their hands, place

a spoonful of batter in their wet palm and squeeze gently; the batter oozes up out of the top of their closed fist into a bubble. They then drop this bubble of batter into the hot oil, wet their hands in a bowl of cold water, and repeat the process. Although I've tried this amusing technique, I can't do it as fast as they can and can't see the reason to get all messed up; they come out the same way when using a teaspoon. You can probably fry 8 to 10 puffs at one time, no matter what method you prefer to use.

4. Keep turning puffs with a slotted spoon until they are lightly browned on all sides (about 3 minutes on each side). Remove with slotted spoon and place on paper towels to drain. Break one open to make sure that the inside is cooked. If it isn't, give them another minute in the hot oil.

5. While puffs are draining, heat honey and water and dip each puff into it quickly. Place on a platter. Sprinkle with cinnamon and serve 6 to 8 hot puffs on a dessert plate for each guest. Dribble any remaining syrup over each portion.

ALTERNATE TOPPING

Instead of honey syrup, roll drained Loukoumathes in cinnamon sugar.

DEEP-FRIED SWEET PASTRY
Thíples

YIELD: 4 to 5 dozen
TIME: Approximately 3 hours

Thiples are delicate pastry strips that are quickly deep-fried, drained, then sprinkled with cinnamon, chopped nuts, and honey. They will literally crumble in your mouth with each bite, and they will crumble if pierced with a fork, so use your fingers to eat them. They are fun to make as well as eat, especially if formed in varying shapes and sizes.

A word of warning: Whereas guests may be shy and eat only two or three Thiples apiece after dinner, if there are children in your household a heaping platterful of glistening Thiples can disappear right before your eyes.

3 eggs, separated, at room
temperature
1 teaspoon baking powder
2 tablespoons orange juice
¼ cup light vegetable oil
2¼ cups sifted all-purpose
flour
Approximately 4 cups
vegetable oil or shortening

2 cups honey (Hymettus or
other fine quality)
1 cup water
1½ cups finely chopped
walnuts, pecans, or
almonds
Ground cinnamon

1. Beat egg whites with baking powder until stiff.

2. Beat egg yolks lightly, add to egg whites, and beat until creamy.

3. Add orange juice, ¼ cup vegetable oil, and flour. Finish by kneading well (at least 15 minutes if kneading by hand on a lightly floured board or 4 minutes in bowl if using dough hook). Dough will be a bit sticky.

4. Form dough into 8 balls. Refrigerate for at least 1 hour, then roll out 1 ball of dough at a time to paper thinness, using a floured rolling pin on a board or a lightly floured pastry cloth.

5. Cut dough with a knife into rectangles about 3 inches long and 2 inches wide. Fold to form a triangle and press with your fingers to stick. If you like, besides the triangles, you could make other shapes with the strips, such as loose knots, bows, pleats, or rosettes (see page 181).

6. Heat 3 to 4 inches of oil to 360° in a deep-fat fryer or large heavy saucepan. (If you do not have a frying thermometer, oil is ready when very hot but not smoking.) When oil is ready, carefully drop in Thiples, one or two at a time; fry until golden but not brown. This will take about a minute for each side. Using a slotted spoon, gently transfer each fried pastry to a large tray lined with paper towels. Repeat with the rest. Remove pot from heat and skim out any crumbs to prevent smoking up the kitchen. Roll out a ball of dough, and make shapes; reheat oil and fry. Thiples are so light you can keep piling layer upon layer, putting paper towels between each layer to absorb any excess oil.

7. Put honey and water on to boil for 3 minutes and set aside.

8. Arrange a layer of Thiples on a large platter and dribble a tablespoon of the warm honey syrup over each. Sprinkle with chopped nuts and cinnamon. Arrange another layer on top and continue until all of the fried and drained Thiples are sprinkled with honey, nuts, and cinnamon. Most of the syrup will eventually drip down onto the platter, but it can be poured over the Thiples again when serving on individual plates. Serve at room temperature or cold. If covered loosely with foil, they will keep for several days.

TO MAKE ROSETTES

Roll out a ball of dough and cut it into strips 16 by 2 inches. Pierce one end of a strip with a fork; immerse in hot oil and start twirling fork (see illustration). Using a second fork, mold loose end of strip around first fork to form a rosette or roll. Pastry

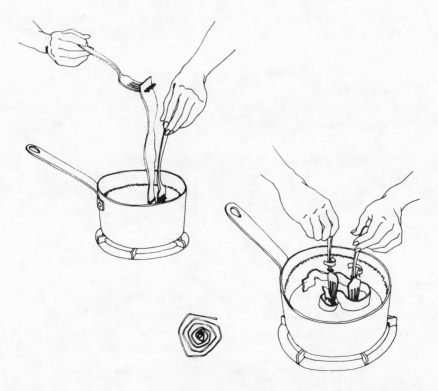

will be bubbling and cooking all the time. The shape will set in a few seconds, and you can remove the first fork. Fry until golden on both sides, remove with slotted spoon, drain on paper towels, and repeat. As soon as you get the hang of it you can turn out a rosette a minute (depending on the thickness of the rolled-out dough).

WALNUT CAKE
Karithópeta

YIELD: 35 small pieces
TIME: 1¼ hours

One of the favorite Greek desserts is called Karithopeta (*karithi* meaning nut and *peta* meaning pie or cake). It's a moist, dark-brown cake with an ambrosial quality that men in particular seem to prefer over many others.

½ pound unsalted butter, at room temperature
3 cups sugar
2 teaspoons vanilla extract
8 medium eggs, at room temperature
1 teaspoon baking powder
½ teaspoon baking soda
2 teaspoons ground cinnamon

1 cup uncooked regular (not instant) farina or cream of wheat
1 cup all-purpose flour
½ cup milk
2 cups coarsely chopped walnuts
3 cups water
1 cup honey
½ stick cinnamon
1 slice orange with peel
1 teaspoon lemon juice

1. Butter a pan 13 by 9 by 2 inches. Preheat oven to 375°.
2. Cream the ½ pound butter and 1 cup sugar until light and fluffy. Add vanilla and eggs and continue beating for 2 minutes. Add baking powder, baking soda, and ground cinnamon, and beat for another 2 minutes.
3. Slowly beat in the farina or cream of wheat, flour, milk, and walnuts.
4. Pour batter into prepared pan. Smooth top with a spatula and bake for 40 minutes.

5. Make syrup while cake is baking. Combine remaining 2 cups sugar and rest of ingredients in a saucepan. Stir until it comes to a boil, then reduce heat and simmer until cake is finished.

6. Remove cinnamon stick and orange slice from syrup. Then pour very slowly, a cup at a time, over the entire cake. Wait for syrup to be absorbed before pouring the next cup. Allow cake to cool slightly before cutting into squares or diamond-shaped pieces. Let sit for at least 4 hours before serving.

VARIATION: LIQUEUR OR RUM SYRUP

2 cups sugar
4½ cups water
1 stick cinnamon
1 slice lemon with peel
½ cup fruit liqueur or dark rum

Combine sugar, water, cinnamon, and lemon slice. Stir until mixture comes to a boil. Lower heat and simmer for 15 minutes. Remove from heat and stir in liqueur or rum.

ALMOND PASTRY CAKE
Kopenhághi

YIELD: 30 servings
TIME: 2½ hours

This rich pastry cake bears the name of the capital city of Denmark. The royal Greek baker created this pastry in 1863 to honor the Danish King George I upon his coronation as the King of Greece.

It has a shortbread crust on the bottom, sponge cake with crushed almonds in the center, and Phyllo pastry sheets on top. The entire pastry is then bathed in a flavorful syrup. It is time-consuming and expensive but a truly exquisite dessert. This recipe easily serves 30 people and can be made ahead of time for a party.

MAKING SHORTBREAD CRUST

½ pound unsalted butter,
at room temperature
½ cup confectioner's sugar or
superfine granulated sugar
2 egg yolks, at room
temperature

1 teaspoon finely grated
orange rind
1 ounce fine Cognac
½ teaspoon vanilla extract
Approximately 1½ cups
all-purpose flour

1. In an electric mixer bowl cream butter and sugar for several minutes at medium speed until light and fluffy. Beat in egg yolks and continue beating for another 10 minutes. Add grated orange rind, Cognac, and vanilla, and continue beating for 5 minutes.

2. Stir in flour gradually, mixing with your hand or dough hook to make a very soft dough. Knead dough for 10 minutes on floured surface or 4 minutes in bowl if using dough hook.

3. Butter a baking pan (14 by 10 by 2 inches) and preheat oven to 350°. Lay the soft pastry dough in the bottom of the buttered pan. Pat evenly and smoothly. (Some chefs like to bring dough up all around the pan, a little higher than the edges of the pan, but this is not necessary.)

4. Prick well with a fork and bake in oven for 15 minutes or until lightly golden. Remove pan from oven and allow to cool in pan.

MAKING FILLING AND
ASSEMBLING PHYLLO

8 eggs, separated, at
room temperature
½ cup granulated sugar
1 teaspoon baking powder
2½ cups finely chopped,
toasted, blanched almonds
(see page 175)

1 teaspoon ground cinnamon
1 teaspoon almond extract
1 ounce fine Cognac
½ pound Phyllo, at room
temperature (see page 9)
¼ pound unsalted butter,
melted and kept warm

1. Beat egg yolks in large mixing bowl of electric mixer until thick and creamy. Add sugar and baking powder and beat for 2 more minutes. Remove beaters and wash them thoroughly.

2. Fold in chopped almonds, cinnamon, almond extract, and Cognac.

3. In another bowl, beat egg whites with clean beaters until stiff but not dry. Using a rubber spatula or your hands, gently fold egg whites into mixture in the large bowl. Preheat oven to 350°.

4. Pour mixture gently on top of the cooled baked pastry crust you prepared earlier. Lay Phyllo lightly on top of the filling, a sheet at a time, brushing melted butter over each sheet. Work quickly and with a light hand so that the cake filling does not lose the air beaten into it. If sheets of Phyllo are larger than pan and stick up over edges, butter these edges as well and fold or push them gently down around mixture to retain filling before laying on the next pastry sheet. This will give your pastry a neat look when baked and out of the oven (never trim Phyllo the way you would a pie crust). Brush the last top sheet of Phyllo and the pushed-down edges of pastry with remaining melted butter.

5. Using a sharp pointed knife, cut 3 lines each about 3 inches long through the Phyllo (not through the filling). Sprinkle entire pan with 10 drops warm water to prevent Phyllo from curling up while it is baking. Place pan in preheated 350° oven and bake for 45 minutes. At the end of that time, insert a thin sharp knife into the center of the cake right down into the filling. If the knife comes out clean, remove pan from oven. If knife is not clean, bake for 10 to 15 minutes longer. The top of the pastry should be a deep burnished gold. Remove pan from oven and set aside.

MAKING SYRUP

3½ cups water	4 thin slices orange with
3 cups sugar	peel
1 stick cinnamon	4 thin slices lemon with peel
8 whole cloves	1 teaspoon lemon juice

1. Combine ingredients in a large pot and bring to a boil. Turn heat down and simmer for 30 minutes. Strain syrup.

2. Pour hot syrup over cooled cake, slowly and evenly; this will take you 15 minutes or longer. If the cake seems to be swimming in syrup, stop and wait for it to be absorbed. Allow cake to cool for 4 hours before cutting into diamond, square, or

triangular-shaped pieces (see illustrations, page 170). Serve at room temperature. This cake does not have to be refrigerated for several days.

FREEZING

If you want to freeze the cake, do it before baking and pouring on the syrup. Wrap entire pan of unbaked cake and seal tightly. Place in freezer. Bake uncovered frozen cake in a preheated 350° oven for 1½ hours; then proceed with syrup as instructed on page 185.

GRECIAN SUGAR CAKE
Ravaní

YIELD: 20 large servings
TIME: 1 hour

This delicious concoction is based on cream of wheat and has a sugar syrup flavored with lemon juice poured over it. The result is a light, fluffy, truly sweet cake and one you can make ahead for company. The recipe makes a large one-layer cake that serves 20 to 30 easily, depending on the size of the pieces.

3 cups water
2¾ cups sugar
1 tablespoon lemon juice
½ pound unsalted butter
5 medium eggs, beaten
1 cup uncooked regular (not instant) cream of wheat or farina

2 cups self-rising flour
3 teaspoons baking powder
2 teaspoons vanilla extract
Whipped cream (optional)
Chopped nuts (optional)

1. Make the syrup first by combining water with 2 cups of the sugar and the lemon juice. Boil in small saucepan over medium heat 15 minutes. Set aside to cool. Syrup should be watery, not sticky.

2. Melt butter over low heat (do not brown). Transfer to large bowl and add remaining ¾ cup sugar. Cream until light. Beat in beaten eggs.

3. Stir cream of wheat or farina with flour and baking powder. Combine thoroughly with egg and sugar mixture. Add vanilla. Mix well with beater or wooden spoon. Batter will be golden yellow with an oatmeal consistency at this point.

4. Set oven at 350°. Butter a pan 14 by 10 by 2 inches or use two small pans. Batter needs at least 1 inch space to rise in pan. Smooth batter out in pan and place on middle oven shelf.

5. Bake 30 to 35 minutes. Cake should be medium brown on top, and toothpick when inserted should come out clean. Cut hot cake into squares or diamond shapes right in pan. Pour some cooled syrup over hot cake slowly and evenly. When absorbed, pour a little more over cake. Repeat until syrup is used up.

6. Allow cake to cool before serving. Room temperature is best. Whipped cream and chopped nuts can be used for topping, but are not necessary.

VARIATION

To make Flaming Rum Cake Ravani substitute 2 teaspoons rum for vanilla in batter. Just before serving finished cake, heat ¼ cup rum over low heat for 2 minutes and pour slowly over top of cake. Ignite with match and enter room with flaming cake.

WHITE SHORTBREAD COOKIES
Kourabiéthes

YIELD: Approximately 4 dozen
TIME: 2½ hours

Kourabiethes are one of the most popular of Greek desserts, among non-Greeks as well as Greeks. In Greece they appear at weddings, birthdays, name days, christenings, and all holidays.

These snowy white cookies dusted with confectioner's sugar have a shortbread quality and must be handled delicately. Throughout the Turkish occupation of Greece, the Greeks were forced to shape these cookies into the familiar Turkish crescent. Once Greece regained its independence, the cookies were shaped into tiny balls, thick slices, or little pears.

1 egg yolk
¼ cup strained orange juice
1 pound confectioner's sugar
1 ounce (2 tablespoons) Ouzo
   or fine Cognac
1 pound unsalted butter,
   melted and slightly cooled

¼ cup finely ground, toasted,
   blanched almonds (see
   page 175)
4 cups all-purpose flour
½ cup cornstarch
Approximately 4 dozen
   whole cloves

1. Put egg yolk, orange juice, ¼ cup confectioner's sugar, and Ouzo or Cognac into a blender container or electric mixer bowl. Blend for 2 seconds in blender or several minutes if using mixer.

2. Add melted butter and ground almonds. Blend for 2 more seconds or for 5 minutes if using mixer.

3. Sift flour and cornstarch into a large bowl.

4. Add mixture from blender and mix with a spoon for 5 minutes to form a soft dough.

5. Knead gently for 15 minutes on a clean surface or for 4 minutes in bowl if using dough hook; then refrigerate for 15 minutes.

6. Form into balls about the size of a very small egg; do not press or flatten them, since they don't rise during baking; as you form them, place cookies on ungreased baking sheets ½ inch apart.

7. Preheat oven to 350°.

8. When you have filled baking sheets with cookies, insert a clove in the center of each. Bake about 30 minutes. Since these cookies do not brown easily, break one open to determine when they are fully baked—you should not be able to see a butter line in the middle of the cookie.

9. Sift 1½ cups confectioner's sugar into a large baking pan, covering the bottom thickly.

10. When cookies are cool enough to handle, remove carefully to the baking pan and place them side by side as close as possible (do not place them on top of one another at this stage). Sift all the remaining confectioner's sugar on top and sides of the cookies. Allow them to sit undisturbed for 6 hours or overnight before transferring to a colorful platter. They will remain fresh for 2 or 3 weeks unrefrigerated.

11. When serving, you may pile layers of cookies to form a mound. Sift loose confectioner's sugar from baking pan over each layer.

TO FREEZE BAKED COOKIES

Allow baked Kourabiethes to cool. Line a cookie sheet with plastic and place Kourabiethes flat, not touching, and freeze until firm. Remove and stack in plastic container or bag, seal and return to freezer. To defrost: Allow cookies to thaw at room temperature for 2 to 3 hours or until a toothpick easily pierces the cookies. Dust liberally with confectioner's sugar and serve.

TO FREEZE UNBAKED COOKIES

As you form each cookie, place on plastic-lined cookie sheet. Do not stack and do not let them touch. Freeze until firm. Remove and stack in plastic container or bag, seal, and return to freezer. Place frozen unbaked Kourabiethes on ungreased cookie sheet and bake in preheated 350° for 45 minutes or for 1 hour until lightly browned if you like them crisp. Dust liberally with confectioner's sugar and serve.

VARIATIONS ON SHAPES

Other than little ball shapes you could form them into little pear shapes, a clove at the end of each to represent the stalk. Or roll dough into a round log and cut diagonally into ½-inch slices. Insert a clove into each slice.

PHOENICIAN HONEY COOKIES
Phoenékia, Melomakárona

YIELD: Approximately 3 dozen
TIME: 2½ hours

Phoenekia, or Melomakarona as they are also called, date back to the fourteenth century. They are rather large, semisoft cookies, fragrant with spices yet delicate in flavor. After baking, they are dipped in a hot syrup made of water and honey and sprinkled with finely chopped walnuts.

½ pound unsalted butter
1 egg yolk
¼ cup orange juice
2 teaspoons baking soda
2 tablespoons 7-star Metaxa Brandy or finest brandy available
½ cup sugar
¼ cup light vegetable oil
3½ cups all-purpose flour
½ cup uncooked regular (not instant) farina or cream of wheat

½ teaspoon powdered cloves
¼ teaspoon nutmeg
1 teaspoon ground cinnamon
2 teaspoons baking powder
⅛ teaspoon salt
½ teaspoon grated orange rind
¼ cup flour (if needed)
½ cup finely chopped or coarsely ground walnuts
2 cups honey
1 cup boiling water

1. Melt butter over low heat and allow to cool slightly.

2. Put egg yolk, orange juice, baking soda, brandy, and sugar into blender container or mixing bowl and blend or mix for 1 minute or several minutes over medium speed if using electric mixer. Add butter and oil and continue blending or mixing until batter is thick and creamy.

3. Sift flour, farina or cream of wheat, spices, baking powder, and salt into a large bowl. Add grated orange rind.

4. Pour batter into the bowl and mix with a spoon. Knead for 15 minutes or until smooth on lightly floured surface or 4 minutes in bowl if using dough hook. The thorough mixing of spices will turn dough a rich beige color. The dough should not be sticky—if so, add ¼ cup flour and mix in thoroughly.

5. Take about a tablespoon of dough into floured hands and shape into a small round cake or an egg shape. If you wish to fill the cookies with nuts rather than sprinkle them as is traditional, add a small amount of chopped nuts in the center of each cookie, then press it closed.

6. Place cookies as you make them on an ungreased cookie sheet. Do not crowd them. Press top of each slightly with tines of a fork to make a little design if you have enclosed chopped nuts.

7. Bake in preheated 350° oven for 25 minutes or until well browned.

8. While first batch is baking, bring honey and water to a boil in a small saucepan and then allow it to simmer slowly.

9. When cookies are done, remove them to cake rack to cool. They will harden as they cool.

10. Dip *cooled* cookies a few at a time into simmering hot syrup for about 1 minute. Turn them over and allow them to remain in syrup for another full minute. Remove with a slotted spoon to a spare baking sheet lined with foil and, unless you've filled them with nuts, sprinkle immediately with chopped walnuts.

11. Allow Phoenekia to drain and cool overnight on baking sheets before serving. You can keep them for several days without refrigeration; just wrap baking sheets loosely with waxed paper or foil. If you wish to store cookies for about 10 days, place them in airtight tins.

FREEZING

After cookies are baked (but before the syrup-dipping), allow them to cool. Freeze flat on cookie sheets. When frozen, pack in containers with sheets of plastic wrap between layers and return to freezer. Thaw at room temperature for 1 hour and proceed with syrup as explained above.

MINOAN KOLOURIA
Koulourákia

YIELD: Approximately 5 dozen large cookies
TIME: 2 hours for simple shapes;
4 hours for intricate shapes

These cookies were always shaped like small snakes by the Minoans. This ancient culture on Crete worshiped the snake for its healing powers. As the centuries wore on, other shapes were added to the figure S that is the snake. Now there are also braided circles, hairpin twists, figure eights, twisted wreaths, horseshoe shapes, Greek letters, and fat little circles. Greek pastry chefs, however, still usually form Koulouria like snakes. These are delightful with morning coffee or afternoon tea. In Greece, they are baked especially at Easter.

9 cups all-purpose flour
3 tablespoons baking powder
⅛ teaspoon salt
2 cups sugar
8 medium eggs, at room temperature
1 pound unsalted butter, melted and slightly cooled
¼ cup orange juice

1 tablespoon vanilla extract
1 heaping teaspoon ground Mastiha (see page 41) or 4 tablespoons brandy or Ouzo
Almond slivers or green glazed citrus fruit (optional)
Sesame seeds (optional)

1. Combine flour, baking powder, salt, and sugar, and sift into a large mixing bowl.

2. Break the eggs directly into the flour mixture.

3. Add melted butter, orange juice, vanilla, and Mastiha or brandy, and mix well.

4. Remove dough from bowl and knead on a lightly floured surface for 15 minutes or use dough hook for 4 minutes. Dough should be stiff enough for you to break off a piece the size of a small apple and roll it on a floured board into a long rope the circumference of a pencil.

5. Cut dough ropes into 4-inch lengths. Braid three of these 4-inch ropes together for large braid-shaped cookies (see illustration). Or twist each rope into S shapes for the little snake design (adding an almond sliver or a piece of glazed fruit for an eye if you wish) or make figure eights or fat little circles. Two little ropes twisted together make wreaths. If bored, you can start forming Greek letters, which I always did as a child. At Easter form little crosses. You could, of course, use a cookie cutter if you're in a hurry: Roll out pieces of dough, using a lightly floured rolling pin, about ¼ inch thick. Use assortment of cookie cutters to make various shapes.

6. Place cookies as you form them directly onto a buttered cookie sheet or pan. Try to fill each sheet with cookies approximately the same size so you won't have smaller shapes baking faster than larger ones. Leave at least 1 inch of space around each cookie.

7. Preheat oven to 350°. For the glaze, beat the egg whites with a fork and brush each cookie well. Sprinkle with sesame seeds if you like.

8. Bake cookies until lightly golden, 25 to 30 minutes, depending on what size you have made them. While they are baking, shape remaining dough and place cookies on the next sheet.

SPICED BISCUITS
Paxemáthia

YIELD: Approximately 2 dozen
TIME: 2 hours

These toasted spicy biscuits slightly resemble rusks or Zwieback. They are delightful with tea, coffee, or hot chocolate. Greeks usually serve Paxemathia as a snack with a wedge of Kasseri or Myzithra cheese.

Paxemathia are simple to make and practical to have on hand. Place cooled biscuits in a tin or a plastic bag and they will keep unrefrigerated for about 3 weeks.

1½ sticks unsalted butter, at room temperature
¾ cup sugar
3 large eggs, beaten
1 tablespoon salad oil
½ cup blanched, toasted almonds (see page 175), finely chopped or ground, or finely chopped walnuts

1½ teaspoons toasted anise seeds, crushed or ground or 1 tablespoon pure anise extract
2¾ cups all-purpose flour
½ teaspoon baking powder
1 teaspoon baking soda

1. Cream butter until light and fluffy and gradually beat in sugar.

2. Beat in beaten eggs, salad oil, nuts, and anise seeds or extract.

3. Sift together flour, baking powder, and baking soda; mix into butter and sugar mixture.

4. Preheat oven to 350°. Lightly butter 1 large baking sheet about 17½ by 11 inches.

5. Pat dough into two loaves about 1 inch high and 1½ inches wide. Don't place loaves too close together, as they spread while baking (the sticky batter will spread to fill entire baking sheet).

6. Bake for 30 minutes. Remove baking sheet from oven and allow it to cool undisturbed for 15 minutes.

7. Using a sharp knife, slice each loaf diagonally into slices ½ inch to ¾ inch thick. You can serve them as soft as this for afternoon tea with jam or dry them into the traditional "hard" biscuits. Lower oven temperature to 250°. Turn biscuits on their sides on baking sheet and dry slowly in oven for an additional 50 minutes, turning biscuits over once. Allow Paxemathia to cool completely, then place them in a tin or a plastic bag and use as needed.

TO TOAST ANISE SEEDS

Place them in a small buttered ovenproof dish and toast in pre-heated 350° oven until golden and fragrant, shaking them occasionally. This takes about 10 to 12 minutes. Crush with a rolling pin between layers of waxed paper.

ROSEWATER HALVA
Halvás Me Anthónero

YIELD: 6 servings
TIME: 30 minutes

This simple but exotic dessert goes back to the travels of Alexander the Great. Originally it was prepared with olive oil and honey. The consistency is a little like marzipan. It is sliced like cake, however, and eaten with a fork.

1 cup milk	½ cup unsalted pistachio or
1 cup water	pine nuts (optional)
1 cup sugar	1 cup uncooked regular
1½ teaspoons rosewater or	(not instant) farina or
vanilla extract	cream of wheat
¼ pound unsalted butter	Powdered cinnamon

1. Boil milk, water, and sugar gently with pan uncovered for 15 minutes. Add rosewater or vanilla and remove from heat.

2. Melt butter in a large heavy frying pan. If using nuts, sauté them in the butter. Do not allow butter to brown.

3. Add farina or cream of wheat and cook over low heat, stirring constantly, for 15 minutes. Do not allow mixture to become too brown.

4. Slowly add hot milk mixture, guarding your face, for it will spatter for a minute.

5. Stir mixture over low heat until it gets very thick and comes away from the sides of the pan (this will take about 5 minutes). You will know it is ready when the mixture holds together and you can easily mass it on one side of the pan.

6. Gently pack into a 2-cup mold and set aside to cool for 1 hour.

7. Unmold onto a pretty plate, sprinkle with cinnamon, and serve. Halvas can be refrigerated and served the next day, but it should come to room temperature before being served. It seems to taste much better that way.

VARIATION

To make Almond Halva: Substitute 1½ teaspoons almond extract for rosewater and ½ cup slivered toasted almonds for pistachio nuts.

GRAPE PUDDING
Moustalevriá

YIELD: 6 servings
TIME: 20 minutes

This is an easy variation on the traditional pudding that calls for wine must, which is crushed grape pulp.

4 heaping tablespoons cornstarch
½ cup cold water
4 cups grape juice
Whipped cream or powdered cinnamon and toasted sesame seeds

1. Beat cornstarch in cold water with wire whisk until perfectly smooth; set aside.

2. Bring grape juice to a boil slowly over medium heat.

3. Add cold cornstarch mixture slowly to boiling grape juice, stirring constantly for 1 minute. When pudding comes to a boil, remove from heat and stir with whisk until slightly cooled.

4. Pour into small sherbet or wine glasses and refrigerate for at least 3 hours.

5. Just before serving, garnish with whipped cream or a sprinkling of cinnamon and toasted sesame seeds.

RICE PUDDING
Rizógalo

YIELD: 4 servings
TIME: 1½ hours

Geographically Greece belongs as much to the West as to the East, but the Greeks' fondness for rice is decidedly Eastern.

I've noticed that almost everyone likes rice pudding. Is it because our mothers made it often when we were children?

For an out-of-this-world rice pudding, try this Greek version.

⅓ cup water
Dash salt
⅓ cup long-grain rice
1 quart milk
¾ cup sugar

4 tablespoons butter
(optional)
2 eggs, at room temperature
1 teaspoon vanilla extract
Powdered cinnamon

1. Bring water to a boil in small covered saucepan, then add salt and rice. Lower heat and cook rice until water is absorbed by rice (about 4 minutes). Remove from heat, still covered.

2. Rinse large pot with boiling water and scald milk.

3. Add parboiled rice and stir. Lower heat and simmer until rice is very soft and tender (about 35 minutes), stirring often to make sure rice doesn't stick.

4. When rice has cooked, slowly add sugar, mixing gently so that sugar will dissolve completely. Remove pot from heat, add butter if you wish, and stir. (The optional butter makes the desert very rich; do not use it if dessert follows a heavy meal.) Allow to cool for 20 minutes at room temperature.

5. Beat eggs well and stir 1 cup of the cooled rice mixture into them.

6. Pour into the big pot and place over low heat. Stir continually until pudding becomes golden and creamy (about 15 minutes). Add vanilla, stir, and remove from heat.

7. Pour pudding into serving dishes or parfait glasses. Sprinkle lightly with cinnamon. Chill in refrigerator before serving.

CHESTNUT PURÉE PUDDING
Kástana Pouré

YIELD: 4 servings
TIME: 2 hours

When I think of Versailles, I don't picture the palace or the grand mirrors, but walking with my dogs through the lovely gardens in the fall, ankle deep in chestnuts.

Greece abounds with chestnuts, and they are used in myriad ways in soufflés, as sandwich fillings, as garnishes for poultry, in meat stews, and chestnut croquettes. They are even used in soups. A crowning achievement of Greek cuisine is this elegant chestnut pudding.

When the chestnut season comes I hope you will try this most unusual dessert. Of course, you can also make it with canned chestnut purée. And don't count calories; just sit down and enjoy the pudding.

2 pounds raw chestnuts or
    2 cans (15½ ounces each)
    unsweetened chestnut
    purée
1 teaspoon vanilla extract
½ cup brandy or rum
3 teaspoons confectioner's
    sugar

2 cups heavy cream
½ cup fresh orange juice
2 tablespoons Curaçao or
    Créme de Vanille liqueur
Bittersweet chocolate
Chopped pistachio nuts
    (optional)

1. If using raw chestnuts, make a cut in each chestnut with a sharp knife and boil in water to cover until chestnuts are very tender, about 45 minutes. If using canned chestnut purée, start recipe at step 3.

2. Drain and, while still fairly hot, peel chestnuts and remove inner skin. Try to enlist help with the peeling and remember that chestnuts are infinitely easier to peel when hot. Mash or put through a ricer.

3. Add vanilla, brandy or rum, and confectioner's sugar to mashed chestnuts or purée. Mix well and refrigerate.

4. Beat heavy cream until stiff, gradually adding orange juice and liqueur. Add chestnut mixture and beat all together thoroughly. Place in attractive serving bowl or individual sherbet glasses and refrigerate overnight. Grate bittersweet chocolate over the top just before serving. In some areas of Greece chopped pistachio nuts are added to the topping.

GREEK CHOCOLATE MOUSSE
Créma Chocoláta

YIELD: 6 servings
TIME: 30 minutes

Mrs. Clarence W. Hall, a neighbor of mine who has traveled widely, tasted this recipe in Greece and liked it so much she asked the chef how it was made. She calls it simply Greek Chocolate Mousse. We tested it one day and it is quite good.

1 envelope (1 tablespoon) unflavored gelatin
¼ cup cold water
1½ squares unsweetened chocolate, melted, or 4 tablespoons cocoa
⅓ cup sugar
¼ teaspoon salt
¼ cup boiling water

3 eggs yolks, slightly beaten
Dash cinnamon
1 tablespoon fine Greek brandy or 1 teaspoon vanilla extract
3 egg whites, beaten till peaks are glistening and wavy

1. Soften gelatin in cold water for 5 minutes.
2. Combine chocolate, sugar, and salt in boiling water. Bring just to boiling point and add softened gelatin. Stir until dissolved and remove from heat. Refrigerate for 15 minutes. Add beaten egg yolks, cinnamon, and brandy and beat this thickened mixture well with a whisk.
3. Fold in the stiffly beaten egg whites thoroughly. Pour mousse into a 3-cup mold that has been rinsed in cold water. Chill for two hours. Serve with sweetened whipped cream.

GRAPEFRUIT OR ORANGE RIND PRESERVES
Frápa Glykó

YIELD: 1 quart
TIME: 45 minutes preparation;
4½ hours cooking

The Greeks make sour cherry preserves, and preserves of the tiniest eggplants imaginable, stuffed with almonds; from the island of Chios comes an exotic orange and lemon blossom preserve; and from other parts of Greece come quince jelly and rose petal jam and, of course, all kinds of citrus rind preserves.

Since grapefruits and oranges are so plentiful in this country throughout the year, I have chosen the following recipe to include in this book. The next time you are eating grapefruit or oranges that are particularly thick-skinned, put the rinds aside for making "spoon sweets." (The skins will keep refrigerated for 2 to 3 days if you put them in a plastic bag.)

In Greece the very old custom of offering "spoon sweets" to guests is still practiced. After formal greetings, the hostess brings in a tray bearing a crystal bowl of preserves, glasses of cold water, spoons, and delicate glasses of liqueur (usually brandy).

The guest takes a spoonful of preserve and eats it. He then drinks some of the water and puts the empty spoon into the glass. Picking up the liqueur, he drinks a toast to the family's health. Once these formalities are over, everyone begins to relax. Coffee and pastries will be served later on.

The preserves are never served in individual dishes. My husband, while dining with Archbishop Athenagoras in New York, was told that this is not merely a sign of Greek hospitality but also a silent sign that since everyone eats from the same bowl, the food is not poisoned. This legend goes back centuries; no one seems to know the exact circumstances that started it.

These preserves go beautifully with roasts or broiled meats. You cannot combine orange and grapefruit rinds—make the preserves separately. You could also make this with thick-skinned lemons. Use 10 to 12 of them, but make sure after washing lemons that you grate skins lightly to remove the bitterness.

6 grapefruits or 8 thick-
skinned oranges (whole
or shells)

⅛ teaspoon baking soda

4 cups sugar

1 cup light corn syrup

½ teaspoon cream of tartar

½ cup light rum or brandy

1. If starting with whole oranges or whole grapefruits: Wash them first, then score skins in 4 to 6 sections. Peel off scored strips (see illustration) trimming off most of the white pulp. These will be medium-size rolls when complete. If starting with leftover orange or grapefruit halves: Wash and cut empty orange or grapefruit shells into 4 or 6 sections. Trim off remaining fruit pulp in each quarter with sharp knife. These will be smaller rolls when complete.

2. Thread a large needle with strong thread, doubled, and make a knot at the end. Roll each strip of rind tightly into a roll and pass the needle and thread through it. Thread another. When you have about 15 tight rolls on each necklace, cut thread and tie the two ends together. Repeat this until you have used

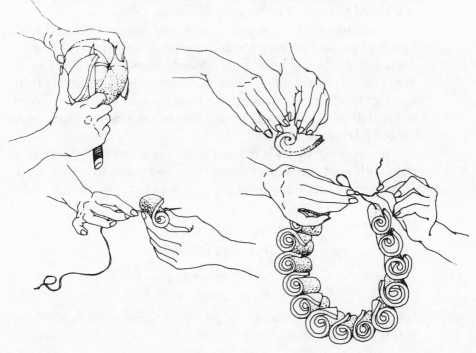

up all the rinds. If you don't care about fancy rolled shapes, cut rind into 1-inch pieces or thin strips, marmalade style. Ignore needle-and-thread instructions and continue.

3. Place rinds in a large pot and cover with water. Add baking soda and bring to a boil. Reduce heat, cover, and simmer for 1 hour. Drain.

4. Add fresh water, bring to a boil, reduce heat, and cover. Simmer for another hour, then drain.

5. Add fresh water for the third time, bring to a boil, reduce heat, and cover. Simmer for 1 final hour and drain. These three water baths eliminate all the bitterness in the rinds. Place the rinds on paper towels and drain well. If you have made necklaces, remove the threads (rinds will have formed into nice little rolls).

6. Wash pot and add sugar, corn syrup, cream of tartar, and 2 cups water. Cook uncovered at medium boil until consistency of honey (about 35 minutes, or 220° on a candy thermometer).

7. Add rinds to syrup and simmer uncovered for 25 minutes. Remove pot from heat and allow to sit undisturbed for 5 hours or overnight in order for the syrup to become thinner.

8. Return uncovered pot to heat and bring to a rapid boil. Reduce heat and simmer for 20 minutes or until syrup becomes thick and rinds are beautifully glazed. Remove pot from heat. Add rum or brandy and gently mix with wooden spoon. Pour into sterilized jars (to prevent jars from breaking when hot syrup is poured, place a spoon in jar before pouring). When cool, tighten lids and refrigerate.

9. Serve Greek style in bowl as a "spoon sweet" or American style with roasts or broiled meats. It is preferable to wait a week or two before serving, to give the rum time to permeate the rinds.

CRETAN GRAPES
Stafíllia Tis Crétis

YIELD: 6 servings
TIME: 40 minutes

When grapes are in season the people of Crete often serve them in this unusual fashion.

If you do not wish to use wine or liqueur, dip each cluster into slightly beaten egg whites instead, then continue as below.

Serve with slices of Kasseri cheese as a snack or plain as a dessert.

    2 pounds seedless grapes
    ¾ cup Mavrodaphne wine or Ouzo or créme de menthe
    1 cup confectioner's sugar

1. Wash grapes thoroughly and drain. Cut stems to make small clusters.

2. Dip each cluster of grapes into wine or liqueur and dust grapes generously with confectioner's sugar. Place on cookie sheet and set in freezer for 30 minutes. Then refrigerate until ready to serve.

APPENDIXES

Greek Ceremonies and Special Foods

In the following section, I talk about Easter and its customs and about personal church services. I also include recipes for special religious foods. Covering all of the Greek customs and holidays would fill another book, since the Greeks have a ritual attachment for just about every event in life, as well as death.

Easter

Easter is by far the most important event in the Greek Orthodox Church, and the traditions of celebration are still widely observed, from major cities to the smallest of towns. It is the one time of year when Greeks abroad try to come home. Ceremonial traditions are observed even before Lent.

Apokries is the three-week period that precedes Lent. The first two weeks are spent scrubbing and cleaning just about everything in sight. In many small villages not only do the houses receive their annual coat of whitewash, but the streets as well, so that they too will sparkle on Easter morning.

The last week of Apokries is a period of festive parties and parades, laughter and good eating. Young and old dress up in gaudy costumes, and the effect is much like the New Orleans Mardi Gras.

Food is restricted on only two days of this three-week period. The second Friday is a day of fasting, since it precedes All Souls' Day (*Psihosavato*), and Lenten dishes are prepared. The final Sunday, the Agony (*Tirini*), is meatless, with cheese dishes predominating.

March 25 is called *Evangelismos* and is a day of great importance in the Greek calendar. A feast day of the Annunciation, of the Virgin Mary, it also commemorates National Greek Independence Day. After the liturgy, special prayers are given to God for freeing the Greeks on this day in 1821 from the oppressive rule of the Ottoman Turks. The Greeks were free for the first time in almost four hundred years. Although Evangelismos is within the Lenten period, because of the celebration of Greece's independence the Church traditionally permits fish and other seafood to be eaten on this day.

Palm Sunday (*Vaion*) is a happy day. This is the Sunday preceding Holy Week. The day commemorates Christ's entrance into Jerusalem, when his path was strewn with palms. After the liturgy, palms are distributed and the eating of fish for that one day is permitted.

Holy Week: The Julian calendar determines the date of Easter. Greek Easter must always follow the Jewish Passover. The early Christians observed strict fasting during Lent. They ate no meat or fish, and even staples such as eggs, butter, cream, milk, and cheese were forbidden. They improvised a special bread made only of flour and water and shaped it to resemble two arms folded in prayer. Today this has come to be known as the pretzel. The Greeks place hard twisted pretzels between two layers of waxed paper and crush them with a rolling pin to the consistency of wheat grains. This is then used as a tasty topping for Lenten fish, cooked vegetables, or baked macaroni. Little pretzels float in bowls of lentil soup, making an interesting variation for the faithful.

Although the Greek Orthodox Church prescribes severe fasting for the entire forty days before Easter, most Greeks fast only during the last fourteen days. In the United States, Greek-Americans on the whole fast only during Holy Week.

Each day during Holy Week, the events of Christ's life are relived. On Holy Thursday night twelve excerpts of the four Gospels are read, relating Christ's Passion. This is also the day the eggs are to be dyed—deep red, to symbolize Christ's blood.

We were in Athens a few years ago during Lent, and by the time Easter arrived, I was amazed at the feeling of tension that existed. The highly imaginative Greeks really relive the tragic happenings in Jerusalem nearly two thousand years ago. Good Friday, the day of mourning, was unbelievably quiet in the normally raucous capital. It is such a day of sadness that it is the only day of the year when the Divine Liturgy may not be celebrated. During Lamentation Service on Friday evening, the priest and choir chant Byzantine hymns around the *Epitaphios* (sepulcher, which signifies the burial of Christ). The parishioners file past this symbolic tomb, which is decorated with hundreds of beautiful spring flowers.

Holy Saturday: After the solemnity of Good Friday, Holy Saturday is filled with bustling activity in preparation for the Resurrection. The streets start to fill with flags, banners, and bands. Rocket and fireworks displays are prepared to soar from rooftops of large hotels and buildings.

The congregations both in Greece and in the United States gather in their churches or cathedrals shortly before midnight to await the Resurrection, each person holding an unlighted candle. A few minutes before twelve, all lights except the perpetual flame inside the altar are extinguished and the church is plunged into darkness and silence—the darkness of the tomb. Then, exactly at midnight, the priest lights his candle from the perpetual flame and calls out, "Christos Anesti" (Christ is risen). He starts lighting the candles of those nearest him, who in turn light the candles of those nearest them; in a few minutes the entire church is filled with flickering candlelight. The priest, choir, and congregation all join in singing the beautiful Byzantine chant *Christos Anesti,* which is followed by the Resurrection Liturgy. Outside at midnight, buildings are floodlit, sirens wail, and the church bells begin to peal.

As the congregation leaves the church, the priest gives each one of the faithful a dyed red egg and says "Christos Anesti." One replies, "Alethos Anesti" (Truly, He is risen), and then takes a piece of holy bread from a tray held by an altar boy. The congregation leaves with their candles still lighted.

Even though Greeks in the United States do not have the fireworks, the church bells, or the bands, Easter midnight is still a happy time. And in both countries before one enters the house one pauses to form a cross of candle smoke over the top of the doorframe. This mark remains throughout the year and means that the spirit of the Resurrection has been brought into the home. The still-flaming candles are then placed on the table, and the fast is broken with the Resurrection meal—Easter Soup (Mayeritsa), Easter Bread (Lambropsomo), Greek cheeses, an assortment of cookies (Koulourakia), and, of course, the red eggs. Retsina is served.

Because not everyone can afford to buy spring lamb, the Easter day meal is a communal affair in the smaller Greek villages. On Easter morning, tables and chairs are set up around the town square for all. Shallow trenches are dug and filled with glowing embers. Young spring lambs are put on spits over the trenches and slowly rotated by hand for many hours. The lamb is sprinkled with a little salt and wild oregano and basted from time to time with lemon juice and olive oil to keep it from drying out. Occasionally the cavity of the lamb is stuffed with Feta cheese. Everyone gathers spring flowers and decorates all the tables. When the lamb is ready, the village priest blesses the food and everyone sits down to share the Easter meal. One year friends of mine, John and Mary Koukos, were driving through such a village when they were invited to stop and eat dinner with the town. This being their very first time in Greece, they were not only delighted but overwhelmed as well by the experience. It is this kind of generous, spontaneous hospitality that is so characteristic of the Greeks.

When John and Mary returned home they had a permanent, electrically rotating spit built over a shallow trench on their property in Connecticut. Because it's much cooler in New England during Easter than it is in Greece, John orders a young lamb for Labor Day to mark the end of summer. All of their friends are invited, and we celebrate Easter all over again in the tradition of a very small Greek village.

During Easter week, red eggs are also dyed at home, traditionally on Holy Thursday. They are used for decorating the Easter breads, and a bowl of them is kept for offering to friends—the eggs themselves symbolic of Christ's Resurrection. And recently Greeks are beginning to make beautiful hand-decorated multi-colored eggs as gifts. The traditional red dye is imported to the United States and may be purchased at any Greek-American grocery store. Using 2 packets to color 18 eggs will give you the traditional deep red color of Greek Easter eggs.

During Easter week wherever you go you will be offered an egg from bowls filled with red eggs. When you have picked one up, someone will come toward you with his egg in hand and challenge you.

This cracking of eggs indicates the loosening of bonds and the start of a new life. This tradition continues throughout the week and is played by everyone from elderly "no-nonsense" relatives to giggling schoolchildren.

You hold the egg of your choosing in your hand with the pointed end up. The other person holds his egg over yours, pointed end down. As he lightly taps your egg, he says, "Christos Anesti" (Christ is risen), and you reply, "Alithos Anesti" (Truly, He is risen). If your egg cracks, he wins. If his egg cracks, you are the winner, and you go on to challenge someone else. (I'm sure this is the reason egg salad caught on for the period follow-ing Easter.) Youngsters usually rush their cracked egg to the kitchen and come back to choose a "harder" egg from the bowl.

Weddings and Christenings

Almonds, among the earliest cultivated goods of the Old World, figure in Greek religious ceremonies such as Memorial Services, weddings, and christenings. These are called Koufeta, the candy-coated Jordan almonds.

Weddings in Greece are wonderfully elaborate affairs. A

friend once remarked during the ceremony, "It looks like a Darryl Zanuck production." He wasn't exaggerating. A Greek Orthodox wedding is a long and beautiful ceremony reminiscent of a royal coronation. Even the humblest of churches will have a dramatic background of icons, shimmering candlelight, ancient chants, and burning incense.

The bride and groom exchange double rings and sip wine from a golden goblet. Elaborate crowns of orange blossoms joined by one ribbon are crossed over their heads three times, giving the blessings of the Holy Trinity to the new partnership. Wearing their crowns still joined by the ribbon and holding tall luminous candles emblazoned with gold and tied with white satin ribbons, they carefully follow the priest around the altar three times.

When guests begin to leave the church, or at the reception that follows, they are offered Koufeta by a member of the wedding party.

The Greek Orthodox baptismal ceremony is also an impressive one. All of the child's clothes are removed and discarded. The priest submerges the naked infant three times in a huge brass or silver cauldron filled with warm water. The child is then dried and anointed with olive oil by the priest, as were the ancient kings when crowned. This symbolizes that the child too is entering a new kingdom, the Kingdom of God. The oil symbolically prevents the devil from grasping the child. The godparents then dress the child in completely new clothes and a gold cross, their gift to the small new Christian, and he or she is given communion. To become a godparent in the Greek church is to take a moral vow that you will take that child as your own if anything should ever happen to the parents.

Whereas a wedding is a majestic and hushed affair, the baptismal is usually the opposite. It really depends upon the age and temperament of the youngster. Most children, especially if they happen to be over a year old, do not enjoy the "public bath and oiling" one bit. (One of my godchildren grabbed the priest so tenaciously by his beard that it took three adults to pry those little hands loose.)

As guests begin to leave the church, or at the reception that follows, they are offered Koufeta by the godparents.

JORDAN CANDY-COATED ALMONDS
Kouféta

Koufeta are usually wrapped in netting and tied with a narrow satin ribbon. This ancient custom of offering Jordan candy-coated almonds denotes a wish for nothing but sweetness in the person's life. The almond is also regarded as a symbol of fertility.

The almonds themselves are available at candy shops or bakeries.

Jordan candy-coated almonds (about 72 per pound; 5 almonds per bouquet)
Nylon netting, in 6-inch squares (1 yard 72 inches wide will make 72 squares)
12-inch lengths of 5/16th-inch-wide satin ribbon
6 to 8 sprigs artificial lilies-of-the-valley, separated (for weddings)
Assorted small plastic favors (for christenings)

For weddings: Use white almonds only, white net, and white satin ribbon. Place 5 almonds in the center of each square piece of netting. Bring corners together, place 1 or 2 blossomed stems from lilies-of-the-valley against the net, and tie ribbon tightly around it, forming a little bouquet.

For boy christenings: Use blue net, blue satin ribbon. You may use all blue almonds or multicolored ones. You may leave the bouquets tied plainly with the blue ribboned bow or tie a little plastic animal or boat around the center of each before making a bow.

For girl christenings: Use pink net, pink satin ribbon. You may use pink almonds or multicolored ones. Tie bouquets plainly with the pink ribboned bow or tie a little artificial flower or animal around the center of each.

Arrange all the little bouquets prettily on a gleaming silver tray and serve one to each guest.

Memorial Services

The *Mnemósinon,* or Memorial Service, is a Greek Orthodox Church rite in memory of a loved one. During the special service,

Kolliva, a tray of sweetened boiled wheat mixed with fruit and nuts, is blessed by the priest. It is then distributed to all present. The eating of Kolliva at the church is to recall to mind the departed soul and to pray for his or her salvation.

The kernels of boiled wheat symbolize the Resurrection, the raisins sweetness, and the pomegranate seeds are symbolic of the abundance of everything good.

According to church tradition, Kolliva is offered at the end of forty days, then six months, then one year after death, and whenever desired thereafter.

In the past, Kolliva was prepared frequently by the family requesting a Memorial Mass. The boiling of the wheat kernels, however, had its difficulties, and the ritual decorating of the tray became so puzzling that second- and third-generation Greek-Americans usually gave up. They often asked the church to find an older member who would prepare it for the forty-day service only. Such pious elderly people are becoming more difficult to locate, however, and this tender custom is almost doomed to extinction. I therefore set out to figure out why our generation was having so much trouble making Kolliva.

After making Kolliva at least ten times, I finally worked out the recipe. It is time-consuming but genuinely good to eat; the wheat will be chewy but soft; the powdered sugar pressed on top won't crack open (as moisture seeps through), and the decorations will be correct.

This exquisite combination of whole wheat, fruit, sugar, and spices would make a nutritious breakfast cereal. Follow the instructions, but omit the ritual decorating of the tray. Place in quart containers and freeze. Defrost each container at room temperature as needed, refrigerating what is not being used. Served chilled with milk or cream, or just eat it plain—this is called Varvara.

MEMORIAL WHEAT
Kólliva

YIELD: Approximately 150 small portions
TIME: 3 days

8 pounds whole-wheat kernels (sold in health food stores or see Shopper's Guide)

3 cups sesame seeds

2 oranges

2 pomegranates (optional)

3 cups finely chopped walnuts or blanched, peeled, and finely chopped almonds

1 pound seedless white raisins

3 pounds granulated sugar

8 tablespoons ground cumin

4 tablespoons ground cinnamon

3 cups unseasoned bread crumbs or graham cracker crumbs or zwieback crumbs

2 pounds confectioner's sugar

6 ounces (¾ cup) silver dragées (tiny silver candy balls)

2½ cups candied white Jordan almonds

1 cup whole blanched and peeled almonds or several tablespoons powdered coffee

150 small glassine bags, approximately 4 by 4 inches

FIRST DAY, THE COOKING

1. Wash wheat carefully several times with warm water (cold water will make kernels harder).

2. Place wheat kernels in a large canning kettle and cover generously with warm water. Bring to a boil, then lower heat to a bare simmer. As froth appears, remove it with a spoon, since it could cause the wheat to sour. Simmer gently from 9 A.M. to 11 P.M. (14 hours), stirring often to prevent sticking. The wheat kernels will split in two. Turn off heat. (Here a prayer is traditionally said over the wheat, asking forgiveness for the souls of *all* the dead.)

3. Strain 3 times, using a large colander, into another pot and reserve the dripping liquid for making Health Fruit Soup (Heelo, see recipe) if you wish.

4. Rinse strained wheat 3 times with warm water, rinsing colander thoroughly each time. Put rinsed drained wheat in colander and allow to drain overnight.

SECOND DAY, THE DRYING
AND OTHER PREPARATIONS

1. Spread many layers of newspapers on a large table or bed. Cover newspapers with 3 clean white ironed sheets. Spread the wheat evenly over the sheets and allow to dry all day and night.

2. Toast sesame seeds in a shallow pan in a preheated 325° oven until lightly golden (about 12 minutes). Crush seeds with rolling pin or blender until pulverized, and set aside.

3. Wash the oranges and grate the rind.

4. Peel the pomegranates and remove the juicy red pods that are the fruit inside; set them aside. Discard peel.

THIRD DAY, THE DAY
YOU TAKE KOLLIVA
TO CHURCH

1. Combine wheat, sesame seeds, grated orange rind, pomegranate pods, nuts, raisins, the 3 pounds of granulated sugar, cumin, and cinnamon, and toss until very well blended. This mixing should take about 10 minutes if doing it by hand or 3 if using a dough hook.

2. Line a large silver serving tray (if you don't have one, ask for one at the Greek church) with waxed paper or aluminum foil, using paper lace doilies to line edges of the tray if you wish. Spread wheat mixture on it, shaping it with your hands so that there is a slight rise in the center.

3. Sprinkle all the bread or cracker crumbs evenly over the wheat; then, using a square piece of folded waxed paper in your hand, pat and press down so that the crumbs will absorb any remaining moisture.

4. Sift the confectioner's sugar over the wheat mixture. It should be at least ¼ inch thick. After all the sugar is sifted on, take your folded piece of wax paper and carefully press all the confectioner's sugar down so that the top of the wheat will be white, smooth, and compact.

5. Cut out a large cardboard cross and make an impression with it in the sugar in the center of the tray. Fill the cross

indentation with silver dragées. On the right side of the tray form
the letters:

IC XC

NIKA

(This means "Jesus Conquers.") Fill the indentations with the
candied white Jordan almonds. On the left side, outline the
initials of the deceased with silver dragées and fill in the indentations with the whole blanched almonds or powdered coffee. A
border may be made using any remaining almonds, dragées, and
powdered coffee if desired. Cover the tray loosely.

You must let the priest know what day you are bringing the
Kolliva in, for he must schedule the Memorial Service following
the end of the liturgy and alert the church committee that their
services will be required. The name of the departed soul is
written on a piece of paper and placed in an envelope. A dona-
tion to the church in memory of the departed is usually included.
This envelope is brought to the church with the tray of Kolliva.

Take the Kolliva (and glassine bags) to the church at least
an hour before services start. It will be placed on the sacramental
table near the altar by the cantor (*psalti*), who will also place
two very large tall candles (*lambathes*), each tied with a black
ribbon, one on each side of the tray. The cantor will light them
when the liturgy is over and the Memorial Service begins.

At the end of the Sunday liturgy the priest will start the
Memorial Service by chanting the *tresayio* (prayers for the salvation of the deceased), during which he will recite aloud the
name of the deceased. He will wave burning incense (*livani*)
over the tray and throughout the church (this is called *theemia-
zee*). The congregation joins in silent prayer throughout this 15-
minute service.

One of the altar boys will then carry the tray to the back
of the church, where several members of the church committee
will distribute the Kolliva into the little glassine bags, using a
small silver scoop. (If you don't have one, the church does.) During this time each parishioner goes to the priest for his blessing
and a piece of holy bread and then starts toward the back of the
church. He will be offered the Kolliva by a member of the church
committee before he departs.

Kolliva is also brought to the church three times during the 40-day Lent period preceding Easter on Saturdays. These Saturdays are called *Psihosavata* (Saturdays of Souls). Anyone who wishes may make Kolliva and take it to church on any of these Saturdays. On the piece of paper he may list the names of *all* departed loved ones to be read aloud during the Memorial Service.

Bread for Church Services

The role of bread in the Greek Orthodox Church has always been important. At every Divine Liturgy, the priest commemorates, reenacts, relives the Last Supper of Christ.

The round loaf of bread called Prosphoron, bread of offering, is leavened; the Latin, or Roman, bread of offering is unleavened. The leavened versus unleavened bread remains one of the minor disagreements between the Greek Patriarch and the Pope of Rome.

Prosphoron is distributed in church to the congregation after each Mass as well as to those receiving Holy Communion. At the end of every service, the priest stands on the steps of the altar and greets each member of the congregation; he offers his hand to be kissed and gives each member a small piece of the bread of offering. The parishioner eats it walking down the center aisle on his way out of the church.

In large cities the bread is baked by a professional baker and delivered to the church because of the enormous sizes of the congregations. In smaller towns and cities throughout the United States the Prosphoron is baked and contributed by a religious woman who is given the honor of making it. The religious seal for the bread is usually only in her possession.

Again I point out that these pious elderly people are becoming harder to find, and it takes a lot of work to knead the bread. I have heard more than once recently the question: "Why don't the younger people start taking turns making the bread?" And the priests now have in their possession more than two or three extra *sfragithes* (religious seals) and are trying to encourage the younger members of the church to start making and contributing this bread.

The wooden seal is stamped only on top of the Prosphoron, and it makes the pattern illustrated here. The center portion of the bread, which is called the "lamb," since it is to become the body of the crucified Christ, is cut out by the priest and placed on the paten, the ceremonial metal plate for the bread. The Greek letters IC and XC are abbreviations for the words "Jesus Christ." The letters NIKA mean "conquers" (see illustration).

The large triangular piece is removed and placed on the paten in honor and commemoration of the Virgin Mary. The nine smaller triangular pieces are removed and also placed on the paten in commemoration of the Angelic Hosts and the Saints of the Orthodox Church.

BREAD OF OFFERING
Prósphoron

YIELD: Approximately 30 small pieces
TIME: 2½ hours rising;
55 minutes baking

In making the Prosphoron you will notice that no shortening, milk, or eggs are permitted in its preparation. That is because it is a communion bread, made in the tradition of the simple bread eaten at the Last Supper.

¼ cup warm water
1 package active dry yeast (¼ ounce) or cake of fresh yeast
2 teaspoons salt
2 cups warm water
6 to 6½ cups all-purpose flour, sifted

1. Rinse a large mixing bowl with warm water. Pour ¼ cup warm water (between 110° and 115° for dry yeast, 95° for fresh yeast) into bowl; add yeast and stir until dissolved. Add salt and warm water. Stir until well blended.

2. Stir in 3 cups of flour, 1 cup at a time. Add fourth cup of flour and beat with wooden spoon until dough is smooth and elastic (rest when you get tired; the dough will be easier to handle after 5- or 10-minute rest intervals). Mix the fifth cup of flour in to make a stiff dough.

3. Sprinkle half of the sixth cup of flour onto the board. Turn out dough onto heavily floured area of board. Keep a coating of flour on the dough as you begin to knead with floured hands. Fold dough toward you with fingers and then push firmly away with heel of your hand. Add more flour to board and knead it in until the dough no longer sticks. Punch it like a prizefighter—slow steady jabs—for 15 minutes *after* putting in the last drop of flour.

4. Kneading is finished when dough is smooth and satiny and nonsticky. Put dough in a warm 4-quart bowl. Cover with a clean dish towel and set in a warm place (about 80°) to rise.

5. Let dough rise until almost doubled in bulk (about 1½ hours at 80°).

6. Punch dough down; squeeze out air bubbles with your hands; shape into 1 large round loaf, turning edges under to make a smooth top. Place loaf on a baking sheet lined with foil or lightly floured. Dust sfragitha (religious seal) lightly with flour; shake off excess. Press seal down *very hard* on top of loaf. Pull up seal gently. Cover bread with a clean dish towel and let rise in a warm place until almost doubled in size (about 1 hour).

7. Bake in preheated 375° oven for 15 minutes; then reduce heat to 350° and bake until golden (not browned), about 40 minutes more.

8. Remove loaf from pan and place on a rack to cool covered with a clean dish towel (this softens the crust somewhat). When fully cooled allow it to remain overnight on top of a dish towel and covered with another one. Wrap in waxed paper, then in foil, and seal in plastic bag. Take it to church or freeze it. To defrost, remove all wrappings and place on rack overnight.

Spices and Herbs
in Greek Cooking

Among the fabled natural beauties of Greece are its crystalline sunlight, sparkling water, locusts drumming in the silvery-green olive groves, and the patches of wild herbs on the rocky hills. Here, briefly, are some of those herbs and spices that figure prominently in Greek cooking.

Basil, a long-respected herb, is very popular; it is particularly wonderful with tomatoes.

Bay leaf, member of the laurel family, is famous both in legend and history. It is used extensively in Greek cooking.

Coriander, native to the Mediterranean, is heavily favored by the Cypriotes.

Dill, which grows abundantly in Greece and used to be carried to ward off spirits, is used extensively in Greek dishes.

Mahlepi, originally from Persia, is the hard small seed of a flowering tree very much like a cherry; it can be found in all the stores listed at the back of the book and the liquid on page 159 can be used in place of it if necessary.

Marjoram grows wild throughout the country. Like basil, it is often used in place of oregano, particularly with meats and fish.

Mastiha, a sweet and unique Greek flavoring derived from the sap of the mastic tree, which grows on the island of Chios; the crystals are pounded into a powder widely used in medicines, liqueurs, candies, cakes, and cookies.

Mint and *oregano* grow wild in Greece, and *parsley,* cultivated, can be raised all year round.

Sage, which is used in sausage or pork dishes, is another herb native to the Mediterranean, as is *saffron,* the world's most expensive spice, the stigma of the *Crocus sativas* blossom. The Greeks call saffron *krocus,* and they use it in pilafs or fish soups.

Savory, also from the Mediterranean, is indispensable in the making of Loukanika, Greek sausages.

Sesame seeds are grown on the island of Kos. In ancient times Greek soldiers used to carry them in their rations—they were recognized even then as a highly nutritious food. Greeks use sesame seeds a great deal, particularly for holiday breads.

And finally there is *thyme,* one of the most abundant of the wild herbs in Greece. Hymettus honey, among the finest in the world, is made by bees attracted to the thyme growing on Mount Hymettus.

Nuts and Seeds

Greece has an abundance of nut trees. This fact and the scarcity of grazing land are the main reasons the nutritious nut is so widely featured in Greek cooking.

The most popular nut is the pistachio, grown on the islands off the coast of Attica. Unlike the dyed red ones found here, they are toasted and sold in their natural off-white or beige color. To toast: Place raw shelled pistachios on a baking sheet and roast in a preheated 375° oven for 10 minutes, shaking them occasionally.

Pistachios, walnuts, and almonds are used in sauces (cooking, not just sweet dessert sauces), poultry stuffings, and stews as well as in cakes and pastries. Walnuts and almonds are also dipped in honey to serve as an accompaniment to wine. Pine nuts, from the stone pine tree, which grows throughout Greece, are also used in stuffings, and almost always in Dolmathes. Chestnuts, higher in starch content than most nuts, are eaten much as we eat potatoes, and they also figure prominently in stuffings.

In many informal tavernas, you will find bowls of ordinary pumpkin, melon, watermelon, squash, or sunflower seeds that have been salted and roasted. These are called *pasatempo* ("to pass the time").

Greeks buy roasted seeds from the *pasatempo* man the way Americans buy peanuts. The *pasatempo* man is a nut vendor who strolls the streets of Greece pushing a contraption that resembles a baby carriage. It is fitted with divided trays covered with glass, and inside these trays are roasted seeds and nuts that the Greeks love to eat.

The next time you have any of these seeds around the kitchen, don't throw them away; make *pasatempo*. Wash and dry the seeds, spread them in a shallow pan, and sprinkle with salt. Bake in a 375° oven for 20 minutes, shaking occasionally. Serve as you would nuts, eating the seed inside the kernel.

The Olives of Athena

Greek children learn early that the gods chose Athena over Poseidon to be the supreme deity of Athens because she caused the first olive tree to grow. Poseidon had merely created a spring.

The olive tree flourishes in the dry, rocky terrain of Greece, making its chief products—olives and olive oil—crucial ones for the Greek economy. The harvest, a brief period in the fall, is a time of hectic work followed by celebration. At this time, the streets of small towns are lined with barrels of olives in brine.

Green olives are those that are picked unripe; the black olives are already ripe. Both must be preserved in brine or in their own oil. When fresh, ripe olives are crushed, one gets the precious olive oil, so essential to Greek cooking. The first pressing produces an oil that is dark green in color and pungent in taste. Second and third pressings have a lighter flavor and aroma and are golden amber in color.

The rest of the tree's products are also used—the oil residue for soap, the pit and pulp for fertilizer, the dead wood of the tree for fires in country kitchens.

Greek Olives Commonly Sold in the United States

KALAMATA OLIVES
The city of Kalamata in Messinia is famous for its large, oblong olives with a smooth purple skin cultivated especially for dining. Sold in jars in a solution of oil and vinegar, Kalamata olives are

firm and juicy with a hint of wine vinegar—they are absolutely delicious. No dinner can be called Greek without some of these on the table.

BLACK OLIVES

These small, round wrinkled olives are oily, slightly bitter, and salty; they are grown throughout most of Greece, although each province prepares them a bit differently. In the United States they are usually sold in bulk, although I have seen jars occasionally in good grocery stores. I grew up with a girl who used to take a pound of these olives to the movies with her each time we went. While the rest of us ate candy she ate black olives and never thought them bitter at all.

BLACK AMPHISSA OLIVES

From the Parnassus region. When recipes refer to large black Greek olives, these are the ones that are meant. They are big, black, juicy, and very tasty, with a slight taste of oil clinging to them.

GREEN OLIVES

These oblong-shaped olives, picked unripe, have a hard green flesh, smooth skin, and slightly bitter flavor. They are not oily. A hint of garlic and oregano prevails. Green olives are sold in bulk as well as in jars.

CURING OLIVES AT HOME
Eliés Tou Spetioú

For you lucky readers who have your own olive tree or who can purchase them "raw," why not cure them yourself, the Greek way? My grandmother bought and prepared olives in this manner right in New York City when I was a child, since she insisted they tasted better if you made them yourself.

I don't know how much better they tasted, but it was always fun to help her prepare the "raw olives," as my sister and I called them. I particularly remember her pounding each olive with a hammer to break the skin before tossing it into the marinade. I suppose cutting a slit in each olive has the same effect, although if my grandmother were here she would insist that you use the hammer.

Green unripe olives are best for this recipe. Multiply all ingredients for however many pounds of olives are available.

1 pound fresh olives	1 small clove garlic,
¾ cup olive oil	finely minced
Salt	1 teaspoon oregano
¼ cup wine vinegar	1 large bay leaf

1. Wash the olives well, and place them in a crock large enough to hold them easily. Cover with a solution of salt water, 1 cup salt to each quart water.

2. Place a heavy plate on top of olives to keep them submerged. Do not refrigerate—just put in a cool, shaded spot for 2 weeks.

3. Drain and rinse olives well with lots of cold running water. Cut a tiny slit in each olive or hit each olive with a hammer.

4. Fill a sterilized jar with olives.

5. Mix remaining ingredients, pour into jar of olives, and shake gently to blend. Allow olives to marinate for at least 2 weeks before using. Every time you want to use a few olives, shake jar gently to mix oil and vinegar. Keep refrigerated once you have placed them in the marinade. They will remain juicy and keep for months.

The Pleasures of Greek Cheeses

In the ancient days, Greeks considered cheese to be an aphrodisiac. Among Greek-Americans the most popular and most accessible cheeses are Feta, Kasseri, Kefalograviera, Kefalotyri, Kopanisti, and Myzithra. Buy at least ½ pound of each and experiment. For a late-evening snack try a wedge of Greek cheese, a glass of wine, and some biscuits. At your next party serve some Greek cheeses with cocktails.

FETA

Feta is the most popular of all the Greek cheeses. Many American markets and cheese stores now carry it. It is a well-salted, white, semisoft cheese that crumbles easily. It is eaten fresh and is widely used in Greek cooking.

Feta is eaten daily by most Greek people, served with fruit and crumbled into salads and scrambled eggs. The famous Tiropetes (Cheese Triangle Puffs; see recipe) would not be the same if this wonderful cheese were not used in the filling.

Feta is made from goat's milk, sheep's milk, or even cow's milk, and this makes for a slight difference in taste. Now many countries make a cheese they call Feta. Some of it is good (especially that from Italy and Yugoslavia, which tend to use goat's or sheep's milk), some fair, and some hardly bears any resemblance to real Feta at all.

Some shopkeepers (there are a few unscrupulous ones around) tell you all Feta is imported from Greece. Insist on seeing the label to make sure it is Greek if buying Feta for the first time. If you know what Feta tastes like, ask for a sliver to taste before buying Feta from another country.

Feta is often sold packed in jars or tins containing a saltwater solution which keeps it fresh and moist. Always remember to *rinse* Feta before using, to rid it of excessive saltiness.

Occasionally Feta is imported in large barrels of salt solution, and the grocer will cut you a piece. It's less expensive to buy it like this, but if buying more than you will use immediately, you must make your own solution when you get the Feta home. Put the cheese in a wide-mouthed jar and fill with salted water (1 teaspoon salt for each cup of water). Screw top on jar and refrigerate. It will stay fresh for months. See the recipe on page 129 for a marvelous soufflé featuring Feta.

KASSERI

Kasseri, a very popular, firm golden cheese, is available here. It is mild in flavor and glistens with drops of butter. This cheese is a sheer delight. It is also used in Greek cooking (see recipe for Saganaki).

KEFALOGRAVIERA

Sometimes called Gravieri, Kefalograviera is made in Crete and resembles Agrafa or Gruyère in that it is rich and creamy. It tastes a bit like a good Swiss cheese. Perfect at the end of a meal with fresh fruits.

KEFALOTYRI

Kefalotyri is a popular hard cheese used mostly grated. It is pale yellow in color and well salted. It gets its name from its shape, which is like a head (*kefali*). It is widely exported to this country. Cheese of this type is made also from goat's milk in the Ozark region in Arkansas.

KOPANISTI

Kopanisti is a blue mold cheese with a sharp, peppery flavor. Fresh, whole milk is coagulated as in making Feta, but the co-agulation period is longer and therefore the curd is firm. The cheese is ready to eat after ripening for one or two months. Imported to the United States and usually packed into crocks or jars when sold as a spread. Marvelous for canapés.

I grew up visiting Florence Galas, a family friend who made the best Kopanisti I ever tasted. She used to keep it stored for 8 weeks in the garage where it was cool. This is how she made it then and now, and believe me it is better than any sold commercially.

HOMEMADE KOPANISTI
Kopanistí Tou Spetioú

YIELD: About 3 pounds
TIME: 30 minutes preparation;
8 weeks aging

2 pounds Feta cheese (rinsed and crumbled)
¾ pound blue cheese or Danish blue cheese (crumbled)
¼ pound softened butter
1 pound cottage cheese (mashed with a fork until smooth)

1 tablespoon oregano
1 tablespoon thyme
1 tablespoon freshly ground black pepper
2 tablespoons olive oil

1. Mix all above ingredients except olive oil to make a smooth paste.

2. Place into crock or jar and pour 2 tablespoons olive oil on top. To prevent too much mold from forming, store in a cool place for 8 weeks without disturbing.

3. Mix all together including the small amount of mold that will have formed on top. Place into small covered jars and refrigerate.

4. Always mix before serving.

MYZITHRA

There are two types of Myzithra. One is a soft bland cottage cheese type called Hlori Myzithra. The very popular Myzithra is the other one, a semisoft cheese that is grayish white in color. It has a most unusual flavor, which is difficult to describe except to say you either like it or you don't. I happen to like it and eat it with rolls and coffee in the morning or grated on top of Browned Butter Sauce (see recipe) over pasta. My husband, on the other hand, has never acquired a taste for it. It is imported to the United States, as are small heads of fine Myzithra from Italy.

The Hellenic Spirit in Wines, Liqueurs and Coffee

My mother's mother, whom we children grew up calling Yiayia (Grandmama), was a sparkling little lady and we loved her dearly. She worked in the fur industry and traveled back and forth from Europe the way some Americans go to Florida. After World War II, however, the family decided she should come and live with us.

We had just got our first television set and were quite excited. Yiayia watched for a moment, then silently got up and disappeared into her room. When she returned, she was wearing her best dress and shoes, and her hair had been recombed. We thought she had dressed up because she was expecting company. She haughtily told us that she didn't want the people on TV to see her not looking her best. If she could see the news commentator, and he was not a movie but broadcasting live into our living room, then of course, she reasoned, he could also see her.

My sweet little Spartan grandmother. From the way she looked she should have enjoyed soap operas, but she didn't. The only programs she watched were news broadcasts, old Tarzan films, and wrestling matches—she was addicted to these. I can still see her screaming excitedly at those TV wrestling matches, her voice getting sharper and shriller by the moment, yelling in Greek, "Hit him again for me! Twist that leg off! What are you, a man or a sissy?" If her wrestler won, she would defy anyone to tell her that wrestling matches were staged or rehearsed. If her wrestler lost, she was angry and upset, positive that her wrestler was seriously hurt.

Yiayia lived mostly on wine, fruits, and vegetables. Her typical meal was a glass of red wine diluted with a little water into which she would dunk chunks of freshly baked bread. The meal was sometimes accompanied by a few black olives and perhaps a piece of cheese. She laughingly referred to this kind of meal as her "peasant heritage."

One of the most poignant days of my life came when Yiayia decided that she wanted to become an American citizen. She barely spoke English, but she didn't want to die in this beautiful country and not be a citizen. It became an obsession with her. She felt it would not be morally right to be buried on American soil unless you were a true American. She was eighty-seven years old at the time she made this dramatic decision.

We spoke to the local police precinct and they told us that if we could get her to the police station, they would fingerprint her and the first step toward becoming a citizen would be out of the way. My family at that time lived in a four-flight walk-up in New York City.

Yiayia went down all those flights of stairs with members of the family supporting her as well as they could, and then we got into a taxi.

Yiayia was tired and weak but very excited. The policemen couldn't have been nicer. They gently rolled each thin finger over an inkpad and onto a clean card. They smiled and talked to her, and as tired as she was she confidently told them of her wish in broken English.

The police, however, took us to one side and whispered that it was "no use." Yiayia's fragile fingertips were worn smooth with age and the police couldn't get even one print. We all decided not to tell her the truth.

When Yiayia passed on a year later, she believed that the trip to the police station and the trouble of being fingerprinted had made her a citizen and thus she would not violate the sacred soil of the United States when she was buried.

I sincerely feel that the wine Yiayia drank helped her live to such a ripe old age. In memory, we toast you, Yiayia.

Most Greeks prefer to stay with their favorite wine, and a Greek dinner may be accompanied most correctly with only one wine throughout dinner. To a Greek, spirits of any kind should give an added flavor and gusto to life. Drunkenness or loss of self-control is never condoned. Greeks have added water to their wine for centuries as a precaution against too much alcohol during the hot summer months.

The following lists a few of the more popular and accessible wines and spirits from Greece. In the United States Greek wines are much less expensive than French wines, so it will not cost you much to experiment. Ouzo and Metaxa brandy will be the most expensive liqueurs. Most of these are available at the finer liquor stores in the United States.

Wines

DEMESTICA

A dry light wine that comes in both red and white and varies in different parts of Greece. A good table wine and quite inexpensive.

HYMETTUS

A light, dry, relatively inexpensive wine of the Pouilly type, most often served chilled as a table wine. Made from the grapes grown on Mount Hymettus.

MATINEA

A white wine popular with tourists and somewhat like Riesling in taste. Made in the Peloponnesus from the type of grapes the French call Petite Vins.

MAVRODAPHNE

A heavy sweet dessert wine that matures in barrels from four to eight years before being bottled. Ruby red in color, Mavrodaphne is usually served with fruits at the end of a meal or over cracked ice as an apéritif. Vineyards are in Achaia and Patras. It is exported in great quantities and is expensive.

NAOUSSIS BOUTARI

This is my personal favorite. It is very strong, very dry, and almost black in color, comparable to the Médoc wines. It is so dry that your entire mouth feels the sensation; nevertheless, it doesn't mask the flavor of the food you are eating. It is made in Macedonia.

NEMEAN

The best known of the dry red Greek wines. It is referred to as "lion's blood" because of its color and alcoholic strength. Made in the Peloponnesus.

RETSINA

Heavily resinated white, red, or rosé wine made in all parts of Greece.

The origin of retsina wine is interesting. Before bottles or even casks were invented, the Greeks kept their wines in goatskins and poured pitch pine on top in order to seal and preserve them. They eventually got used to the taste of resin or pitch pine and continued to add this flavoring even after the invention of casks and bottles.

Retsina wines have been found intact in the original terracotta containers the ancient Greeks called amphoras. These huge jars were still sealed with the pitch pine even though they were discovered in the bottom of ships wrecked thousands of years ago in the Aegean and Mediterranean.

As a child visiting Sparta, I remember being taken to a private wine press where they were preparing to make retsina wine. The grapes were unloaded through an opening in a wall and fell to the cement floor of a large vat. Men were waiting with bare feet and trousers rolled up to stamp on the grapes. They began to work with the precision of Flamenco dancers, singing louder and louder as the tempo increased. As each supply of grapes was finished, the skins were swept away and another batch of grapes was thrown in.

My younger sister and I were asked to join in the festivities. After scrubbing our feet thoroughly, we were lowered into the huge vat, where we did our own amateur grape trampling for a little while.

One of my dearest friends, Mary Prodis, always serves retsina wines mixed with soda or mineral water. It then tastes like a most unusual champagne.

Retsina is best served chilled and is usually served as an apéritif or as a table wine. I think you will get used to this strange, almost turpentine, taste and like it very much.

The best of the retsina wines are under the brand names of Metaxa or Cambas.

ST. HELENA

A dry, amber-colored wine made from the golden grapes of the Peloponnesus. Very pleasant table wine, served slightly chilled.

SANTO

A strong dessert wine that comes from the volcanic island of Santorini. The Vatican favors wines from this island for its Communion wines.

ZITSA

A very pleasant golden sparkling wine, sometimes referred to as champagne. Made in Epirus.

Liqueurs, Brandies, and Other Spirits

OUZO

In my opinion Ouzo is the only aphrodisiac sold freely and exported widely. Looking like innocent clear water and tasting a bit like Pernod, this apéritif liqueur can run as high as a hundred proof. Distilled from grapes, usually the by-product of wine-making, it is flavored with anise. Ouzo can be taken straight or on the rocks.

The strong licorice flavor and high alcoholic content make Ouzo the most popular drink not only in Greece but throughout the Middle East. In some Arab countries it is made from dates, which give it a slightly different taste. It is called Arak or Raki as well as Ouzo.

Ouzo is made both commercially and in private homes. That made in private homes is fiery stuff and should be treated with utmost respect. The oldtimers who make it themselves usually drink it straight with a water chaser.

Tourists prefer to mix Ouzo with water and add a cube of ice. This makes it white and cloudy, which accounts for its nickname "lion's milk."

Ouzo is by far the favorite of the young Greek sidewalk café crowds. They prefer it poured over ice and sipped very slowly. Mostly used as an apéritif, it has the advantage that it does not paralyze the palate for anything that follows. Of course if you have several, you will happily go numb all over and anything can happen. The Greeks insist you eat appetizers when sipping Ouzo.

MASTIHA

A liqueur flavored with gum mastic and made only on the island of Chios, where the mastic is harvested. You will find references to Mastiha throughout this book, for it is a unique flavoring frequently used in Greek baking. Best over ice before dinner.

CAMBAS VO BRANDY

Twenty-five years old. Expensive and quite good.

CAMBAS VSOP BRANDY

Thirty years old and excellent.

5-STAR METAXA BRANDY

One of the finest brandies in the world. Truly fit for the gods.

7-STAR METAXA BRANDY

This is the best, with a bouquet and smoothness unsurpassed by any other brandy made anywhere. A bottle of this should be treasured like an heirloom.

BEER

Greek beer is a light lager type, and the most popular brand in Greece is called Fix. This beer is made by the firm of Fix, a corruption of the name Fuchs. The Fuchs family have been brewing this beer for generations.

Coffee

Wherever there are Greek people there is an invitation to pause, sip, nibble, and philosophize on just about any subject. Very often this is done over Greek coffee, or Turkish coffee, as it is sometimes called. It is coffee made of imported coffee beans that have been very finely ground or pulverized. Instant coffee cannot be used as a substitute, for it dissolves in water and Greek coffee does not.

Traveling around Europe I picked up a Balkan-type coffee grinder that is quite a conversation piece. I am too lazy to grind my own coffee, however, and prefer to buy the packaged Greek coffee that is sold in ½- or 1-pound cans. I would suggest buying the smaller size, which can be replaced as needed. This is much better than drinking coffee made from beans that are no longer fresh. You can buy Greek coffee at any of the shops stocking Greek groceries. You can also pick up a *breke* there. A *breke* is a small brass pot with a long handle and no cover. It is in this pot that you make true Greek coffee. *Brekes* are inexpensive and come in several sizes. Greek coffee cannot be made properly in large quantities.

You can make the coffee in your kitchen, but it's fun to make it over an alcohol burner right on your dining room table on less formal occasions. Greek coffee is never served with cream or milk. It is served in demitasse cups, which can be quite small. It is ruined if it is stirred once it has been poured into the cups, so no spoons are served with it. When ordering Greek coffee in a restaurant, you must tell the waiter how sweet you want your coffee. If you wish no sugar in it, you say, "Sketo," which means plain. If you want it medium sweet, you say, "Metrio." If you want it very sweet, you say, "Vari glyko."

When you have been served the coffee (always accompanied by a cold glass of water) you will notice that it has a bit of foam on the top of it. This is called *kaimaike* and is supposed to bring good luck. Allow the coffee to cool a bit before sipping, as it is very hot when served. This will also give the coffee grounds a chance to settle into a thick sediment on the bottom of your cup, which *you do not drink.*

GREEK COFFEE
Kafés Ellínikós

YIELD: 2 servings
TIME: 5 minutes

⅔ cup cold water
2 teaspoons sugar (for medium sweetness)
2 heaping teaspoons Greek coffee

1. Using your *breke* or a small enameled saucepan, bring water and sugar to a fast boil. Remove *breke* from heat and stir in the coffee vigorously. Return *breke* to heat. Coffee will boil almost to the top immediately and have a brown foam on top. Just before it overflows, remove from heat and tap the sides of the *breke* three times with a teaspoon until foam subsides a bit.

2. Return *breke* to heat a second time and allow it to boil almost to the top again. Remove from heat and tap again three times.

3. Return to heat for a third, final, time and allow it to almost overflow again. Quickly remove from heat.

4. Using a teaspoon, carefully distribute the foam evenly into the 2 demitasse cups and then slowly fill the cups, being careful not to disturb the foam on top of each cup. Serve at once.

Shopper's Guide

The following is a listing of stores, by states, that stock Greek foods; it is done alphabetically by state and by city. Of course, the list is by no means complete, since there is no central "file" of such stores and all little stores seem to be rapidly disappearing from American life. Those stores marked with an asterisk will have information on other local retailers. You can also find some of the foods in health food stores, the gourmet shops of large department stores, Italian, Armenian, Syrian, and other Middle Eastern groceries, and some supermarkets. Wines and spirits can be found at good liquor stores.

The quickest and easiest way to find a source near you is to call a Greek Orthodox Church. Since the church is the center of Greek ethnic and cultural life, there will always be someone there who can guide you to the nearest grocery store that sells Greek specialties. You will usually find a Greek Orthodox Church listed in the telephone directory.

ALABAMA

Bruno's Food Store; 1218 South Sixth Ave.; Birmingham; main office; 2620 13th W. *(several stores)*

Cash Produce Co.; 2216 Morris Ave.; Birmingham

Sarris Import Co.; 201 18th St.; South Birmingham *(imported cheeses, olives, and olive oil)*

Lignos Grocery; 160 Government St.; Mobile

ALASKA
Bob's Distributing Co.; 355 E. 76th Ave.; Anchorage*

ARIZONA
Food for Health Co., Inc.; P.O. Box 23122; 3839 West Indian Rd.;
Phoenix*

CALIFORNIA
Sunnyland Bulghur Co.; 1435 Gerhart St.; Fresno
Athens Liquor Store, 12000 South Figueroa; Los Angeles
Nassraway's Pastry Shop; 4864 Melrose Ave.; Los Angeles
G. B. Ratto & Co.; International Grocers-Importers; 821 Washington St.;
Oakland
Daldas Grocery; 199 Eddy St.; San Francisco
Istanbul Pastries & Imported Foods; 900 North Point; San Francisco
Macy's; Stockton and O'Farrell; San Francisco

COLORADO
Colorado Specialty Foods Corporation; 4430 Glencoe St.; Denver*
Economy Greek Market; 973 Broadway; Denver

CONNECTICUT
Cap 'n' Cork Package Store; Danbury Shopping Center; Danbury
Dimyan's Market; 116 Elm St.; Danbury *(well stocked and the Dimyan
brothers will answer any questions you might have)*
The Sesame Seed; 68 West Wooster St.; Danbury *(huge sacks of nuts,
olives, seeds, spices, and all kinds of Greek cheese)*
Gourmet Galley; 900 Greenwich Ave.; Greenwich *(full line of Greek
products as well as pastries and cooked Greek foods to take out)*
Milano Super Market Inc.; 879 Dixwell Ave.; Hamden
North Street Market; 96 North St.; New Britain
Vittoria Import Co.; 35 Lafayette St.; New Britain
Greek Village; 316 Elm St.; New Haven
Achorn's Liquor Shop; 7 Veterans Plaza; New Milford *(for help in
selecting Greek wines and liquors, see Hans Wessels)*
Gourmet Galley; Post Road East; Westport *(full line of Greek products
as well as pastries and cooked Greek foods to take out)*

DISTRICT OF COLUMBIA
Acropolis Food Market; 1206 Underwood St., N.W.; Washington
Marjack Co. Inc.; 1816 Half St., S.W.; Washington*
Greek-Arabic Grocery; 1206 Underwood, N.W.; Washington

FLORIDA

IGA Market; 9807 Gulf Drive; Anna Maria Island *(finest imported Feta cheese)*

Chop 'n' Block; 5906 Manatee Ave. W.; Bradenton

Joseph's Imported Food Co.; Fields Ave.; Jacksonville

Soup Ta Nuts *(health and gourmet store);* 6842 Gulf of Mexico Drive; Longboat Key Island

Joseph Baratta; 2503 S.W. Eighth St.; Miami

Near East Bakery; 878 S.W. Eighth St.; Miami

Steve's Superette; 1629 West Garden St.; Pensacola

Maas Bros., Inc. *(department store);* 3rd St. and 1st Ave. North; St. Petersburg

Angel's Market; 455 Athens St.; Tarpon Springs

Barbers Food Store; 815 Dodecanese Blvd.; Tarpon Springs *(west end of the sponge docks; open Sundays; one of the most complete shops in Florida; see Mrs. Barber)*

Perry's Pastry Shop; 610 Athens E. St.; Tarpon Springs *(fine pastries and breads)*

GEORGIA

Big Apple Stores *(general office);* 600 Selig Drive, S.W.; Atlanta

George's Deli; 1014 North Highland Ave., N.E.; Atlanta

Snack N Shop Deli, Pasa Sara Road; Decatur

HAWAII

Gourmet Bazaar; International Market Place; Honolulu

ILLINOIS

Columbus Food Market; 324 N. Bell; Chicago

Delphi Supermarket; 2655 W. Lawrence; Chicago

Health Foods Inc.; 155 W. Higgins Rd.; Des Plains*

INDIANA

Athens Imported Food Store; 222 E. Market; Indianapolis

Mrs. Joseph Sabb; 22 Judith Lane; Terre Haute

Kassis Imports; 2318½ Wabash Ave.; Terre Haute

IOWA

Italian Importing Co.; 1st St. and 6th Ave.; Des Moines *(retail, whole-sale, Greek, Spanish, and Italian items)*

KENTUCKY
Arimes Market; 216 Walton Ave.; Lexington
Central Liquor Dispensary; 429 East Fifth St.; Lexington *(the finest assortment of Greek wines and liquors; ask for "Mama Bess")*
Thomas & Sons Co.; 309 E. Jefferson St.; Louisville

LOUISIANA
Central Grocery Co.; 823 Decatur St.; New Orleans

MAINE
Model Food Importers; 115 Middle St.; Portland
Boucouvalas Bros. Supermarket; Common and Middle Streets; Saco

MARYLAND
H & H Imported Foods Inc.; 409 W. Lexington Ave.; Baltimore
Steve Panos Grocery; 15 Preston St.; Baltimore

MASSACHUSETTS
Hellas Bakery; 194 Hurley; Cambridge
Syrian Grocery Import Co.; 270 Shawmut Ave.; Boston
Chiungas Importers; 302 Market St.; Lowell
Demoulas Supermarket; 80 Dummer St.; Lowell
Giavis Market; 391 Market St.; Lowell
Blatsos Fruits & Groceries; 124 Broad St.; Lynn
Olympia Market; 617 Main St.; Worcester

MICHIGAN
Big Ten Party Store; 1928 Packard Rd.; Ann Arbor
Delmar & Co.; 501 Monroe St.; Detroit

MINNESOTA
The Great Plains Distributing Co.; 5270 W. 74th; Edina*
The Pavo Health Foods Co.; 57 South Ninth St.; Minneapolis

MISSISSIPPI
George M. Nassour; 909 Cherry St.; Vicksburg

MISSOURI
Italo-American Importing Co.; 5851 Elizabeth St.; St. Louis

MONTANA
Hepperle's Store; Box 117; Plevna

NEBRASKA

H & H Distributing Co.; 102 Gateway Shopping Center; Lincoln*
Leon's Food Mart, Inc.; 2200 Winthrop Road; Lincoln

NEVADA

The Louis Cononelos Co.; 4 Cononelos Food Center; McGill
Walter Heiser Candy Co.; 2550 Comstock Dr.; Reno*

NEW HAMPSHIRE

Joseph's Bros.; 196 Lake Ave.; Manchester
Liamos Market; 295 Lake St.; Nashua
Youngsville Market; 1536 Candia Rd.; Manchester

NEW JERSEY

Andrew's Deli; 305 Sewell Ave.; Asbury Park
Apollo Strudel & Filo Leaves Co.; Mr. Kontis; 56 Cortland Ave.; Dumont
    (fine Phyllo, made on premises; and distributor of Apollo Filo brand)
Central Food Stores; 63 Main St.; Hackensack
Liberty Food Mkt.; 1006 Clinton Ave.; Irvington
Gacos Deli; 378 Summit Ave.; Jersey City
International Food Market; 347 Broad Ave.; Leonia
A. Sahadi Company (main distributor in U.S.); 200 Carol Place; Moo-
    nachie
Olympia Foods of All Nations; 906 Kinderkamack Rd.; River Edge
S. Balish & Son Liquors; 522 Morris Ave.; Summit

NEW YORK

Associated Food Stores; 37th St. and 31st Ave.; Astoria
ABC Food and Delicatessen; 36–15 30th Ave.; Astoria
Ditmars & 35th St. Market; 28–07 Ditmars Blvd.; Astoria
Constantines Deli; 205–10 48th Ave.; Bayside
Malko Bros.; Cassatly Co., Inc.; 197 Atlantic Ave.; Brooklyn
    (Oriental groceries, pastries)
Malko Importing Corp.; 184 Atlantic Ave.; Brooklyn
    (wholesale dealers; Oriental and domestic food products)
Sahadi Importing Co., Inc.; 187 Atlantic Ave.; Brooklyn
Sammy's Imported and Domestic Foods; 1348 Hertel Ave.; Buffalo
Freeport Italian American Deli; 52 West Merrick Rd.; Freeport
Dairy Fair Food Corp.; 31 Station Plaza; Hempstead
Athens Liquor Store; 300 W. 40th St.; New York

Eighty-Seven Delicatessen; 1681 First Ave.; New York
   (Phyllo, Tarama, Greek cheeses, olives; ask for Dino or Peter)
Kasson Bros.; 570 Ninth Avenue; New York
Liberty-Oriental Pastry Shop; 281 Audubon Ave., New York
   (homemade pastries and breads)
Macy's *(department store)*; Herald Square; New York
Margaritis Grocery Co.; 390 Eighth Ave.; New York *(very well stocked,
   family-owned for three generations)*
Poseidon Confectionery Shop; 629 Ninth Ave.; New York
   (pastries, bread, and spices)
Sugar N Spice Shop; 8th Ave. at 43rd St.; New York *(pastries)*
Zabar's; 2245 Broadway; New York
V.I.P. Bakery; 80 Route 303; Tappan *(Nick Stellas will prepare Greek
   pastries and holiday breads for you on order)*
International Foods; 183 Lee Rd.; Rochester
C. A. Thanos & Co.; 424 Pearl St.; Syracuse

NORTH CAROLINA
A. C. H. Deas Food Importers; 218 S. Blount St.; Raleigh
College Beverage Shop; 102 Redford; Winston-Salem *(Feta and Phyllo)*

OHIO
Ellis Bakery; 577 Grant St.; Akron *(specializes in Baklava)*
Metropolitan Coffee Co.; 451 E. Cuyahoga Falls; Akron
Nick Yanko's Fine Cuisine; 2761 Market; Akron
O'Neil's Epicure Shop; 226 S. Main; Akron
Shiekh Grocery Co.; 1012 Prospect Ave.; Cleveland

OKLAHOMA
Royal Coffee & Tea Co.; 115 S. Robinson St.; Oklahoma City

OREGON
Maletis Bros.; 100 N.W. 3rd Ave.; Portland

PENNSYLVANIA
Capitol Italian Grocery; 213 Chestnut St.; Harrisburg
Michael's Greek Grocery; 930 Locust St.; Philadelphia
European Grocery Store; 520 Court Pl.; Pittsburgh
Stamoolis Brothers; 202 Penn Ave.; Pittsburgh

RHODE ISLAND
Bond Foods Inc.; 10 Crary St., Providence
Near East Market; 41 Cranston St.; Providence

SOUTH CAROLINA
John P. Liatos; Margaret St.; Charleston

TENNESSEE
Collegedale Distributing Co.; Amos Rd.; Collegedale*
The Cheese Market; 505 Clinch Ave., S.W.; Knoxville
Barzizza Brothers; 351 South Front St.; Memphis

TEXAS
Paletta's Grocery; 202 Recoleta St.; San Antonio
     (a fine variety of Mediterranean specialties)
Kandis Liquors & Imports; 1202 N. Main St.; Victoria

VIRGINIA
Galanides, Inc.; Cooke Ave. and Virginia Beach Blvd.; Norfolk
The New York Deli; 2802 Williamson Rd., Roanoke

WASHINGTON
Nick Carras; 422 N. 48th St.; Seattle
Angelo Merlino & Associates; 2822 Rainier S.; Seattle

WEST VIRGINIA
Haddy's Prime Beef Inc.; 1422 Washington E.; Charleston

WISCONSIN
Topping & Co.; 736 N. Second St.; Milwaukee

Index